A SHEARWATER BOOK

THE WHALING SEASON

THE
WHALING
SEASON

An Inside Account
of the Struggle to Stop
Commercial Whaling

KIERAN MULVANEY

ISLAND PRESS/SHEARWATER BOOKS

Washington / Covelo / London

A SHEARWATER BOOK

Published by Island Press

Copyright © 2003 Kieran Mulvaney

Shearwater Books is a trademark of
The Center for Resource Economics.

Library of Congress Cataloging-in-Publication Data

Mulvaney, Kieran.
  The whaling season : an inside account of the struggle to stop
commercial whaling / Kieran Mulvaney.
     p. cm.
Includes bibliographical references (p.   ).
  ISBN 1-55963-978-4 (hardcover : alk. paper)
  1. Whales—Polar regions. 2. Whaling—Polar regions.
3. Mulvaney, Kieran—Journeys—Polar regions. 4. Greenpeace
International. 5. Wildlife conservation—Polar regions. I. Title.
  QL737.C4M85 2003
  333.95'95—dc21

2003001901

British Cataloguing-in-Publication Data available.

Printed on recycled, acid-free paper ✪

Manufactured in the United States of America
09 08 07 06 05 04 03   10 9 8 7 6 5 4 3 2 1

To

Leslie Busby,
for hiring me;

Anne Dingwall,
for sending me to the Antarctic;

John Frizell,
for being the brains behind it all;

Walt Simpson,
for making it all happen;

and the memory of
David McTaggart,
for his infuriating, inspirational, and deeply missed genius.

"When you kill the greatest,
you do not become the greatest.
You only lose the greatest."

SANDRA LEE
Former New Zealand
Minister of Conservation
53rd Meeting of the
International Whaling
Commission
London, 2001

CONTENTS

The Antarctic, December 2001

Thousands of miles from anywhere, surrounded by icebergs and enshrouded in fog, we waited.

The stillness was interrupted by a minke whale, announcing its presence with an exhalation and a cloud of vapor as its breath collided with the cold Antarctic air. It didn't look particularly large—perhaps twenty to twenty-five feet long, I guessed, from what I could see of its back as it rolled through the water: massive by the standards of most animals but small even for this smallest of all great whale species. Its solitariness made it seem somehow vulnerable as it plowed its lonely path through sea and ice, and I found myself strangely moved by the scene, silently vowing that if we could achieve one thing, it would be to ensure that this whale lived to see another day. We gathered quietly on deck and watched as our companion cruised languidly through the water; it surfaced once, twice, three times, each time farther from us, moving steadily into the distance until we could see it no more and we were once again alone.

It could not know what we suspected: that somewhere just

over the horizon, a fleet of whaling ships was heading toward it, and toward us. Once—sixty, seventy years ago—hundreds of such ships scoured these freezing Antarctic waters, hunting tens of thousands of whales every year, reaping huge profits from the sale of whale oil for use in everything from soap to nitroglycerin. But the scale of the industry was undone by its own rapaciousness: by the dawn of the twenty-first century, almost all the whales were gone from the Antarctic, and the whalers with them. Only one fleet remained to pursue them, defying an international ban on whaling by dubbing its activities "scientific research," hunting minke whales such as the one we had just seen, to cater to a small and shrinking market for their meat, kept determinedly alive by support and subsidies from a Japanese government that yearned to see its whaling industry expand and thrive again.

Barely had the whale vanished from sight than our first target appeared on the radar, eleven miles distant. I stood on the bridge, staring at the radar screen, watching the echo move steadily closer as the ship headed toward us. It was searching for prey, waiting for the fog to clear so it could begin hunting. It was our job to stop it, but not yet. Our prime target, the fleet's mother ship, was still some distance away, and until it was in our sights we needed to avoid detection.

That wasn't going to be easy, caught as we were out in the open, with only the fog to offer us protection. We might be able to hide behind the nearest iceberg, but it was small, and we were on the wrong side of it, the same side as the whale catcher. If we tried to sneak slowly behind the berg, we would become a moving target on the whaler's radar and alert the fleet to our presence. All we could do was sit still in the fog, pretend we were an iceberg ourselves, and hope that we would remain undetected.

If it maintained its trajectory, the catcher would pass five miles south of us. In this fog bank, visibility was no better than two miles. If we didn't move, and the crew on the catcher didn't suspect anything, chances were that they would pass by us and remain completely unaware of our presence. But Antarctic conditions are as capricious as they are hostile, and as the catcher edged nearer, the fog slowly began to lift. Closer and closer the whaling ship came: eight miles, seven miles, six. And as time ticked agonizingly by, the fog steadily parted.

Olivier saw it first. He pointed, directed my gaze toward it, and held the binoculars to my face, but I still couldn't see the outline he had detected through the mist. One by one, others shouted—their eyesight not as sharp as the bosun's but better than mine—as they too spied what Olivier had spotted. As the curtain of fog lifted further, I finally saw it too, that familiar, almost menacing silhouette that, over the last decade, I had come to know so well: long, low in the water, the crow's nest reaching toward the sky, and, sitting atop the high bow, the harpoon cannon.

If we could now see them so clearly, then surely they had seen us too. But the catcher continued steadily on its way; and almost as suddenly as the fog had lifted, it rolled in again, as if tempting us with a brief look at the world beyond before deciding we should see no more. After having the element of surprise nearly snatched from us, it looked as if we had somehow won it back. It seemed scarcely believable, but the catcher appeared not to have seen our ship.

Before we could relax, before the first echo had left the radar, a second emerged at the bottom of the screen, heading directly for us.

"That's it, Kieran," Andy declared. "Game's up. There's no way this guy can miss us."

The words had barely left the captain's mouth when the gods once more threw us a lifeline. The second echo made an abrupt change of course and slowed down. It seemed to be threading its way through a thick patch of ice; as it did so, its path would take it behind an iceberg, blocking its view and affording us the opportunity to duck quickly behind a berg of our own. I exhaled and looked at Andy. The engines started up, and as the second catcher concentrated on finding its way through the ice, we slipped into the shadow of the berg.

Two bullets dodged, and as we caught our breath behind the iceberg and contemplated the next step, the remaining two targets appeared on the radar. One of them, like the two we had somehow seemingly so far evaded, was a catcher: one of the ships that actually searched for, hunted down, and harpooned whales. The other was the grand prize: the *Nisshin Maru*, seventy-five hundred tons of steel, the giant factory ship where the catchers took their bounty, where the whales were cut up, processed, and packaged as cuts of meat for supermarkets and restaurants in Japan, all in the name of science. The *Nisshin Maru* was the heart of the fleet, the one from which the others never strayed too far and to which they constantly had to return. If we could chase down and stick with the factory vessel, then the others would be in our grasp.

But experience gained from years of encounters with the fleet had shown that that would be easier said than done. The *Nisshin Maru* was slower than the catchers, but not by much; and even this relative slowpoke of the whaling fleet could outpace us by several knots. If the factory ship chose to flee as soon as it saw us, there wouldn't be much we could do except keep up until it disappeared from our radar, and then try to find it again. In the past, running had always been their first response: the last thing they wanted was to be caught and filmed hunting whales. However much they criticized the "emotionalism" of their detractors, they knew that color footage of dead and dying whales made for bad PR, and it was something they preferred to avoid. Discretion was the better part of valor, and the whalers generally had no problem embracing it.

And so, even after we picked up their echoes, we waited some more. If we waited too long, the fog might lift, revealing our green hull in bright contrast to the gray and white of ice, sea, and sky; or one of the catchers we had so far avoided might suddenly show up from the other side of an iceberg and blow our cover. If we made our move too soon, they would spot us on their radar while we were still miles away, and their head start would put us out of radar contact in a hurry. For forty minutes we sat and watched the *Nisshin Maru* and the catcher as they inched ever closer, until finally the moment was right: they were within two miles, as close as they were going to get on their current course, and sure enough, the mist was starting to part. I nodded to Andy. The *Arctic Sunrise* sputtered to life and we emerged from our hiding place.

For the first minute or so, the *Nisshin Maru* and its companion continued on their way, seemingly still oblivious to our presence. Then, with a cloud of black smoke, the factory vessel changed direction, turning away from us and speeding up. But almost as soon as it did so, another puff of smoke appeared, and the giant ship slowed down again. Antarctic conditions, which had alternately protected us from discovery and nearly conspired to reveal us at the worst possible moment, were once again working in our favor. The same icy seas that had forced the second catcher to detour and had thus given us the opportunity to hide behind the iceberg were now blocking the escape route of the *Nisshin Maru*. If it turned around now, the whaler would head directly into our path; faced with little choice, it took the plunge and steamed into the ice.

Although equipped with a strengthened bow, the *Nisshin Maru* was not a true icebreaker, and would not be able to bludgeon its way through the thickest floes; the *Arctic Sunrise*, however, was. The playing field was suddenly more even, the whaling ship robbed of its great advantage over us, unable to simply blast over the horizon as we bobbed helplessly in its wake. But if the *Nisshin Maru* could not easily outpace us, it wasn't clear we'd catch up: even icebreakers, save the largest and most powerful—a club in which our little ship, though sturdy and capable, did not belong—must labor their way through the ice floes, pushing them aside or riding on top of them and splitting them open.

The chase was slow and hours in duration, the *Nisshin Maru* looking for leads through the ice and having to force its way through the floes when no pathways were obvious, and the *Sunrise* doing the same, breaking and shoving ice when necessary but taking the path of least resistance when available.

Periodically, the whaler would emit a blast of smoke from its funnel and put on speed as it entered open water, but its advantage would be short-lived as it encountered another patch of ice at the same time as the *Sunrise* broke free of the ice floes from which the *Nisshin Maru* had just escaped.

When both ships were in open water, we launched our two large, rigid-hulled inflatables, each around twenty feet long, in the hope that the speedy boats would be able to catch up to the fleeing whaler more swiftly than our ponderous little icebreaker, but almost as soon as we had put them in the water, the motor died on one of them; we sent the other boat on ahead, but by then the *Nisshin Maru* was back in the ice, and instead of gaining on the factory ship we actually lost ground when forced to retrieve both boats and their crews. After several hours of pursuit, when the respective twists and turns of hunter and hunted had enabled us to close the gap on our quarry, and when the ice was thin and open enough for a small boat to navigate but still plentiful enough that the *Nisshin Maru* could not simply put on full throttle and escape us, we decided to try again with the working inflatable.

The boat, with five people on board, swiftly covered the two miles between us and the factory vessel, and the whaling crew lined up along the rail and stared down at the small gray boat speeding alongside. Our Japanese crew member, Yuko Hirono, called up the *Nisshin Maru* with the inflatable's VHF radio, and her voice flooded the deck of the whaler as the ship's public-address system relayed her explanation of our position, purpose, and goals:

- Although they called their activities "scientific research," we considered them commercial whaling.
- We were opposed to commercial whaling because it has always, without exception, depleted or even decimated whale populations.
- We were not alone: countries from around the world opposed commercial whaling.

- Ours was a strictly nonviolent protest: although we planned to
  document and hinder their activities, we would do nothing to
  harm their persons or endanger their ships.

It was a courtesy call, one that we always made whenever we
first encountered the whaling fleet, an attempt to explain our
position and purpose and emphasize our pacifism. The factory
vessel did not respond—it never had in the past, and we did not
expect it to now—and so the boat returned to the *Sunrise*.

And then, suddenly, the factory ship stopped. The third
catcher, the *Yushin Maru*, which had remained close by the
mother ship throughout the pursuit, drew up alongside to refuel.
The factory ship's crew watched us through binoculars as we
watched them, filmed us as we filmed them. We slowly circled
the two whalers before coming to a halt a half-mile away, waiting
for the whalers' next move.

A few hours later, the *Yushin Maru* slipped slowly away and
off our radar screen. We let it go and kept an eye on the factory
ship. A couple of times in the middle of the night it started up
suddenly and made what appeared to be a halfhearted break for
it, before giving up when the *Sunrise* responded and gave chase.
The next morning the *Nisshin Maru* began steaming slowly to
the southwest. When we had first spotted them the previous
day, the fleet had been heading northeast, and that was almost
certainly the direction they actually planned to go today. The
factory ship, we guessed, was trying to lead us away. So we
decided to head in the opposite direction, northeast. The gambit
paid off: almost immediately, we saw the radar echoes of the
three catchers, waiting for the day to begin.

Its ploy unsuccessful, the *Nisshin Maru* reversed course and
joined the rest of the fleet. They assembled in formation, the
Arctic Sunrise settled in the middle of the pack, and we all
steamed off as one.

They were ready to start whaling. We were ready to stop
them.

CHAPTER ONE

Beginnings

Amsterdam,
September 1991

WALT SIMPSON TOOK A BITE OF HIS SANDWICH, LEANED BACK IN his chair, and looked at me, the faint hints of an incredulous smile gracing his lips as he contemplated the notion that the naive kid in front of him had actually been tapped to help lead an expedition into the coldest, stormiest, most remote waters on Earth. Walt had been a captain and mate on several Greenpeace ships and a member of a good many journeys to sea as a merchant seaman. Now, no longer interested in spending months at a time away from land, he was helping to oversee Greenpeace's maritime adventures from the relative comfort of the organization's international headquarters in Amsterdam. He put his hands behind his head and spoke slowly and quietly, with a soft Southern drawl.

"This is going to be the longest, hardest, most risky, most uncomfortable, most frustrating, most boring—basically the all-round most difficult—trip Greenpeace has ever put together."

He watched me stare nervously at the chart of the Southern Ocean he'd laid out on the table, and smiled some more.

"So," he said. "Still want to go?"

That I was in a position to even contemplate going to Antarctica was the direct result of a circuitous journey that had its origins seven years earlier when—sixteen years old, living in a beach resort town in the west of England, my childhood love of wildlife having morphed first into teenage angst over the state of the environment and then into an aspiration to pursue a career writing about and campaigning on environmental issues—I saw an advertisement for a magazine.

If I hadn't seen that ad—for a publication called *BBC Wildlife*, produced by the same department of the British Broadcasting Corporation responsible for the company's famed wildlife documentaries on television—I wouldn't have picked up a copy at my local newsstand. I'd have missed its lead article, a critical analysis of zoos, by a writer named John May, and wouldn't have been prompted to consider the debate surrounding the issue of whether animals should be kept in captivity as one worthy of research and writing. I wouldn't have picked up the subsequent issue of the same magazine and seen, in the heavy mailbag of readers' letters in response to May's article, one from Bill Travers and Virginia McKenna, the husband-and-wife acting team famous for their roles in the movie *Born Free* and now leading an anti-zoo pressure group called Zoo Check. I wouldn't have written them to ask for further information on the controversy surrounding zoos. And they, in turn, wouldn't have put me in touch with a man named Bill Jordan.

A gray-haired, soft-spoken Ulsterman, Bill Jordan was an experienced environmentalist and veterinarian. He had been a leading light in the Royal Society for the Prevention of Cruelty to Animals and personal veterinary adviser to the shah of Iran; he had coauthored a seminal critique of conditions in British zoos, *The Last Great Wild Beast Show*, and was now director of an organization called the People's Trust for Endangered Species. He proved remarkably responsive to my constant inquiries: so much so that, instead of merely fielding my questions about zoos, he saw some hint of promise in my persistence and interest and took me under his wing. I went with him when he gave talks and lectures to local conservation groups; I edited a newsletter about the trust's activities around the world; and I soaked up the advice he gave me on how to evolve from an aspiring writer to a successful one. It was under Bill's tutelage that I first began to write articles and see them appear in print.

Around the time that my first articles were being published, a note came in the mail. It was from another People's Trust alumnus, Sean Whyte. I had told him earlier about my zoo project, and now Sean had dropped me a line, mentioning that he had traveled frequently to the United States and had photos of several of the larger zoos and wildlife parks there. Did I want to come and take a look?

So I made the forty-minute train journey to the home that Sean shared with his wife, Margaret, and over coffee we talked about zoos, about conservation, about the People's Trust, about whales and whaling. I mentioned that as part of my research into zoos, I had begun studying dolphin shows; to understand dolphin shows, I needed to understand dolphins; and to understand dolphins I had been doing a lot of research on them and their larger cousins, the whales—research that I had found so interesting that it was pushing my putative zoo project to the sidelines.

Much of the early research on whales had been conducted by scientists wading through the entrails and carcasses of specimens on the deck of whaling ships. But in recent decades, a dedicated and growing band of researchers had been working in their subjects' natural habitat, taking photographs and lowering hydrophones from boats, and even diving into the water to watch and film whales in their element. With each passing year, it seemed, something new was being added to the whale and dolphin knowledge base, be it that several species of dolphins live in complex social groups, communicating through clicks and whistles; or that humpback whales sing long, haunting songs; or that the low moans of a blue whale are the deepest, loudest noises made by any living thing on Earth; or that the giant testicles of male right whales are the size of small cars; or that sperm whales have the largest brains on the planet, dive to depths in excess of three thousand feet, and possibly stun the giant squid with which they do battle by shouting at them very, very loudly.

I began visiting Sean and Margaret regularly, and on each occasion we sooner or later ended up talking enthusiastically about our mutual interest—not just about our enthusiasm for them, but also the numerous threats that many different species of whales and dolphins faced around the world.

Commercial whaling, long seen as the greatest threat to whale populations, was substantially reduced from its heyday and was continuing to decline. But declining did not mean deceased, and although an international moratorium on commercial whaling was scheduled to take effect in 1986, Japan, Norway, and the Soviet Union had announced their intention to carry on whaling anyway, while Iceland and South Korea looked as if they would try to continue by using a loophole that allowed countries to kill whales for "scientific research."

But in many ways, commercial whaling was now the least of the problems various whales and dolphins faced. Tens of thousands were drowning every year in the huge drift nets used by commercial fisheries, or were caught and killed in tuna nets because they swam with yellowfin tuna in the Eastern Pacific. Similar numbers were being hunted for food around the world, in such varied places as Japan, Sri Lanka, and the Faeroe Islands. Others were being put on display in shows around the world. And everywhere, it seemed, they were being contaminated by the pollutants that were being dumped and pumped into the seas.

Yet in Britain at least, relatively little was being done to help them. There was Greenpeace, of course, which for more than ten years had been confronting whaling ships at sea and which we looked up to as the preeminent defender of the world's whales. There were other, smaller groups like our own People's Trust. But there was, so far as we were aware, not a single organization in the United Kingdom devoted solely to the conservation of all the world's species of whales and dolphins.

Sean and I began to throw around the idea of doing something about that, of starting our own organization. We were two people; we had no way of putting together anything to match the feats of Greenpeace, no chance of being in a position to force changes of policy or directly bring about an end to whaling. But we were enthusiastic, and we knew the issues. I was a writer and Sean had had a successful career in business and retail; between us, we felt we would be able to attract enough funding and contacts to start an organization that could educate, inform, network, and possibly even mobilize people across Britain who were interested in cetaceans.

And so the Whale Conservation Society was born. Its origins were humble: a typewriter in my bedroom; sheets of paper spread across my parents' living room floor, on which I planned and plotted our first newsletters; and stacks of envelopes on Sean and Margaret's dining room table, into which we stuffed the flyers we had printed up, advising of our society's imminent arrival.

We picked June 5, 1987—World Environment Day—as our official launch date. A week later, one of the country's leading newspapers, *The Guardian*, published an article I had written exposing the sham of "scientific" whaling, which was rapidly becoming the favored way of avoiding the moratorium. The first issue of what we hoped would be a regular and authoritative publication—an eight-page broadsheet we called the *International Whale Bulletin*—carried a front-page article along the same lines. We sent out copies to local media, to experts we knew, and to the few people who had to that point responded to the flyers we had mailed. And we took the rest with us to Bournemouth, on the southern coast of England, where the International Whaling Commission (IWC), the body that regulated whaling and had voted for the moratorium, was holding its annual meeting. Nongovernmental organizations are allowed to attend IWC meetings as observers, and so we paid our membership dues and I went to my first International Whaling Commission meeting as the observer from the Whale Conservation Society.

The evening before the meeting started, WCS held a reception, complete with a reading of a new poem by the writer and actor Heathcote Williams. Entitled *Whale Nation*, it had been published in the alternative British press and was winning attention as a piece of performance art. Few people came to our inaugural reception—I believe there was a conflict with some other event and we were, after all, the new kids on the block—but it didn't really matter. Sir Peter Scott, founder of the World Wildlife Fund and son of the polar explorer Robert Falcon Scott, had agreed to endorse us and even serve as our president, bestowing upon us an instant aura of gravitas and respectability; a couple of days later, at the end of a long day of IWC discussions, I found myself in exalted company indeed, standing alongside Sir Peter and esteemed whale scientist Roger Payne and addressing local supporters of Greenpeace and Friends of the Earth.

From those beginnings, WCS went from strength to strength. Supporting the conservation and welfare of whales and dolphins was something of a no-brainer in England, and positioning ourselves as the only cetacean conservation organization in the country meant we soon began to attract a lot of support. I was regularly called and quoted by newspapers, radio, and television, asked to comment mostly on commercial whaling but also on captivity, the hunting of dolphins, pollution, and other related issues. Geography worked to my advantage: my hometown of Weston-super-Mare was just thirty minutes away from Bristol, site of the BBC's famed Natural History Unit. Accordingly, I was frequently asked to the studios to pontificate on some issue or contribute to some program or other. In addition, having pestered the editor since I had pulled that first copy off the shelf of a local newsstand three years earlier, I finally began seeing my articles appear in *BBC Wildlife* magazine.

Early in 1988, I made my first solo foreign trip, to Costa Rica, as a delegate to the General Assembly of the International Union for Conservation of Nature and Natural Resources* (IUCN), a giant gathering of governments and nongovernmental organizations. Later that year, I was back at the IWC annual meeting, this time in Auckland, New Zealand. A few weeks after I returned to Great Britain, I was asked to take part in a nationally televised discussion on whales, whaling, and the environment—a program prompted by the publication, in coffee-table format, of Heathcote Williams's *Whale Nation*—where I found myself alongside some of my greatest idols, including Jim Lovelock, originator of the influential Gaia hypothesis (which essentially postulates that Earth is one giant megaorganism) and Petra Kelly, leader of the German Green Party.

The Whale Conservation Society was riding high. By late 1988, we had changed the organization's name to the Whale and Dolphin Conservation Society (WDCS), to better reflect our concern for *all* dolphin and whale species; we had attracted more than two thousand dues-paying members; we had hired a leading London publicity and public-relations firm; and we had begun publishing a new color magazine called *Sonar*.

Others had been paying attention to us and what we were doing, and when I returned from Auckland, I was approached to work for Greenpeace. Various Greenpeace campaigners I had encountered at the IWC and assorted other meetings over the past twelve months had banded together to try to persuade me to join a small unit coordinating Greenpeace's IWC work, to zassist with the European end of the organization's global dolphin campaigns, and to help write a book on dolphins—which, coincidentally, was being edited by John May, whose *BBC Wildlife* article on zoos had helped steer me down the path that had brought me to this point. I would be based at the organization's international headquarters, presently sited in England but soon to be moving to Amsterdam.

In response to Sean's concerns that my departure would mean

---

* Now called the World Conservation Union—but, confusingly, still abbreviated as IUCN.

the end of WDCS, I insisted (correctly, as it turned out) that he'd be able to keep it going, attract talented new people, and go from strength to strength. To be honest, though, that wasn't foremost in my mind. I was twenty years old, I had been given a dream offer, and I was really thinking only of myself. It was a chance to join a big, glamorous organization, leave Weston-super-Mare, move to Amsterdam, and write a book—just about everything I could have wanted—and I intended to take it. Early in 1989, I piled my belongings into a truck and headed off to start my new life with Greenpeace.

Long before I joined the organization, Greenpeace had become synonymous with the campaign to end commercial whaling, and images of its boat-driving activists blocking the line of harpooners' fire were icons of the movement. But the organization had been born out of a very different event: the detonation, on November 6, 1971, of a five-megaton nuclear bomb.

Code-named Cannikin, the explosion was the third in a series of underground nuclear tests, all conducted on the remote island of Amchitka in the Aleutian chain, an archipelago that curves its way like a necklace from Alaska almost to the Kamchatka Peninsula and separates the North Pacific from the Bering Sea. When the first test, Long Shot, took place on October 29, 1965, it did so to relatively little outcry; by the time the Atomic Energy Commission announced plans for a second, larger test, code-named Milrow, in 1969, opposition had begun to mount.

Ranks of anti-nuclear protesters were swelled by Vietnam dissenters and people afraid that the test's location, in the middle of a mosaic of fault lines, could prompt an earthquake as massive as the magnitude 9.2 temblor that had ripped through south-central Alaska in 1964, devastating several towns in the state and powering tsunamis that crashed along the shores of Oregon, California, Hawaii, and Japan. The day before the detonation, ten thousand protesters, most of them Canadian, massed at the Douglas Border crossing between British Columbia and

Washington State to give voice to their fears. DON'T MAKE A WAVE, their placards read; IT'S YOUR FAULT IF OUR FAULT GOES.

After Milrow's detonation, three participants in the Douglas Border crossing protest—Jim Bohlen, a forty-three-year-old American who had fled to Vancouver with his family when his son became eligible for the draft; Irving Stowe, a converted Quaker who had entered self-imposed exile in the same city for the same reason; and Paul Cote, a young Canadian lawyer—sat down to try to organize opposition to Cannikin. Borrowing from the sentiments expressed on the signs at Douglas Border, they fashioned themselves the Don't Make a Wave Committee, attracted other like-minded would-be protesters and, following the Quaker tradition of "bearing witness"—a form of passive resistance that involved traveling to the scene of an objectionable activity and registering opposition simply by being there—they hit upon the idea of chartering a boat and sailing it to the test site. Shortly after the notion had been agreed upon, Irving Stowe signed off a meeting of the Don't Make a Wave Committee and its supporters by flashing the V sign and saying, "Peace." Bill Darnell, the youngest person at the table, offered that it should be something more, a union of peace and ecology: "Make it a green peace," he suggested. To Bohlen, that sounded like a good idea. If they managed to find a boat, he declared, they would call it Green Peace.

They did indeed find a vessel—the *Phyllis Cormack*, a thirty-year-old, eighty-foot-long halibut seiner—and on September 15, 1971, the first-ever Greenpeace voyage set sail for Amchitka. They didn't succeed in stopping the test; a combination of the weather, the U.S. Coast Guard, and onboard tensions prevented them from actually reaching the test site. But the protesters demonstrated considerable media savvy, to the point of inviting three journalists—Robert Hunter of the *Vancouver Sun*, whose columns criticizing the nuclear tests had been an inspiration for the Douglas Border crossing; Canadian Broadcast Corporation freelancer Ben Metcalfe; and Bob Cummings, publisher of the counterculture newspaper the *Georgia Straight*—

onto the *Phyllis Cormack*. The journalists in effect became part of the crew; indeed, Hunter in particular would play an important role in the nascent Greenpeace. Of more immediate import, their dispatches allowed people in Canada and the United States to follow the activists' adventures as they happened, enabling the expedition to generate enormous amounts of media attention—so much so that, when the vessel returned to British Columbia, it was to a hero's welcome.

The Cannikin test went ahead as planned, but it was a Pyrrhic victory, as *Time* magazine noted: "Seldom, if ever, had so many Canadians felt so deep a sense of resentment and anger over a single U.S. action. . . . For once the cries of protest were not confined to the radical Left, but came from a broad spectrum of Canadian society distressed by the environmental risks and the other possible hazards of the test." The Greenpeace action, *Time* editorialized, was the "most vigorous" protest "ever lodged against nuclear testing, both in the U.S. and overseas." Four months later, the Atomic Energy Commission announced that, "for political and other reasons," there would be no more testing at Amchitka.

It was not the first time someone had sailed a ship to a test site; the Quakers had tried it twice before, to protest nuclear testing at Bikini Atoll in the South Pacific. But the first Greenpeace voyage deliberately sought to avoid the mistakes the Quakers had made. For one, the Quakers used American boats with American crews, which allowed them to be easily and swiftly arrested by U.S. authorities before they came close to reaching the atoll; the *Phyllis Cormack*, and the people on board, were Canadian, a fact that protected them unless or until they entered U.S. territorial waters. For another, the Quakers were content with merely bearing witness; Greenpeace was not. That was the reason for including Hunter, Metcalfe, and Cummings; the goal was to hit the mainstream, underground, and broadcast media all at once, with the idea that not only would the crew of the *Phyllis Cormack* bear witness to the test, but the whole world would vicariously bear witness with them. In so doing, the strategy of that first voyage became a template Greenpeace would follow and fine-tune over the years: even if a specific action or voyage itself didn't succeed in preventing the activity it was protesting, it would aim to shine a media spotlight so bright that others would pay attention to what was happening and take up the cause, leading to a groundswell of public response that ideally would ultimately compel national or international change.

After Amchitka, the Don't Make a Wave Committee was formally renamed the Greenpeace Foundation. With anti-nuclear protest still its watchword, the group recruited Canadian expatriate David McTaggart to lead a crew from New Zealand to the South Pacific atoll of Moruroa, site of the French government's nuclear test program. In many ways it was a venture even more daring and challenging than sailing to the Aleutians—not only because of the greater distance, but because French nuclear tests, unlike those of the United States, were "atmospheric," or above-ground: each explosion blasted a vast cloud of radioactive fallout, and anyone in the direct path of that cloud—Greenpeace protesters included—would be in the gravest danger.

When McTaggart's thirty-eight-foot ketch *Vega* arrived off Moruroa in the middle of June 1972, it was swarmed by French warships. As it struggled to close in on the atoll, minesweepers and cruisers bore down on it, turning away at the last minute and missing the overmatched boat's hull by just a few feet. Day and night the harassment continued, frightening and exhausting the Greenpeace crew, until finally, after more than two weeks, the minesweeper *La Paimpolaise* rammed the *Vega* in the stern, crippling the ketch and ending the protest.

The following year, funded largely by the limited advance he received for writing a book about his experiences, McTaggart and the *Vega* returned. This time the French didn't wait before making their move: on August 15, shortly after the *Vega* arrived off the test site, three warships descended, an inflatable boat dispatched from one of the ships sped toward the ketch, and a complement of commandos boarded, beating McTaggart and another crew member so severely that McTaggart's right eye was permanently damaged. French authorities denied an assault had taken place, but one of the *Vega* crew, Ann-Marie Horne, succeeded in photographing the attack and smuggling the film off the boat. When the photographs were released to wire services, the accompanying outrage proved a major embarrassment for Paris. Shortly afterward, France announced to the U.N. General Assembly that, after one more year, its atmospheric nuclear tests would end.

McTaggart took the French to court, arguing that their actions in impeding, ramming, and boarding his vessel were in violation of the Law of the Sea. Back in Vancouver, other Greenpeace members looked at photos of the *Vega* actions and began to consider other, quite different opportunities. For several months Paul Spong, a New Zealand–born whale researcher living in British Columbia, had been urging the organization to extend its unique brand of peaceful confrontation to take on the commercial whaling industry, but had met opposition from those who had been attracted to the cause purely by the anti-nuclear issue and who argued that getting sidetracked into saving whales would spread too thin the organization's extremely limited resources. Even after Spong managed to break down that resistance, there remained the difficult question of exactly what Greenpeace could do to stop the whalers. The answer came when Spong and Robert Hunter noted that the commando raid on the *Vega* had been made infinitely easier by the use of fast, inflatable boats called Zodiacs. These boats were maneuverable, stable, and easily launched from a ship. In *Warriors of the Rainbow: A Chronicle of the Greenpeace Movement*, Hunter wrote that the plan he and Spong devised

> was as old as the passivist notion of throwing yourself on the tracks in front of a troop train, except that there was more hardware involved. We'd take a boat out to sea, find the whalers, put the high-speed rubber Zodiacs in the water, and race in front of the harpoons, making a clear shot at the whales impossible without

a good chance of a human being getting blasted in the process. We would become living shields.

On June 18, 1975, the *Phyllis Cormack* left Vancouver Island in search of a Soviet whaling fleet known to be operating some-where in the region. After a little more than a week, about fifty miles west of Eureka, California, it found what it was looking for, and the Greenpeace crew raced their inflatable boats into position. As the whale catcher *Vlastny* closed in on a group of sperm whales, one inflatable sped in front of its bow while another filmed the action. Suddenly there was a loud crack as the *Vlastny* fired its harpoon directly over the heads of the inflatable's crew and into the back of a whale right next to them. The harpoon's grenade exploded inside the whale and the cable lashed less than five feet from the Zodiac. The whole incident was captured on film, and response among media and public was phenomenal. Photos and footage ran in newspapers and on tele-vision screens around the world, and the *New York Times* was moved to remark, "For the first time in the history of whaling, human beings had put their lives on the line for whales."

The following year, Greenpeace returned to action against the Soviet fleet, which was again hunting sperm whales, primarily for their oil. In 1977, at-sea actions against the Soviets were complemented by Zodiac-based protests against the last remaining whaling station in Australia. By 1978, the campaign had spread to Europe, where a new ship—a converted trawler that Greenpeace dubbed the *Rainbow Warrior*—steamed into the North Atlantic to combat the hunting of fin whales by Iceland. Two years later the *Warrior* was seized by authorities while interfering with a Spanish whaling fleet, and was detained for five months until it was able to escape under cover of darkness. Three years later it narrowly avoided capture again, desperately evading Soviet warships and fleeing to U.S. waters after docu-menting that the meat of gray whales hunted off Siberia, sup-posedly for the subsistence needs of the region's indigenous peoples, was in fact being used to feed mink in Soviet fur farms.

There had been public interest in "saving the whales," and a concerted political effort to limit or end commercial whaling, long before Greenpeace. Indeed, the International Whaling Commission first voted on a commercial whaling moratorium in 1972, three years before the *Phyllis Cormack* first set out in search of the Soviets. But Greenpeace's actions dramatized and emotionalized the campaign as never before, and mobilized ever greater numbers of people to speak out in defense of whales and against whaling. Many of those newly mobilized people found an outlet for their concerns in Greenpeace, and as a result the organization rapidly grew.

Commercial whaling had become Greenpeace's signature campaign, but it was far from its only issue. The organization continued to oppose nuclear testing, and over the years expanded its portfolio to include, at different times, seal hunting, kangaroo culling, nuclear power, the dumping of hazardous waste at sea, and the production of toxic chemicals. From a small group of idealists in Vancouver, Greenpeace had spread around the world. In the late 1970s and early 1980s, David McTaggart stitched together the patchwork of independent offices into one truly global organization, with a coordinating international headquarters at the hub. Its direct actions no longer existed in a vacuum but were instead integral components of broader, multifaceted campaigns geared toward changing or creating national legislation or international treaties; scientists and suit-clad lobbyists were as representative of the organization as were activists driving inflatable boats.

Greenpeace had emerged in the early 1970s, at a time of powerful social change, and had both ridden that wave and helped shape it. In Europe and the English-speaking world, environmental policies grew from a counterculture cause célèbre to a mainstream political concern, and a wide range of organizations evolved that both responded to that concern and further fanned the flames of public opinion. By virtue of its name recognition and its unique ability to combine lobbying with research and education (or, depending on your perspective, propaganda) while simultaneously conducting daring protest actions, Greenpeace earned itself a place at the head of the table.

The extent to which, in the space of less than fifteen years, Greenpeace grew from a determined yet effective bunch of hippies, New Agers, and pacifists to a genuinely potent force was perhaps best highlighted by an incident that in many ways remains the organization's defining—albeit most tragic— episode.

On July 10, 1985, the *Rainbow Warrior* was in Auckland, having just completed a remarkable voyage to Rongelap atoll. In the path of fallout from U.S. atmospheric nuclear tests in the 1950s, Rongelap had become drenched in radioactive contamination, and the rates of cancers and birth defects had become disproportionately high; at the request of the island's parliament, the *Warrior* had evacuated the entire population to uninhabited Mejato, 120 miles away. The Rongelap evacuation, however, was just one part of the *Warrior*'s South Pacific journey; its next stop would be leading a peace convoy to Moruroa where, although French atmospheric testing had ended after David McTaggart's *Vega* voyages in the 1970s, underground nuclear detonations still continued. The use of Moruroa was becoming a political flashpoint among France's restive South Pacific colonies, and Paris was anxious about the possible consequences.

At 11:38 P.M., a massive explosion rocked the *Rainbow Warrior*, ripping a hole the size of a car in the ship's side and causing it to lurch upward and sideways. Minutes later came a second explosion, and the remaining crew scrambled onto the wharf—all except photographer Fernando Pereira, who was trapped below and drowned.

The cause was sabotage, an attempt by the French government to prevent the *Warrior*'s voyage. The two secret service agents responsible for planting the mines on the ship's hull were arrested by New Zealand authorities; without enough concrete evidence to charge them with murder, however, a deal was struck whereby, after a trial of just thirty-four minutes, they pled guilty to manslaughter and willful damage and were each given concurrent sentences of ten years on the first charge and seven on the second. Under extreme political pressure from Paris, New Zealand allowed them to serve their sentences at the French military base at Hao Atoll; two years later, they were repatriated and later awarded medals for their services to the republic.

An initial government inquiry in Paris denied evidence of any French involvement; it took dogged investigations by the French media and Greenpeace to establish the contrary. On September 19, 1985, two months after the bombing, the head of the French secret service was fired and Defense Minister Charles Hernu resigned; three days later Prime Minister Laurent Fabius appeared on national television to admit that the bombing had indeed been conducted by French agents acting under government orders to prevent the *Warrior*'s voyage.

Greenpeace had lost its flagship, and one of its own had been murdered. But the French plan had backfired. The Moruroa protest went ahead, with a different ship, and as a result of the sabotage garnered far more world attention than it otherwise might have. "You Can't Sink a Rainbow," Greenpeace's publicity materials defiantly proclaimed; and indeed, following the loss of the *Warrior*, the organization gained more attention and clout than it ever could have imagined. Whether you viewed it in a positive light or not, by the time I arrived in early 1989, Greenpeace, though a financial midget compared to those it opposed, was a political force to be reckoned with.

Working for Greenpeace was, for me, a culture shock. For the first time in my life, I was surrounded by a community of activists, people who, if anything, knew more about the issues than I did. But few of them were motivated by the same feelings.

For one thing, protecting whales and dolphins was just one part of Greenpeace's work. Its other concerns included nuclear testing and nuclear power, the production and trade of toxic waste, ozone depletion, global warming, the threat of mining in Antarctica, overexploitation of fish stocks—the range of issues was wide and, it seemed, constantly growing. To my surprise, some staffers in these other areas were dismissive of the whaling campaign, regarding it as a minor issue given the numbers of whales being killed, and even an issue that could interfere with the organization's efforts to establish positive links with other groups, individuals, and officials in countries such as Norway and Japan, where anti-whaling efforts had generated hostility and suspicion.

Even the folks who worked on whale and dolphin issues came at them from a different direction than I had. I had initially largely been inspired by my fascination with dolphins and whales, their possible intelligence, their evident beauty, and the fact that, as I saw it, there was no longer any need for commercial whaling, or for whales and dolphins to be killed, mostly in extremely cruel fashion, as was happening around the world. At least in the international headquarters where I worked, people generally accepted that that kind of approach wouldn't get us very far. For one thing, value judgments of that nature were highly subjective. They might play well with the media and public in Britain or Germany, but they wouldn't make a dent in countries such as Japan or Norway—the very countries where progress was most needed.

As a consequence, rather than blustering moral outrage, our campaigns were couched in more concrete terms, concentrating on such matters as population statistics and broader environmental issues. Rather than focusing merely on the fact that dolphins and whales were being killed and caught, we looked for the reasons why, to place the problems in a larger context. When we addressed the tens of thousands of dolphins being caught by tuna fisheries or in drift nets, we tried to look beyond the fact that dolphins were dying and to consider the social, political, and economic imperatives that all but obliged commercial fisheries to use such destructive technologies. When dolphins started dying in massive numbers along America's eastern seaboard, or in the Mediterranean, we did more than focus on a single pollutant or other cause that could be responsible, but instead looked at their plight as symptomatic of a marine ecosystem that had been put under too much stress by the scale of human activities.

It was challenging, fascinating, and fun. Nobody else was looking at the issues in this way, and by the end of 1990, we even had a beautifully illustrated *Greenpeace Book of Dolphins* to advance our cause. We had the definite sense that we were going places, breaking new ground, confronting preconceived notions. I met, worked, and exchanged views and opinions with Greenpeace campaigners from countries and cultures around the world. I traveled to conferences and meetings in Europe, the United States, and beyond.

But there was a downside. When I had been at the Whale and Dolphin Conservation Society, I had effectively been able to set my own agenda; work on what I wanted, when I wanted; establish policy; and talk to the media. Now I was part of a much larger organization, and although that meant the work I did was, in the long term, likely to be much more effective, I also had a lot less freedom and autonomy, and spent a lot more time writing memos and attending internal meetings than crafting articles or briefing reporters. For a creative person like me, that was frustrating.

Working for Greenpeace could also be less immediately rewarding, because the goals were that much bigger and consequently much more difficult and time-consuming to reach. At the Whale and Dolphin Conservation Society, our task had been relatively simple: keep cetacean issues in the media and the public eye. Every time a magazine published one of my articles, or I appeared on television, or a newspaper covered a topic following a lead from me or Sean, we had a sense of achievement, a visible sign of a job being done. Not that Greenpeace was shy of attracting media attention—indeed, it had made its name by courting the media more ruthlessly and effectively than any environmental organization before or since. But that was mostly the job of the national offices, which were generally extremely defensive about the folks from International muscling into their patch. Our task was more to bring about change in, and adoption of, regional and global legislation and conventions to protect cetaceans, and those were wheels that turned very slowly indeed.

Over time, I moved steadily away from working purely on cetacean issues and somehow ended up as a kind of writer-in-residence, which sounded fine in principle but in practice meant that I spent my time crafting proposals, writing interminable internal policy reviews that were swiftly forgotten, and editing fifty-page reports to correct them for grammar. This was not what I was about. I wasn't getting very much out of Greenpeace, and Greenpeace wasn't getting very much out of me. I was being wasted. By the time I had been with the organization for two years, I needed some kind of inspiration. Out of the blue, it was handed to me on a plate.

It was the chance of a lifetime, everything I could possibly have hoped for. I had been complaining that my work was dull and repetitive, that I needed a challenge. And here it was.

And yet, when Greenpeace Communications—the organization's London-based media arm—called to tell me about a planned Antarctic whaling campaign and to ask if I wanted to be the media coordinator on board, my initial response was to pass. I was too busy, I said; I had too many other things going on that I couldn't leave for three months. In reality, what I didn't want to leave for three months was my girlfriend—or, to be more honest, my soon-to-be-ex-girlfriend. Our relationship had clearly been sliding downhill for some time but, showing the obliviousness to reality characteristic of infatuation, I still believed it had a chance. Even when she announced she wanted me out of our apartment, I still refused to concede defeat; if I had one last chance, I figured, I could still make something of it. Leaving for a quarter of the year or more, especially over Christmas—even if on a heroic, whale-saving mission to the Antarctic—would make the situation hopeless.

But then, one night after work, I found myself sitting in the bar across the street from our office with my boss, Anne Dingwall. A native of British Columbia, Anne had worked for

Greenpeace for close to fifteen years, in San Francisco, Washington, and Moscow, and was now in Amsterdam, running the organization's work on oceans.

It was one of those typical September evenings in Amsterdam: dark, wet, and cold. We sat in the protective warmth of the Café de Lelie and stared at our beers.

"So," I said at length, "I was asked to go on this Antarctic trip, you know."

"Yeah," said Anne, "I know."

We looked at our beers some more.

"I said no," I said.

"Uh huh."

"I mean, the last thing I want to do right now is be on a ship bobbing around the ocean over Christmas."

"Yeah, right. Like you haven't got enough things to do."

"Yeah, right."

And there it might have stayed, if it hadn't been for another of those curious twists of fate. I wonder sometimes how different my life might have turned out if a friend of ours, a cheerful guy named J. R. Yeager, hadn't also decided to seek shelter from the wind and rain in that same bar that night. As it was, he did, and came and sat next to us. We said hello to each other and Anne and I went back to staring at our beers again.

"Say," J. R. piped up. "Do either of you guys drink Jägermeister?"

"Do I, hell!" I exclaimed. "It's a disgusting, dangerous, demon drink. Had it a couple of times, haven't touched the stuff since. Never again."

So he bought me a Jägermeister, and I drank it.

"Of course," I said to Anne, shuddering as the liqueur barged its way down my throat, "I can understand *why* I was asked to go."

"Oh sure, you're the best qualified for the job, really. But that's exactly why you've got so much else to do."

Hmm, I nodded.

Obviously, J. R. had decided the first Jägermeister had gone down too quickly. Next thing I knew, another small glass of the potent brown syrup was sitting on the bar in front of me. It was beginning to interfere with the aesthetics of the place, so I did the decent thing and drank it—and the next one that magically appeared. I blinked a couple of times, refocused my eyes, and leaned toward Anne.

"Come to think of it," I slurred, "it would be a pretty damn good idea for me to go along."

"Well, yeah. You're the best writer we've got, you've got some ship experience, and you know the issue inside out."

"Yeah!" I exclaimed, merging the two blurred images of Anne into one and waving an uncertain finger into the air. "You're right."

I don't actually remember anything after the fourth or fifth glass of Jägermeister, but the next morning, aboard a train on my way to a meeting in Brussels, I had the curious feeling that I had committed myself to something. I had a worrying, if vague, recollection of banging my fist on the bar and *demanding* to go to the Antarctic. I reassured myself with the thought that Anne must have been drinking too, so whatever I had said would probably have been forgotten. But then, of course, Anne hadn't had any Jägermeister. I began to wonder if I had fallen victim to some kind of elaborate plot.

Whether I had or not, Anne certainly hadn't forgotten. By the time I arrived in Brussels—and called Anne to see how things were going in my absence and what was new and, oh, by the way, I hadn't actually insisted on going to the Antarctic last night, had I?—plans were already being made for my involvement in the campaign.

Shortly afterward, my one remaining, feeble argument against going collapsed with a deafening crash. I had barely moved all my belongings out of the apartment I had shared with my girlfriend when someone I'd considered one of my best friends, someone who'd been the boyfriend of another of my best friends, moved in. Even I had to concede that this was not a good sign.

I had no reason to stay, and nowhere else to go. The day I returned from my trip to Brussels, I found myself standing at Walt Simpson's desk, staring at a chart of the Southern Ocean. A couple of weeks later, I was on a plane to Singapore, where I would board a ship to take me to the Antarctic.

CHAPTER TWO

South from Singapore

THE PLAN, IN PRINCIPLE, WAS SIMPLE.

The MV *Greenpeace* and its crew would be in Singapore, awaiting news that four Japanese whaling ships had left port. It would then head south to the Lombok Strait (a narrow stretch of water between the Indonesian islands of Lombok and Bali, through which the whalers pass on their way to the whaling grounds), intercept them, follow them down to the Antarctic and spend about sixty days chasing after them and attempting to stop them from killing whales.

The number of whales the fleet was planning to kill—up to 330—was not, by itself, anything like enough to threaten the Southern Ocean population of minke whales that the whalers were targeting, ostensibly for "scientific research." But that was only the tip of the iceberg. The Japanese government had made clear that its goal was to bring about a return to full-scale commercial whaling as soon as possible, allowing it to jettison its few hundred "scientific samples" in favor of a commercial quota of two or three thousand. Although an international moratorium on commercial whaling had been in effect for five years since 1986, we saw increasing signs that the resolve of some previously staunchly conservationist nations within the International Whaling Commission was beginning to weaken. We needed to strike a blow against a resurgence of the whaling industry while it still had only a toe in the door.

The Antarctic whaling grounds were a long way from the rest of the world. There would be little point in heading down there by ourselves to look for the fleet if nobody knew we were there. So we would do all we could to drum up as much publicity and media interest as possible. We wanted the presence of the *Greenpeace* in the Antarctic to call attention to the fact that whaling ships were down there also, labeling their activities scientific research but in fact doing little different from nakedly commercial whaling: they would be killing whales, cutting them up, and processing them, with the meat of those whales destined for supermarkets and restaurants in Japan where the choicest cuts would be bought and consumed as a delicacy by those who could afford them.

We would be at sea close to three months, twenty-eight of us crammed together on a thirty-two-year-old converted oceangoing tug and salvage vessel called, simply, the MV *Greenpeace*: burly and black, sturdy but slow, it measured roughly two hundred feet in length and was possessed of such an independent will in matters of maneuverability that it had earned the nickname "Black Pig." It had been in the Greenpeace fleet for six years; acquired and refitted in 1985 to take Greenpeace to Antarctica, it was pressed into service earlier than planned, and in a different part of the world, substituting for the stricken *Rainbow Warrior* in leading the peace convoy to the French nuclear test site at Moruroa.

As the *Greenpeace* approached Moruroa that September, accompanied by the other members of the flotilla, French warships had kept a close and watchful eye. The warships had instructions to ram members of the peace convoy if necessary, as they had done in the past with the *Vega*, and the French had experimented with ways of fouling the propeller of the *Green-peace*. But the *Greenpeace* was not intended to enter the exclusion zone around Moruroa; that would have invited arrest, a step Greenpeace could not afford with the expedition to Antarctica imminent.

As it happened, the *Greenpeace* was forced to head to Papeete for repairs when one of its generators broke down. French authorities refused it access to the Tahitian port, and it had no option but to return to New Zealand.

Weeks later, the ship left Auckland for the Antarctic. The goal was an ambitious one: to set up a permanent base on Antarctica, the first such undertaking by a nongovernmental organization. The purpose was to draw attention to the fact that a growing number of countries were establishing a presence in the Antarctic, in many cases damaging the fragile environment and, of yet greater concern, preparing for the possibility of opening the frozen wilderness to drilling for oil and other minerals. The mission faced critics and skeptics, inside the organization and beyond. It was too difficult, they said; setting up a base in the Antarctic—even getting through the ice to reach the continent—required knowledge, experience, planning, and logistical support of the highest order. It was just too risky.

Undaunted, Greenpeace pressed ahead with its plans. But its goals were, indeed, to be unfulfilled. The 1985–86 season saw the thickest sea ice around Antarctica in thirty years and, despite waiting several weeks for the ice to clear, the *Greenpeace* was unable to find a way through to the continent and was forced to turn back.

The following year, the *Greenpeace* tried again. This time, the Ross Sea opened up obligingly, but at one stage, as the *Green-peace* pushed through the pack ice to the southwestern edge of Ross Island where the base was to be set up, it looked as if the ship might still become trapped. Nonessential personnel were flown ashore by helicopter until the danger had passed.

But pass it did, and shortly after midnight on January 25, 1987, the ship reached McMurdo Sound and began setting up the Greenpeace base. Within weeks it was complete: a lurid yellow-green hut with "Greenpeace" emblazoned across one wall. Until, that is, the middle letters were removed one night, leaving the name "Grace"—a gesture to Grace O'Sullivan, one of the *Greenpeace* crew, who had also been aboard the *Rainbow Warrior* before it was sunk. Although later officially referred to as World Park Base, it would always, to many in Greenpeace, remain Grace Base.

The *Greenpeace* made one more expedition to Antarctica before being replaced, for the 1988–89 season, by the MV *Gondwana*, a 1,400-ton, 200-foot German-built supply vessel better suited to the thick ice of the Antarctic. The name "*Gondwana*" came from Gondwanaland, the ancient southern "supercontinent" from which Antarctica was born. The *Greenpeace* had originally been slated to receive the name, but it was ultimately rejected as too esoteric. Presumably, the world had grown more sophisticated in the intervening four years.

Relieved of its duties in the Antarctic, the *Greenpeace* proved its worth on campaigns around the world. In December 1989, it was rammed by the U.S. Navy while protesting the test of a Trident II missile. Ten months later, it was boarded by armed crew members from a KGB-operated icebreaker, objecting to Greenpeace's opposition to Soviet nuclear testing in the Arctic. In early 1991, the *Greenpeace* returned to the Arctic for a campaign against overfishing in the Barents Sea, before heading south, via Amsterdam, to Spain and then on to the Persian Gulf for a grueling two-month tour monitoring the environmental impacts of the war that followed Iraq's invasion of Kuwait. From there, it sailed through the Suez Canal toward southeast Asia until October 1991, when it made its way to Singapore and wound up tucked away in some God-forsaken dockyard in the southeast of nowhere. It was an inauspicious place from which to start.

Entrance to the lounge on the *Greenpeace* was through either of two doors, one on the port and one on the starboard side, each taking the entrant down a small set of tributary steps and in turn to a wide main staircase that led into the lounge proper. The stairs were unnecessarily grand, like a truncated piece of scenery from *Titanic*, a legacy of the ship's previous incarnation as a kind of floating hotel for pilots who guided ships into port. The *Greenpeace* remained a comfortable ship, but the trappings of luxury were long since gone. Directly ahead of the stairs stood an unadorned round table encircled by a half-dozen chairs; ahead and to the left, a collection of old armchairs and sofas sat in front of a television set and several rows of books haphazardly stacked on shelves, the whole scene looking not unlike, in the memorable words of a visiting journalist, a student squat.

We hauled our gear up the gangway and into the lounge and stood at the bottom of the stairs surveying the scene in front of us. A large, irate German took one look at the suitcases, camera bags, computers, and video equipment that had suddenly taken over half of the lounge and turned to us with a piercing look.

"Fucking Jesus!" exclaimed the German, who was Hanno, the ship's bosun. "How many of you are there?"

Six, we told him.

"Six? *Six?* Fucking Jesus. You have enough luggage for fifteen. Where you going to put it? This is fucking small ship."

We pointed out that the collection included a lot of computer and photographic equipment that we needed to do our work for the next few months. We couldn't exactly leave it behind. Hanno wasn't impressed.

"We have computer on board already, we have camera. Here, on board, now. Why you need more?"

He waddled off to find us some cabins, muttering as he went, leaving us all sweating quietly in the Singapore heat. But upsetting Hanno had its advantages. Eager to confine as many of our excessive belongings as possible to one part of the ship, he put the four of us with the most equipment—photographer Robin Culley, video cameraman Alex de Waal, logistics coordinator Athel von Koettlitz, and me, the media coordinator—in one of the ship's largest cabins, a six-berth on the lower deck. Secreted in the bowels of the ship, it was without natural light and possessed only the most rudimentary air circulation. But it was large, with its own washbasin and a table where I immediately set up my computer. Perhaps most importantly, being below the waterline and positioned roughly amidships, it would likely be the most stable place in times of rough weather.

In the ship's pre-Greenpeace incarnation this cabin had been the crew mess, and sealed somewhere behind a wall there remained the dumbwaiter that carried food down from the galley. At one stage after Greenpeace took charge, it had been used as the campaign office, but that function had recently been moved to the forecastle deck; one explanation, possibly apocryphal, was that when the *Greenpeace* went to the Gulf, the campaigners felt it might be safer to have their office above the waterline.

As I unpacked my bags and looked for linen for my bunk, I began to wonder just what I was doing here. Narrow beds, communal bathrooms, fixed mealtimes: it reminded me too much of boarding school. I had hated boarding school, especially having to share what I considered my private space with a bunch of other people I wouldn't normally have even passed the time of day with. I hadn't much enjoyed sharing a group house, either, and now here I was committing myself to the ultimate group-house experience, with twenty-seven other people and, worse, once we left Singapore, not a hope of ever being able to leave. I thought of Amsterdam, of my new, girlfriend-less apartment, of my friends. I pictured them sitting in cozy bars, sheltered from the cold, dark winter evenings, or walking along the canals.

Everybody else on board, it seemed, already had a job to do, knew where and how to do it, and pretty much knew each other. Me, I needed time to get my bearings. I was too shy and uncertain of my position to force my way into things, so for the first few days I decided to blend into the background, watching how people interacted and how things were done. I made mental lists of the people I'd spoken to and those I hadn't, and found myself imagining which of them would turn out to be my closest friends on the voyage ahead and with whom, if anyone, I'd end up butting heads.

Fortunately, I wasn't entirely among strangers. A couple of the crew who were scheduled to arrive in the next couple of weeks had been with me on board another Greenpeace ship, the *Sirius*, when I'd been part of a campaign against French drift nets earlier in the year. And there was Athel, and Naoko.

Athel von Koettlitz was thirty-eight years old, a self-taught engineer by trade, a well-built, slightly brooding, and deliberately mysterious Englishman with a wealth of Greenpeace experience. Thirteen years previously, he'd been kicking around London, not doing much, when a friend asked him if he would help check out an old trawler that Greenpeace wanted to purchase. Athel inspected it, Greenpeace bought it, Athel helped refurbish and refit it. A few months afterward, he was heading for Iceland, taking part in the inaugural anti-whaling campaign of what was now the *Rainbow Warrior*.

A couple of years later he was aboard the *Warrior* again, this time to confront whalers from Spain, when the Spanish navy decided to intervene. The *Warrior* was impounded and kept under twenty-four-hour guard at the naval base of El Ferrol. Athel and two others managed to take off in the ship's long-range inflatable and, after a harrowing five-hundred-mile chase across the Bay of Biscay, made it to the island of Jersey in the English Channel. A couple of months later, Athel and six others stole back the ship itself, sneaking it away one night under the navy's nose.

In the ensuing years, Athel tied himself to the stern of a Peruvian whaler, drove a Greenpeace truck from Amsterdam to Moscow, and went with Greenpeace to Antarctica. Now he was the man who, as he put it, was in charge of "making it all happen." His official title was logistics coordinator, but in effect, Athel had largely put the expedition together. He had been involved in administering the budget, hiring the crew, making sure the *Greenpeace* was supplied with the right amount of fuel and carried the necessary equipment for actions and for battling the Antarctic elements. On board, it was his responsibility to make sure that actions were organized, boat crews trained, the captain and mates fully apprised of the campaign team's plans. Athel carried an air of world-weariness, of having "been there and done that," which some on board, understandably resentful of any implied slight to their abilities or expertise, took as unjustified arrogance. But he was more sensitive than his demeanor suggested, and I came to rely on him as a good friend, ally, and drinking mate during the voyage.

Ultimate authority, however, rested in the apparently unassuming person in the cabin next to us. At first glance, Naoko Funahashi gave every impression of living up to the average Westerner's stereotype of a Japanese woman: small, slight, and deeply introverted. But even the slightest scratch of the surface revealed a far more complex and formidable personality. Naoko was a nonconformer, from the most rigorously conformist of societies. Not only had she resisted her parents' admonitions to do the proper female thing—namely, marry a nice, successful man and bear his children—in favor of leading an independent life, but the life she was leading was that of an activist, and an anti-whaling activist at that. It was a role that required amazing inner strength and resolve. For most of us, opposing commercial whaling was no great hardship—indeed, identifying yourself as an anti-whaling campaigner for Greenpeace in the Netherlands was a sure-fire way to get on the good side of the average cab driver or police officer—but, at least in the eyes of the fisheries elite who promoted Japan's whaling policy, Naoko and her comrades were traitors. She regularly had to withstand abuse, mockery, and accusations of being a dupe of Western, anti-Japanese interests.

Athel, Naoko, and I constituted the core campaign team. Between us, we were responsible for our individual elements: Naoko, overall strategy and policy; Athel, implementing the actions when we were in range of the whaling fleet; and me, doing what I could to secure the widest possible coverage of our actions in the world's media. As the expedition's leaders, we were the ones who had to make Greenpeace's investment pay off; we decided where the ship went, what we did when we got there, and when we did it.

But no leaders of any ship-bound expedition, with Greenpeace or otherwise, are in charge to the extent that they like to think they are. We could theorize and direct all we wanted, but it would count for nothing if we couldn't engage the crew and persuade them of the rightness of our cause and the practicality of our plans. Figuratively and literally, we were all in the same boat, facing the same challenges and difficulties. But however much we might want to blur the boundaries, a definite division existed between campaigners and crew.

Crew on Greenpeace ships are generally multinational (ours included seven Britons, six Germans, five Americans, three Dutch, two Swedes, two Japanese, one Irish, one Canadian, and a skipper from New Zealand) and tend to serve for three or four months at a time, their terms overlapping with each other so that there is generally a regular carousel of new and departing members. During those few months, most crews see a number of campaigns come and go, with a campaigner or two jetting in from some office to take up residence on board for anything from a few days to a couple of weeks. For the crew, campaigners can be both a blessing and a curse. On the one hand, if everyone is lucky, the campaign is interesting and productive. On the other, far too few campaigners, from the crew's perspective, fit in well on board, often choosing to bring the secrecy and hierarchy of their office work onto the ship with them, not sharing plans or information with anyone except the captain and rarely trying to enter into the group dynamic.

Our expedition was obviously going to be different from most, in that campaigners and crew had all joined at the same time and would be together on board for several months. But the division would still be there: the crew would be looking after routine duties on the ship, working in shifts in the wheelhouse or galley, on deck or in the engine room, while the campaign team enjoyed much more fluid hours, eschewing "real" work to sit at computers drafting briefings and updates, or talking over the plans for finding and taking on the whalers. If the expedition was going to succeed over the long haul, our relationship with the crew was of paramount importance: we would have to play a full part in ship life, and keep everyone on board as involved and informed in decision-making as possible.

Even then, the ship wasn't going anywhere, or the crew doing anything, unless the captain agreed to it. In our case, that was Bob Graham. A New Zealander in his mid-forties, Bob was a veteran sea dog who regarded Greenpeace campaigners with a mixture of suspicion and contempt. His expressive face could break into a wide, leering grin and almost immediately return to its more natural scowl. He could be charming and friendly one minute, then for no apparent reason start cussing and insulting you with the best Kiwi vocabulary he could muster. His dark moods had earned him the sobriquet "Black Bob"; but he enjoyed intelligent conversation, especially over a stiff drink. He also loved the sea and its wildlife, particularly the albatross, petrels, and other birds that keep a ship company on long ocean voyages. Most of all, he loved Antarctica. He had first sailed to the Antarctic almost twenty years before, had been there virtually every year since, and had been on all the Greenpeace Antarctic expeditions bar one.

"I can honestly say Antarctica changed my life," he said to me over dinner one night. "It possesses you, that place, keeps drawing you back, year after year." He paused, fixed me in the eye, and broke into one of his wide, knowing grins. "I'll tell you something: the twenty-eight people who leave on this trip aren't going to be the same ones who come back."

For weeks we sat in Singapore, first in a beat-up old dockyard in the middle of nowhere, then at an anchorage near the Tiger Balm Gardens and, more importantly to us, a dockside bar called Seafood 88. The paltry air conditioning on board couldn't cope with the humid heat of the tropics, and the stale air induced headaches and sleepless nights. Afternoon naps brought on strange, surreal waking dreams and pillows drenched with sweat. All the time, we waited—for old crew to leave, for new ones to arrive, and, most of all, for news about the whaling fleet.

Information was almost nonexistent. We knew only that the *Nisshin Maru No. 3*, the fleet's factory ship, was almost certainly somewhere around Yokohama and that the catchers were probably farther south, in their home port of Shimonoseki. We could guess, but had no way of knowing, exactly when they would leave port, and could only hope that we would find out about it once they had departed. Naoko had heard unconfirmed reports that the whalers might not even be using the aging *Nisshin Maru No. 3* at all, but a new converted factory trawler instead. If that were the case, there was no guarantee that her spies would be able to pick out an unfamiliar ship from all the other trawlers and fishing vessels in the crowded harbor, and we'd have only the hope that the fisheries newspapers in Japan would report the news when the whaling ship left port.

The weather and the waiting combined to bring out tensions: Athel annoyed Naoko, first by calling a campaign meeting at 2000* every evening and then by missing two of the first three because he was out drinking. In response, Naoko annoyed Athel by refusing to come to any of the others and, when Athel arranged a crew briefing for a Friday evening, unilaterally deciding to move it to the next day.

People were bugged by the smallest things: doors being left open, empty beer cans left on the table, milk not put in the refrigerator, meat eaters depleting the stock of "vegetarians only" food. Nothing serious, really, and all part of the shake-down process. By and large, everyone was getting on well. But it was becoming painfully clear that we all needed to get away from Singapore, get out to sea, and get on with our mission.

---

* Ship's time is kept by the twenty-four-hour clock. Morning hours from midnight to midday are expressed as 0000, 0100, 0200, and so on, all the way to 1200. Afternoon and evening hours from midday to midnight are written as 1300, 1400, 1500, and so on. If a number is greater than 1200, it is after midday but before midnight; if you're having trouble figuring out what time it is, subtract 1200. So, for example, 1730 is 5:30 P.M. (1730−1200=5:30).

All we could do in the meantime was to keep ourselves occupied. I put together briefings for the crew and for Greenpeace offices, and started keeping a journal. Alex, Robin, Athel, and I decorated our cabin, stringing up Christmas lights and pinning a huge decorative fan on the wall. After all, if we were going to spend the best part of four months together in this dark, windowless room, we might as well do our best to make it seem something like home.

When we finally began receiving information about the whalers' whereabouts, it was profoundly contradictory. The catchers were in Shimonoseki, the catchers weren't in Shimonoseki; they were, but Naoko's contact couldn't see them. The *Nisshin Maru No. 3* had been sold to China for scrap; it was in Yokohama, ready to leave for the Antarctic. Finally, on November 11, Naoko received some solid news. The catchers had been seen, freshly painted, in Shimoneseki, and the *Nisshin Maru No. 3* had been spotted in Yokosuka harbor. According to the port authorities, the factory ship would be leaving on the 14th.

We held an impromptu meeting of the campaign team and Bob. As I went to look for Patricia Becher-Ketterer, our campaign assistant, I bumped into one of the crew and discovered the first rule of life on Greenpeace ships: news travels faster than light.

"So what's this I hear, Kieran? Is it true we know where the ships are now?"

I gave a stalling answer, but told the rest of the campaign team that we needed to have a crew meeting as soon as possible. We agreed on a time, and I wrote it on the blackboard. Two other crew members stood watching me.

"What's the meeting about?" they asked. "To tell us that the *NM3* has been found and that it'll probably leave on the 14th?"

Bob did some quick arithmetic, based on the factory ship's likely cruising speed and the amount of time it would take us to get to a point south of the Lombok Strait where we could intercept the fleet. He figured that if the *Nisshin Maru No. 3* left for the Antarctic on the 14th, we would need to depart on the 19th or 20th.

I was waiting for Julia Roberts. We had made a date at a party held by Jane Fonda and Al Gore to honor our return from saving whales. Now I was lying on my bed in my hotel room. There came a knock on the door, and a soft female voice.

"Hello?"

I opened my eyes. It was the afternoon of the 14th, it was hot, I was on a narrow bunk on a ship in Singapore, my pillow was sodden with sweat, and Naoko was not doing a very good impersonation of Julia Roberts. She blinked her eyes and tilted her head, looking at me inquisitively.

"News," she announced. "*Nisshin Maru No. 3* left Yokosuka for Antarctic at eleven-thirty this morning."

I gave her a thumbs-up sign, then let my head fall back onto the pillow. A short while later, she returned.

"More news. It is not the *Nisshin Maru No. 3*. It is another ship, also called *Nisshin Maru*, but much smaller: 7,200 tons. Problem is, Bob believes she can go much faster than us. Maybe fourteen knots."

This was not the kind of news any of us wanted to hear. If we didn't know what the new ship looked like, it could conceivably sail straight past us as we waited for it and we wouldn't even know. If it traveled at fourteen knots, that made it a good three or four knots faster than the old factory ship—and, more importantly, a couple of knots faster than our top speed. At that kind of speed, it might make it to Lombok before we could get there, outrun us on the chase south to the Antarctic, or escape us in the whaling grounds. Even if we could keep it in sight, the extra fuel expended in trying to match its speed might force us to head home after only about thirty days instead of the scheduled eighty.

At dinner, the nervousness brought on by the news showed clearly. I fiddled with the contents of an ashtray before moving on to the slightly less disgusting target of an empty cigarette packet. Robin ran his finger slowly around the edge of a glass. Athel just stared into space.

The following day, a photo of the new *Nisshin Maru* was faxed to us from Japan. It was included in a long newspaper article about the fleet. The ship was a four-year-old converted stern trawler, formerly called the *Chikuzen Maru*. We asked contacts in Auckland and Amsterdam to see what they could find out about it. Early returns suggested the *NM* might have a *cruising* speed of fourteen knots, a couple of knots faster than our very best. But then it seemed that fourteen knots might be its *top* speed; if that were true, given that it would be heavily laden with fuel for the long voyage ahead, it might prove slower still. All, it seemed, was not yet lost. Nonetheless, just to be absolutely certain that we would arrive at Lombok in time, we decided to leave Singapore on November 18, a day or two earlier than planned.

The next few days were a rash of activity as we stocked up on everything we would need for the long journey ahead—culminating, on the morning of departure, with the arrival of the food stores. We worked hard to find places for all our provisions, but with limited success: many boxes remained scattered around the ship, cluttering the hallways and blocking the doors.

At three o'clock, Athel and I were standing at the bottom of the stairs to the bridge when Bob arrived, a mug of coffee in his hand.

"We're all on board," said Athel. "We're all set."

"Right," said Bob, a grin spreading over his face. "Let's go to Antarctica."

A few hours after we set sail, Alex, Robin, and I were sitting in the cabin when Athel came in with some news.

"According to a newspaper report, they plan to hit the whaling grounds on December 4. The *Nisshin Maru* will meet up with the catchers at a point two hundred miles south of Lombok, and that journey will take 'about a week.' In other words, they're going bloody fast and they're going to burn us off. We haven't a hope."

He climbed quietly into his bunk. The rest of us sat in silence.

As evening fell, I stood out on the bridge wing, feeling the wind in my face and watching the *Greenpeace* cut effortlessly through the waves.

Bob appeared, mug in hand as usual.

We looked out at the calm sea, the water turning silver in the evening light. Bob sipped his coffee.

"So the *Nisshin Maru*'s going to outrun us after all?" I asked.

"The way I see it," he replied, "there are three basic choices. The campaign has to make some hard decisions. It depends on how much you lot want to gamble." He smiled and went back into his cabin.

Later, Bob met with the campaign team. "According to these dates," he told us, "the *Nisshin Maru* is going to be doing a steady thirteen knots all the way down. To match that, we'd have to use both engines at virtually full power for the ten days from Lombok to the Antarctic, and even then they'll get away from us."

The *Greenpeace* was an old ship and nobody, he pointed out, had ever used both engines for that length of time. Even if the ship could stand the strain, the effort would double our fuel consumption and cut down the amount of time we could spend in the whaling grounds.

As Bob saw it, we could press on with our original plan anyway—intercept the *Nisshin Maru* at Lombok and hope we could shadow it and the catchers on the long chase down to the Antarctic without using up too much fuel. We could head directly for the point where the factory ship and the catchers were expected to meet. Or we could take a chance, jettison the plan of intercepting them en route, and head straight for the whaling grounds to wait for them there.

Athel and I had liked the idea of meeting the *Nisshin Maru* at Lombok because it would provide a perfect opportunity to kick off the whole voyage with an action. As the factory ship came barreling toward us, we could string our inflatables across its path and deploy a banner calling on the fleet to stop and turn back. We'd be able to send out footage and photos of the meeting, and the chase past the Australian coast down to the Antarctic would probably play for days in the region's media. But if the fleet was traveling at twelve knots or more, an action would be difficult. Besides, even if we did find them easily and did pull off an action, it would hardly make for good media images if we were then left bobbing around helplessly in the whalers' wake as they sped away over the horizon.

Meeting them at the rendezvous point wasn't really an option: we didn't know precisely where it was, and conditions several hundred miles out to sea were likely to make an action difficult. Which left us looking at abandoning our original plans altogether and heading straight to the Antarctic to search for the fleet there. The risks were huge: we were no longer talking in terms of picking them up in a relatively small area of water reasonably close to land, but of hoping to miraculously guess the most likely spot amid a million square miles of open ocean. It would be like being deposited in California and told to find a group of four cars that was somewhere west of the Mississippi. And even if we did find them, they might well outrun us. Still, if they were going to outrun us, it might as well happen in the Antarctic as a few miles south of the equator. At least that way they wouldn't be forewarned of our presence, and the fuel we'd save would allow us to stay in the whaling grounds longer.

We took a deep, collective breath. This was going to be a huge shot in the dark, a lot less certain than our original plans. But circumstances had changed, and we had little choice but to play the hand that had been dealt us. We agreed to consider the decision overnight, but there wasn't really that much to think over. The next morning we all agreed: we'd head straight for the Antarctic.

That first morning at sea was bright, and the sea so calm it was like sailing across glass. Flying fish leapt out of our path, scuttling along the surface of the water on their tails. Jellyfish and sea snakes lazed at the surface. At 0830, with a blast of the whistle, we crossed the equator.

And so we made our way south. Because the area south of Indonesia was known as pirate country, each night saw an extra person on watch, patrolling the deck and looking out for possible bandits. Patricia set up a whale-watching project so that anyone could fill a spare hour or two with time on Monkey Island (the area atop the bridge) or up in the crow's nest, looking for whales and noting the results in a log.

Being at sea seemed to lift everybody's spirits. The sea and sky were both clear and blue, and the cooling sea breeze compensated for the scorching sun. Thom Looney, the overly caffeinated radio operator, bounced around singing "Summer Holiday." The song was appropriate, except that instead of driving around Spain in a bus, we were heading to the Antarctic in a battered old chugalug tug. Even Hanno was in a jovial mood, wandering into the wheelhouse during watch one morning and making a beeline for the glass in Robin's hand.

"Vodka?" he beamed, eyes sparkling.

"Coconut juice," corrected Robin, "with water."

"No shot? Paaah!" He waved his hand dismissively. "Water is for fish and for dogs. Fish are fucking in water, so I never drink it."

The previous night, Hanno had held court at dinner out on the poop deck. It had been a perfect evening: the sun was setting, the moon was full. Dolphins played off the stern. A weary bee-eater alighted on the stern railing before struggling to the banner line. Someone strummed on a guitar, and Athel played his didgeridu. I half-expected to see a rainbow suddenly appear and a flock of doves fly past.

On the morning of November 22, we passed through the Lombok Strait and left Indonesia behind us. We would not see any more land for seventy-seven days.

If we couldn't stage any kind of token blockade at Lombok, I figured we might as well try to go one better. The northern limit of the whaling areas was 55 degrees South; if we could work out where on that line the fleet would enter the whaling grounds, we could sit there and wait for them, perhaps hide behind an iceberg until the last possible moment and then emerge, deploy the inflatables, and block their path. If they wanted to enter the whaling grounds, we'd tell them, they'd have to come past us first.

All of which sounded fine on paper. But we had to figure out where their entry point was likely to be. The area stretched from 70°E, east to 130°E, and from 55°S south to the ice edge— a lot of water to cover, roughly equivalent in area to one-third of the contiguous United States. John Frizell, the coordinator of Greenpeace's whaling campaigns worldwide and the person who'd be providing us with ideas and information throughout the voyage, sent us some details:

> The survey area is stratified into three zones:
>
>   1. North (55S to 60S)
>   2. Middle (60S to 45 nautical miles from ice edge)
>   3. South (within 45nm of ice edge)
>
> Last time, they spent a total of only 5 days in the North Zone, two on arriving and three when leaving.
>
>   They spent 42 days in the South Zone and 31 days in the Middle Zone.

As far as John could deduce, the last time the whalers were in this particular area, they turned south from 60S to a point on the 100E line that was close to the likely ice edge. So we figured our best chance of finding them was to head south down 100E to the ice, and wait for them there.

On December 2, we reached the Antarctic Convergence—the biological boundary of the Antarctic, where the waters of the temperate zone clash with the cold polar currents. As if passing

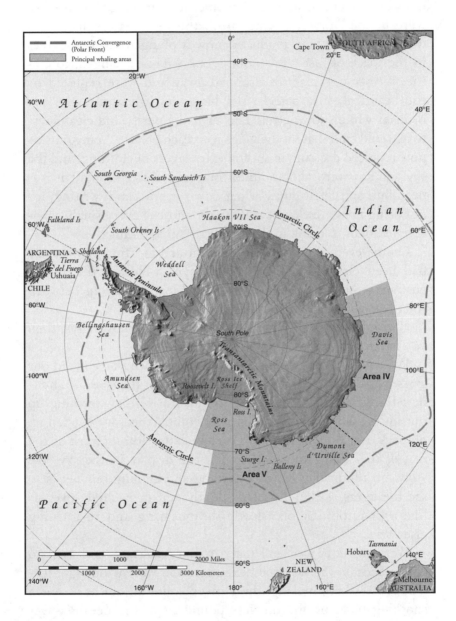

Legend:
- - - - Antarctic Convergence (Polar Front)
☐ Principal whaling areas

Atlantic Ocean

Indian Ocean

Pacific Ocean

Cape Town   SOUTH AFRICA

0°
20°W
40°W
60°W
80°W
100°W
120°W
140°W
160°W
180°
160°E
140°E
120°E
100°E
80°E
60°E
40°E
20°E

40°S
50°S
60°S
70°S
80°S

South Georgia   South Sandwich Is
Falkland Is
South Orkney Is
Haakon VII Sea
Antarctic Circle

ARGENTINA   S. Shetland Is
Tierra del Fuego
Ushuaia
CHILE
Antarctic Peninsula
Weddell Sea

Bellingshausen Sea
South Pole
Davis Sea

Amundsen Sea
Roosevelt I.   Ross Ice Shelf
Transantarctic Mountains
Area IV

Ross I.
Ross Sea
Sturge I.   Balleny Is
Dumont d'Urville Sea
Area V

Tasmania
Hobart
NEW ZEALAND
Melbourne
AUSTRALIA

0   1000   2000 Miles
0   1000   2000   3000 Kilometers

through some kind of border crossing, we disappeared into a mass of fog and mist; when we emerged on the other side, we were in the Antarctic. Until now, the temperature had been dropping steadily but gradually; now it plunged several degrees in the space of just a few hours. The wildlife changed, too, as the warm-water seabirds dropped away and were replaced by the beautiful, tiny petrels: the black-and-white pintado, the brilliant white snow petrel. The air had a purity and cleanliness to it, a cold chill that hit the lungs with each breath. Going outside now required dressing in several extra layers of clothing, and the sky and sea were almost uniformly gray. But I thought it was beautiful, and I felt guilty when down in my cabin writing, for not being up on deck, not making the most of every single available moment to drink in the Antarctic surroundings.

On the evening of the 3rd, I mentioned to Athel that the sky had been clear all day and that maybe we'd see the aurora australis—the "southern lights," caused by interactions between solar particles and the upper atmosphere.

"If you're going to see aurora," said Athel knowingly, "then you have to have a shot or two first."

We poured ourselves a couple of shots of whisky, clinked our glasses, and threw the golden liquid down our throats. We shuddered a little and had another round, the whisky warming up our insides as it slid down. Suitably emboldened, we headed up on deck, not bothering to put on any extra clothing, just as the rest of the ship gathered to watch the display in the sky. We stood on the bridge wings, shivering and craning our necks to see the lights as they hovered silently and menacingly over us like a phantom, before slowly disappearing and re-forming elsewhere.

We were now well and truly in the Antarctic, and as if to commemorate the fact, the next afternoon we saw our first iceberg. It was breathtaking: three caves hollowed out of it, one a shocking blue, by the timeless pounding of the ocean; waves crashing over its base; and so tall we could hardly see the top for the low-slung clouds that sprinkled snow over us as we stood out on deck to gaze in awe. Even Bob, grizzled veteran of count-less Antarctic vistas, had to admit that, for a first berg, it "wasn't bad."

At 2130 on the evening of the 5th, we reached the ice edge. The cloud line curled steadily away from the horizon, and ahead we could see a white glow—known as "ice blink"—as the light of the setting sun reflected off the ice. As we drew closer, the indistinct haze separated itself into sea and sky, and the ice edge itself—small, loose pieces of brash ice, rising and falling with the gently undulating waves—emerged from the mist. Some penguins porpoised through the water off the starboard bow. As we cruised along, the temperature dropped below freezing. The wind that came screaming off the ice sliced through us, numbing our fingers and faces and making it feel fifteen or twenty degrees colder.

We were a long, long way from anywhere, all alone. It was like the end of the world.

CHAPTER THREE

Life and Death at the End of the Earth

SINGAPORE WAS HALF A WORLD AND FIFTY DEGREES FAHRENHEIT behind us. We were surrounded by icebergs and enveloped in a thin gray mist. Were it not for the knowledge that the whaling fleet was just a couple of days over the horizon, we might have imagined ourselves the most isolated people on Earth.

If we didn't qualify for that title, our location at least put us in the running. Antarctica is, among other superlatives, the most distant of all continents: the nearest landmass, South America, is 450 miles across the dangerous Drake Passage from the relatively northerly archipelago known as the Antarctic Peninsula; but more representative of Antarctica's isolation is its distance from other neighbors—1,500 miles from Australia, 2,500 from Africa.

Surrounding the continent is a ring of sea ice—literally, the frozen surface of the sea. The extent of sea ice varies from season to season, year to year; on average, in summer, it covers about 1.5 million square miles, expanding in winter to encompass five times that area. Beyond the sea ice, the Southern Ocean is a swirling mass of wind, waves, and an almost constant parade of low-pressure systems that have earned it a reputation as perhaps the fiercest and least hospitable of all the world's seas.

The Antarctic's remoteness and its fearsome conditions conspired to keep humans away from its forbidding frozen expanse for most of recorded history, but it was the subject of speculation and pontification for millennia before, on January 17, 1773, Captain James Cook finally crossed the Antarctic Circle—the line of longitude south of which the sun does not set at the height of summer nor rise in midwinter.

Aristotle had been perhaps the first to propose Antarctica's existence, on the grounds that the northern landmass that surrounded the Mediterranean Sea had to be counterbalanced by one to the south. Certainly, he was the first to bestow upon it its present moniker, offering that as the land to the north lay beneath the constellation of Arktos, the bear, so this southern realm must be the opposite—*Antarktikos*. About five hundred years later, Ptolemy asserted that this southern part of the world was fertile and populous. But as the Greek tradition of knowledge and learning gave way to clouds of dogma, and Earth was deemed to be flat rather than spherical, speculation on the Antarctic's existence—let alone the prospect of its being inhabited by people who by the nature of their isolation "shared neither the sin of Adam nor the redemption of Christ"—was declared a heresy. Only centuries later did voyages of exploration begin to part the veil of ignorance over the southern realm. By the late sixteenth century, some of these voyages, such as those by Ferdinand Magellan and Francis Drake, reached the tip of South America, and in the seventeenth century, Dutch seaman Abel Tasman sailed south of Australia and discovered the island, Tasmania, that now bears his name. On occasion, some of these expeditions found their ships blown yet farther south by violent storms; the reports they brought back were invariably of "prodigious seas" and "islands of ice," of winds that "were such as if the bowels of the earth had set all at liberty," and waves that "were rowled up from the depths." And yet, despite such consistently negative assessments, there persisted a belief in Ptolemy's vision of a fertile, populated paradise.

If Cook's voyage was dispatched in pursuit of this Shangri-La, it definitively dashed any hopes of its existence. Cook was not able to reach the continent itself; thick pack ice prevented that. But he saw enough to provide a bleak review of the region's prospects: "Thick fogs, Snow storms, Intense Cold and every other thing that can render Navigation dangerous one has to encounter and these difficulties are greatly heightened by the inexpressible horrid aspect of the Country, a Country doomed by Nature never once to feel the warmth of the suns rays, but to lie for ever buried under everlasting snow and ice."

Toward the end of Cook's expedition, the explorers had a brief surge of enthusiasm and optimism when their ships encountered land in the southernmost reaches of the South Atlantic. Perhaps, finally, they had found the fabled southern continent after all? Alas, no. It proved to be an island, dubbed South Georgia, and Cook was as dismissive of it as he was of the region as a whole. "The Wild rocks raised their lofty summits till they were lost in the Clouds," he wrote, "and the vallies laid buried in everlasting Snow. Not a tree or shrub was to be seen, not even big enough to make a tooth-pick."

But if Cook's damning observations laid to rest the notion of tropical bounty to be had in the Antarctic, they hinted at riches of a different kind. The seas and beaches of South Georgia, noted Cook, were host to huge numbers of fur seals. "The shores," he wrote, "swarmed with young cubs."

Within years, American and British sealing ships had descended on the island, seeking bounty for the rich fur trade. In 1800, twenty-six years after the hitherto all-but-undisturbed island had been visited by Cook, British and American sealers killed 122,000 seals over a period of just four months. One vessel alone, the *Aspasia*, sailed for home with the pelts of 57,000 seals in its hold. Twenty-two years later, sealing captain James Weddell estimated that "not less than 1 million 200 thousand seals" had been killed on the island in just a few decades. "These animals," he wrote, "are now almost extinct."

But that was no immediate problem for the sealers, because exploitation was fueling exploration, and vice versa: the discovery of more coastal areas and islands prompted new floods of sealers, who in turn found new lands with yet more populations of fur seals, ripe for exploitation. Where the populations of South Georgia had led the way, so others followed: four years after the discovery of the South Shetland Islands in 1819, British and American sealers had killed more than 300,000 of the islands' fur seals. Only another six years had gone by when W. H. B. Webster, surgeon on board the HMS *Chanticleer*, wrote, "The harvest of the seas has been so effectually reaped, that not a single fur seal was seen by us during our visit to the South Shetland group; and although it is but a few years back since countless multitudes covered the shores, the ruthless spirit of barbarism slaughtered young and old alike, so as to destroy the race."

Within a matter of decades, it was all but over. When the smoke lifted, around three million fur seals and one million elephant seals had died, including pups unable to survive after their mothers had been killed.

Once the industry had exhausted itself with the scale of its slaughter, interest in the Antarctic waned and a kind of calm returned to the area. But it was not to last for long. In the early years of the twentieth century, a new wave of humanity descended on Antarctica and the Southern Ocean. Part of that wave was the so-called "Heroic Age" of Antarctic exploration: men such as Roald Amundsen, Robert Falcon Scott, and Ernest Shackleton, whose efforts to combat the fiercest of elements in pursuit of geographical and scientific knowledge, personal gain, and national glory have become engraved in history. But others, far greater in number, came, like the sealers before them, in search of commercial profit. They were looking for whales.

There are approximately eighty species of whales, dolphins, and porpoises in the world. The agreed-upon number regularly fluctuates, as taxonomists debate whether one recognized species should in fact be two (or two species contracted to one), and as new species continue to be identified, even in the twenty-first century. Collectively, these eighty-or-so species are members of the mammalian order known as cetaceans, in the same way that humans, the great apes, monkeys, and lemurs are collectively known as primates. Although they live in the sea (or, in the case of some dolphin species, rivers and estuaries), they are not, as Herman Melville once opined, "spouting fish with a horizontal tail," but mammals, like us: they are warm-blooded; they must come to the surface to breathe air; and they give birth to live young that suckle their mothers.

Cetacean nomenclature can be confusing. Some species of "whale"—specifically, pilot whales and killer whales—are in fact large dolphins. Many Americans refer to all dolphins generically as "porpoises," whereas that name is more properly reserved for six, mostly coastal, species of small size (not more than eight feet, and sometimes as little as four and a half feet), with snub noses and spade-shaped teeth. (Hawaiian restaurants that list "dolphin" on their menu are in fact offering a fish, the so-called dolphin-fish, otherwise known as dorado or mahimahi.)

Scientific classification offers greater clarity. Cetaceans are essentially divided into two principal groups, or suborders. Most species are in one group, the odontocetes, or toothed whales. The odontocetes include some of the most familiar of cetacean species, such as the bottlenose dolphin (star of dolphin shows and *Flipper*); the aforementioned killer whale, or orca; the sperm whale; and the bizarre narwhal, the "unicorn of the seas," males of which sport a long, spiraled tusk up to ten feet in length. They include, also, the least familiar of all: the elusive and little-known beaked whales, some species of which have never been seen alive and are known only from skulls or carcasses washed up on the shore. It is the beaked whales that, more than any others, continue to contribute to the total known number of cetacean species; the most recent find was made in 2002, following DNA analysis of marine mammals that had washed ashore along the California coast.

The distinguishing feature of the other group, the mysticetes or baleen whales, is that they have no teeth; instead, hanging from their upper jaws are large plates of baleen—commonly known as whalebone, but in fact made from keratin, the same substance as in our fingernails. The baleen plates act as sieves: the whales take giant mouthfuls of water and force them out through the baleen, which traps the microscopic organisms known as plankton on which mysticetes primarily—or, depending on the species, almost exclusively—feed. Baleen whales are massive; with the exception of the sperm whale, which tips the scales at an impressive forty-five tons and reaches more than fifty feet in length, none of the odontocetes comes close in size to the largest of the baleen whales. Even the very smallest mysticete, the pygmy right whale, which is smaller than several beaked and bottlenose whales and the orca, is, at roughly twenty feet and four tons, comparable in size to the largest land animal, the African elephant. The blue whale, the largest of the baleen whales—indeed, the largest animal ever to have lived on Earth—is so big that that same elephant could fit on its tongue.

Baleen whales have borne the brunt of commercial whaling through the centuries. Although other toothed cetaceans have been, or still are, hunted around the world, caught in fishing nets (sometimes in huge numbers), or facing some other environmental impacts, only the sperm whale (and, to a lesser extent, two species of beaked whales) has been subject to prolonged pursuit by the whaling industry. In contrast, every single baleen-bearing species, with the exception of the aforementioned pygmy right, has been relentlessly persecuted, often to the point of extirpation of individual populations or even, in at least one case—the Atlantic gray whale—outright extinction.

It is not known for certain when the first commercial whaling enterprise was established, but credit—or blame—is generally given to the Basques, a seagoing people of indeterminate origin who inhabited the Bay of Biscay region, straddling what is now the border of France and Spain. At some stage around the year 1000 c.e., the Basques began systematically hunting a species of whale that was considered the "right" whale to hunt because it swam slowly and close to shore, contained plenty of oil, and obligingly floated at the surface when killed. It is still known as the right whale today.

It is uncertain how many right whales the Basques hunted. Some authors have suggested that each of the villages from which whaling was conducted took only two or three whales a year, which would not have been enough to deplete the population. Perhaps, then, they killed greater numbers, or perhaps the mere act of whaling was enough to disturb the whales and force them to move elsewhere; either way, within a few centuries, right whales had disappeared from the Bay of Biscay, and they have never returned.

The Basques headed westward, into the open ocean, all the way to the waters off Newfoundland and Labrador, and continued their pursuit of the right whale, selling its products, primarily oil for lighting and heating, throughout Europe. In many respects, notes writer Richard Ellis, "the Basques were the advance guard of what would eventually become an all-out war on the whales." The first sustained assault of that war was launched by the British and the Dutch, who began hunting bowheads—more massive cousins of the right whales—in the Atlantic Arctic in the seventeenth and eighteenth centuries. American whalers did likewise in the Western Arctic from the mid-1800s; Yankee whalers had by that stage already become well established in their pursuit of sperm whales across the Atlantic, Pacific, and Indian Oceans.

By the late nineteenth century, commercial whaling was on its knees. The emergence of petroleum had undercut the need for whale oil, although the fashion for whalebone corsets breathed renewed life into the whaling industry and spelled particular misfortune for the already heavily depleted bowhead whales, which possess the largest mouths and thus the longest baleen plates of all mysticetes. Most damaging of all, however, was the industry's own rapaciousness: whale populations had been so massively depleted throughout the traditional hunting grounds that in many cases there simply were not enough whales remaining to make the search for them sufficiently profitable.

In the late nineteenth century, a series of whaling expeditions were launched in a region where previously no whales had been hunted but where reports from explorers suggested an abundance: the Antarctic. Each of these first voyages was an unmitigated disaster, succeeding in catching just one immature right whale among them: although a plentitude of whales indeed inhabited the region, the bulk of them were not the right whales, which the hunters sought, but were rorquals, which were most definitely not the "right" whales to hunt at all.

The rorquals are a family of baleen whales including the blue, fin, sei, Bryde's, humpback, and minke whales, all of which, save the mostly tropical Bryde's whale, are found in the Antarctic. They are generally sleeker and more streamlined than rights and bowheads, but their defining characteristic is pleated throat grooves that enable them to massively distend their already cavernous mouths and thus take in even more water, and more food, at a time. Their meat and blubber is thinner than that of right whales, and they do not float when killed; what really put them out of reach of whalers, however, was that they are very fast swimmers—too fast for the whaling boats of the time.

That all changed with two developments that, combined, effectively sounded the death knell for the rorquals of the Antarctic and ultimately ushered in the most intense and devastating period in the history of commercial whaling. One was the ascendancy of steam-powered ships, fast and powerful enough to keep up with the speediest of whales; the other was the invention by Norwegian Svend Føyn of a bow-mounted harpoon cannon, replacing the hand-thrown harpoons that had previously been used and ensuring that the whales, once killed, did not sink.

The first commercial whaling operation in the Antarctic was established by Norwegian captain Carl Anton Larsen on South Georgia in 1904. A few days before Christmas that year, his men shot their first whale—a humpback—and after one full season had killed almost two hundred. Humpbacks were the first of the rorquals to be targeted, as they are the slowest, and tend to be more coastal and thus easier to catch from shore stations. They also offered themselves up as easy targets: gunners reported that they could practically steam up to the whales and drop their harpoons on them. It was even easier if they came across a mated pair, as when one was killed, the other would refuse to leave its side and thus also became an easy victim. During its first twelve months, Larsen's company shot 183 whales—149 humpbacks, 16 fins, 11 blues, and 7 rights. Other companies followed in Larsen's footsteps, and whaling on South Georgia grew so quickly that in 1910 the amount of whale oil brought out of the island exceeded the entire global total of the previous three years. At the end of their first decade of operation, South Georgia whalers had killed a recorded 1,738 blue whales, 4,776 fin whales, and 21,894 humpback whales—more than half the number of humpbacks that are alive throughout the world today.

The slaughter had only just begun. The majority of rorquals, less coastal in their habits than humpbacks, remained out of reach as long as whaling ships were obliged to return their catches to shore stations to be processed. To reach them, a means needed to be developed to process those whales at sea, and once again it was Carl Anton Larsen who led the way. In the Antarctic summer of 1923–24, Larsen skippered the factory ship *Sir James Clark Ross* on the first whaling trip to the forbidding, icy Ross Sea. Two years later the *Lancing*, an improved type of factory ship equipped with a stern slipway up which whales could be hauled, left Norway for the Antarctic, heralding a new era of pelagic, or open-ocean, whaling. By 1930, Antarctic whaling had spread from its small beginnings on South Georgia to a huge and growing industry throughout the Southern Ocean.

In the ensuing decades, factory ships swarmed across the ocean, and shore stations expanded along the coastlines of South Georgia and places such as Deception Island in the South Shetlands. By 1934, the average annual kill was more than 30,000 whales; by the beginning of the following decade it was more than 40,000. In the greatest single season of slaughter ever visited on the world's whales, over 45,000 whales were killed in 1937–38 alone.

The consequences were all too predictable. Within decades, whale populations in the Antarctic, like those of the fur and elephant seals before them, had collapsed. In 1931, more than a thousand blue whales were killed off South Georgia alone. In 1965, throughout the whole Southern Ocean, the entire global commercial whaling fleet could find and kill only twenty. Only then, when it was too late, did the International Whaling Commission step in and grant protection to the blue whale.

Where the blue whale went, so followed the fin, and then the sei until, by the early 1970s, the whalers were turning their attention to the minke whale, previously considered too small to be worth hunting and, at around thirty feet, the smallest of the so-called great whales (a designation applied to the sperm whale and all the mysticetes except the pygmy right whale).

Opposition to commercial whaling was beginning to grow, however, reflective of a burgeoning sensitivity to environmental issues. Members of the International Whaling Commission's Scientific Committee had been pleading for several years for greater restrictions, lower quotas, and even complete protection of some species and populations. Now this concern was reaching out into the broader public, where a discomfort with the obvious decimation of whale populations was joined by a groundswell of feeling for the whales themselves. The size of cetacean brains as well as certain aspects of their behavior were leading to speculation that they might be highly intelligent. In 1970, scientist Roger Payne released a recordings of the haunting, melodic songs of humpback whales—considered so beautiful that they were included on the *Sounds of Earth* record that accompanied the *Voyager* spacecraft out of the solar system.

The 1972 U.N. Conference on the Human Environment adopted a resolution calling for a ten-year moratorium on commercial whaling. A burgeoning "Save the Whales" movement became a beacon for growing concern about the state of the global environment. By confronting the whalers at sea, Greenpeace both became part of this movement and caused it to grow exponentially.

Finally, in 1982, the IWC, which by now contained more ex-whaling and nonwhaling nations than whaling countries, agreed to an indefinite moratorium on commercial whaling. The moratorium was scheduled to take effect in the 1985–86 Antarctic season and last at least until such time as the commission's scientists were able to devise a significantly improved management regime for commercial whaling.

Between 1975, when Greenpeace first took to the seas against Soviet whalers in the North Pacific, and 1986, when the moratorium became official, the number of whaling countries steadily diminished. One by one, Australia, Chile, Peru, Spain, and ultimately even the Soviet Union hung up their harpoons: partly because of the moratorium, partly because of international opprobrium and campaigns such as those waged by Greenpeace and other environmental organizations, in one case (Australia) because a government commission had decided that commercial whaling was unethical, but largely because the numbers of whales were no longer sufficient to make commercial whaling profitable for those countries.

But the moratorium did not bring commercial whaling to a close. For one thing, IWC rules allow a member state that objects to a commission decision to be exempt from it if it lodges that objection formally within ninety days of the decision; Japan, Norway, Peru, and the Soviet Union all lodged objections to the moratorium. Peru withdrew its objection in 1986. The Soviet Union did not withdraw its objection, and its successor state, the Russian Federation, has maintained it; but the USSR stopped whaling in 1987, and Russia has not resumed the practice. Norway continues to hunt minke whales in the Northeast Atlantic, and Japan openly maintained its commercial whaling program in the Antarctic for two seasons until, under pressure from the United States, its objection was withdrawn.

That withdrawal did not mean an end to Japan's whaling in the Antarctic, however. Instead, immediately upon officially ending its commercial whaling program, Japan announced that it would be sending its whaling fleet back to the Southern Ocean to hunt a reduced number of whales for purposes of "scientific research."

In so doing, Japan was taking advantage of Article VIII of the 1946 International Convention for the Regulation of Whaling (ICRW), the legal document on which the IWC is based, which states that "any Contracting Government may grant to any of its nationals a special permit authorizing that national to kill, take or treat whales for purposes of scientific research subject to such restrictions as numbers and subject to such other conditions as the Contracting Government thinks fit." The convention was drafted at a time when, even though concern about overexploitation of whale populations was growing within the scientific community, it was considered far more acceptable than now to learn about whales—or indeed, any other wildlife—by hunting down a certain number, measuring them, and cutting them open to see what was inside; but even if Article VIII was written with honest intentions, it has been subject to abuse, or attempted abuse, almost since the first IWC meeting in 1949.

In 1956, the United Kingdom informed the commission that it intended to take twelve baleen whales of unspecified species "for the purpose of testing an electric harpoon." Norway objected, arguing that this did not fall within the ambit of Article VIII, and the proposal was withdrawn. That same year, the Soviet Union announced that it had issued permits to hunt baleen whales outside the permitted whaling season, a blatant attempt to effectively prolong its season and in effect increase its quota. In the 1960s, the number of permits issued increased substantially, as several countries, notably Australia, New Zealand, and South Africa, responded to severe restrictions in the quotas of the baleen whales on which their industry depended by using Article VIII as a pretext to hunt sperm whales, for which the IWC did not then set catch limits.

The United States, despite its latter-day reputation as a defender of whales and opponent of whaling, was for a time one of the more egregious abusers of Article VIII, killing a total of 316 gray whales for "scientific research" in 1959–64 and 1966–69; Eastern Pacific gray whales, which had at one point been considered almost extinct, were increasing in number, and the California-based shore whaling industry, which had suffered from the collapse of baleen whale populations, saw the grays as a way to remain in operation. The effort failed: in 1971, two years after the "scientific whaling" program ended, the last American commercial whaling operation closed for good.

And so it continued. In 1975, Japan began a three-year "research study" of Bryde's whales in the northern Indian Ocean and the South Pacific; the effort was strongly criticized by the IWC Scientific Committee, which noted that, instead of random "sampling," the whalers concentrated on larger individuals— which are more profitable—and that, of 225 whales taken during the first year of the study, the most basic of scientific studies (the measurement of body proportions) was conducted on just 40. In 1980, Peru submitted a permit request for two to three blue whales; in 1981, Chile proposed a "scientific" catch of 100 sei whales; that same year, the Danish Faeroe Islands briefly began using scientific permits to hunt fin whales.

The most extensive misuse of Article VIII, however, began with the moratorium decision, with Iceland and South Korea first out of the blocks. Iceland's original proposal, circulated internally in 1985 but not submitted to the IWC, called for the catching of 80 fin whales, 80 minke whales, and 40 sei whales, as well as an annual take of 10 blue whales and 10 humpbacks to "facilitate studies on what happens to over-exploited whale species after many years of protection." The version ultimately presented to the commission removed all references to blues and humpbacks, and the permits for minke whales were never issued. Over a four-year period, from 1986 to 1989, Iceland killed 312 fin whales and 70 seis for "scientific research," and has not hunted whales commercially since, despite repeated—

almost constant—threats to do so. (As I write this, in February 2003, the prospect of Iceland truly returning to whaling looks more serious: see the Epilogue for details.) The Korean proposal was almost laughable in its lack of detail, proposing only to catch 200 minke whales annually for four years in order to obtain "important results." Washington applied diplomatic pressure, and the Korean proposal, and its commercial whaling program, quietly disappeared.

Norway would ultimately also join the scientific whaling club for a while, with a four-year hunt of minkes lasting from 1992 to 1995. The element of the Norwegian program that attracted the most attention, and generated the most sarcasm, was the statement that five of the 35 minke whales targeted for the first year of the program would not be killed but anesthetized, until it was pointed out in the IWC Scientific Committee that whales are voluntary breathers—that is, unlike most mammals such as ourselves, every breath they take is a conscious effort—so anesthetizing a whale is therefore the same as killing it. At the end of the program, Norway dropped the pretense and returned to hunting whales in open violation of the moratorium.

Since the moratorium decision, however, the most determined and consistent abuser of Article VIII has been the whaling industry in Japan. In 1984, two years before the moratorium was scheduled to come into effect, the Whaling Council, an advisory panel to the Fisheries Agency of Japan (FAJ)—a bureau of the powerful Ministry of Agriculture, Forestry and Fisheries, and the prime architect of Japan's whaling policy—recommended that Japan cease commercial whaling in the Antarctic and instead adopt a program of "research whaling," with the meat to be sold on the market as usual. An article carried by the Asahi News Service later that year commented, "The government and ndustry have considered various strategies to continue whaling, such as continu[ing] to catch whales under the guise of 'investigative whaling,' although the catch would still be sold and eaten. . . ." In 1985 Moriyoshi Sato, minister of agriculture, forestry and fisheries, promised that "the Government will do its utmost to find out ways to maintain the nation's whaling in the form of research or other forms."

That promise first took shape in 1987, when Japan submitted to the IWC a proposal to hunt a total of 825 minkes and 50 sperm whales a year under Article VIII. When both the Scientific Committee and the commission itself raised objections, Japan scaled it back, sparing the sperm whales and electing instead to prosecute an annual hunt of up to 330 minke whales.

The IWC could do little about any of this. Article VIII specifically states that "the killing, taking and treating of whales in accordance with the provisions of this Article shall be exempt from the operation of this Convention." In other words, an IWC member state can assign itself as many whales as it wants, for as long as it wants, in the interest of scientific research. Ever since it first became clear that Article VIII was vulnerable to manipulation, numerous proposals had been put before the commission to bring it under tighter control—suggestions that the Scientific Committee be allowed to define "scientific research"; that the commission should be able to approve all permits before they were issued; that no population of whales should be hunted by scientific whalers until it had been subject to thorough sightings surveys to determine its size and conservation status (i.e., whether the population was depleted or endangered)—but none gained traction. The IWC did agree in 1979 that the Scientific Committee should review any planned permits before they were actually issued; in 1986 the commission awarded itself the authority to pass resolutions concerning any research whaling program, and in 1987 it used that new authority to pass a resolution criticizing Japan's planned scientific whaling and asking the Japanese government not to issue the permits. But all those measures were nonbinding, and so, despite the criticism, Japan went ahead as planned.

That first "scientific whaling" season, 1987–88, was uneventful. But in the following year, for a short while at least, the whaling fleet found itself with some unexpected and unwelcome company.

On January 25 1989, the Greenpeace ship *Gondwana* was in the middle of its inaugural voyage to the Antarctic. Only a matter of days before, its crew had been involved in a series of tense confrontations with construction workers at the French base of Dumont d'Urville, on the Antarctic coast due south of Australia, where the building of a hard-rock airstrip—a process that involved dynamiting and leveling five small islands—was, coincidentally, killing hundreds of the area's emperor penguins and cutting off the rest from their breeding grounds; after a brief stop at the Soviet research station of Leningradskaya, those on board the *Gondwana* were looking forward to heading for the Ross Sea and the welcome of World Park Base, which the crew of the *Greenpeace* had set up in 1987. But campaigners and crew were also hoping to intercept the whaling fleet and, just a day out of Leningradskaya, they did.

Shortly after the Greenpeace ship appeared, the fleet scattered. But despite plowing into heavy seas, the *Nisshin Maru No. 3* couldn't shake the pursuing *Gondwana* off its tail. Unable to escape, the whalers resigned themselves to continuing with their program; for several days, the distant waters of the Southern Ocean played silent witness to a dramatic game of chase, as the *Nisshin Maru No. 3* and its catchers tried to kill the whales they wanted and the *Gondwana* and its inflatables tried to hinder them. At one stage, *Gondwana* captain Arne Sørensen maneuvered his ship close enough to the stern of the factory vessel to block the slipway and prevent the catchers from offloading any whales. The strategies weren't always effective, though: one whale was harpooned under the *Gondwana*'s bow, and the assembled Greenpeace crew could only watch as it thrashed around helplessly.

In late November 1990, the *Gondwana* intercepted the *Nisshin Maru No. 3* in the Tasman Sea, on its way south to the whaling grounds. Greenpeace crew dropped into the water from helicopters in a desperate effort to block the factory ship's path, but were picked up and tossed to one side by the giant bow wave. When the *Gondwana* found the fleet again in the whaling area, the whalers deployed a new tactic: knowing that the *Gondwana* could not stay with them for long, factory ship and catchers simply shut down their operations for several days and waited until the Greenpeace vessel, obliged to meet other commitments, was forced to move on.

It seemed like the whalers had effectively won. For all the efforts of environmentalists back on land, the whalers' use of the research loophole meant that their activities were within the letter, if not the spirit, of the law. And as long as Greenpeace could stay for only a week, all the whalers had to do whenever the *Gondwana* arrived was to stop hunting for a while and pick it up again as soon as their antagonists had left.

The whalers alternated the area of the Antarctic in which they hunted: one year operating in the Ross Sea region south of New Zealand, the next year whaling several hundred miles to the west. It was for this second whaling area that the *Nisshin Maru* and catchers were heading as they steamed south in 1991; they would have known that the *Gondwana* was in New Zealand, preparing to sail as usual for the Ross Sea and Grace Base, and as a result they presumably felt confident they would avoid any trouble this year. What they didn't realize was that another Greenpeace ship was already in the Antarctic waiting for them, and that, instead of having to move on to other things after a week or two, this ship was planning to stick with the whalers for a good two months.

CHAPTER FOUR

Cat-and-Mouse Among the Icebergs

I SAT ON DECK FOR HOURS AT A TIME, WAITING FOR THE WHALERS to show up, peering through the fog for the first signs of the fleet. I sheltered from the icy wind by hunching up in the lee of an inflatable or behind a stack of fuel drums, drowning out the engine noise by listening to music through my headphones, and staring at the albatross hanging regally off the ship's stern. Sometimes, when several of the giant birds were accompanying us at a time, I would pick just one, focusing on it intently and never moving my gaze as it hovered above me and then, apparently without moving a muscle, caught a thermal, soaring up alongside the ship, then down toward the water and back to where it started, all the time seemingly doing nothing except spreading its huge black wings out wide.

I tried to picture what our first encounter with the fleet would be like. I had dramatic visions of a catcher chasing down a hapless whale and then, just as the whale was too exhausted to flee anymore and its hunter was on the verge of delivering the coup de grâce, an inflatable appearing from nowhere and, with a blast of the whistle, the MV *Greenpeace* roaring into vision from behind an iceberg, churning up a powerful wake as it turned dramatically toward the factory ship.

When it came, the actual sighting could scarcely have been more different from my vision or, frankly, more embarrassing. A number of people, acting on a suggestion from Athel that they should grow accustomed to waddling around in several layers of cold-weather clothing, were standing out on deck and staring absent-mindedly out to sea when somebody noticed something in the distance just beyond a large iceberg.

There, looming out of the mist, was a whaling ship. It was a catcher, the *Toshi Maru No. 18*, on its way to check the location of the ice edge. The people on deck stood looking at the ship for a short while, taking in this development, until it occurred to someone that maybe the bridge ought to be informed. The mate on watch, more concerned about running into the ice that was scattered everywhere, had the radar set for a six-mile range and hadn't even noticed the catcher's approach.

We had been at the ice edge less than two full days, and already we had found the whalers. But this wasn't how I, or any-one else, had imagined it would be. There had been no hiding behind icebergs, no pouncing on an unsuspecting fleet, no launching of inflatables to surprise the whalers in midhunt. A catcher had emerged out of the mist and everyone had stood around on deck and looked at it.

There wasn't much excitement or running around. It was a cold, gray, windy day; the sea was too rough to launch the boats and, even if it hadn't been, there would have been little point in doing so if the fleet wasn't actively whaling. It was all strangely anti-climactic.

The catcher turned north and headed toward us. As it passed us on the starboard side, we lined up on deck to have a good look at it, its gray hull struggling through the heavy swell, its harpoon uncovered and loaded, ready for use. Obviously, the catcher was being sent to give us the once-over, to have a close look and confirm that we weren't the *Gondwana*—and if we weren't the *Gondwana*, then who were we?

After a short while, the *TM18* moved ahead and back in front of us. Figuring that it was probably trying to lead us somewhere—most likely as far from the *Nisshin Maru* as possible—we pulled back to see if it would follow us. It did, for a while, and then it also broke off.

We had been right about where to find them: we had been on the 100E line, on the ice edge, when the *Toshi Maru No. 18* appeared. They would probably still want to start whaling from there, so we decided to patrol up and down the line. Back and forth we went, down to the ice edge, then forty-five miles north to the northern edge of the ice edge zone, before turning around and heading south again. Around midnight, another echo appeared astern of us. The *Toshi Maru No. 18* was behind us again, and it followed us through the night as we patrolled the line.

At first light, the *TM18* could be seen on the horizon. Because we were several knots slower than our shadow, we could do nothing to get away. Through the next day, and the day after, the *TM18* continued to dog us. The gray mist that enveloped the Black Pig reflected the mood I shared with Naoko and Athel as the ship steamed helplessly back and forth. We had been so close to seizing the upper hand right from the first moment; instead, it was the whalers who held the advantage. Thanks to the reports that were doubtless being sent by the catcher off our stern, the rest of the fleet knew exactly where our ship was at all times, and was easily able to stay comfortably out of our radar range; accordingly, we could hazard only the wildest guess as to their whereabouts.

We were growing increasingly irritable. We hadn't slept properly since the catcher first appeared, staying up until all hours figuring out what to do next: Naoko trying to put herself in the heads of the whalers and calculate their next move, Athel attempting to work out some way we could use our inflatable boats to our advantage, and me wondering if we could somehow reap a bit of media capital from our situation. Even when we finally wore ourselves out, our sleep-starved bodies were tossed about in our bunks as the *Greenpeace* was buffeted by a gathering Southern Ocean storm. The wind increased to Force 8, gusting to 9, whipping up big waves and long swells. Pots and pans slid around the galley; drawers came off their runners, spilling their contents on the floor; toilet seats left up came crashing down with a bang.

The waves were great gray mountains; we'd climb up one side, pause at the top, and then plunge down the other side, the water blocking the sky and the pitching of the ship leaving our stomachs somewhere up in the crow's nest. In the wheelhouse, where we could see and anticipate the swells and troughs and hang onto the rails, riding the waves like a rodeo steer, it was exhilarating. One wave grew closer and closer and seemed to explode in front of the bow. A fin whale, previously unseen and now only a few meters from the hull of the ship, disappeared again beneath the water.

We plowed into the waves despite the discomfort, hoping that our relative bulk would prove an advantage over the smaller catcher, enabling us to weather the storm better and perhaps escape our escort. For a brief period it seemed to work, when the *Tōshi Maru No. 18* suddenly stopped and let us get away. But the next day the catcher loomed once more out of the mist and promptly assumed its position off our stern. It was all very depressing. It wasn't meant to be like this.

We continued west, the perpetually miserable Antarctic weather making our journey more difficult. When the storm subsided, the mist settled on us once more. We peered intently through the murk, scanning the water ahead for growlers. Old, weathered pieces of ice, generally around the size of a piano, growlers are normally translucent, difficult to spot, and dangerously hard. If we collided with one of them, looking for whaling ships would be the last thing on our minds.

On December 13, after six days of being shadowed, the catcher problem seemed to resolve itself. For some reason the *TM18* had begun dropping back, so Bob put on an extra couple of knots and turned west into a huge pack of icebergs. Visibility was poor, and echoes were all over the radar screen. It would be virtually impossible for the catcher to pick us out; of course, we wouldn't be able to tell the catcher from the icebergs, either. But as the day wore on, it became clear that we had left the *Toshi Maru No. 18* behind.

We'd been moving in a vaguely westerly direction for some days; Athel and I wondered if the *TM18* hadn't simply gone as far west as it had been told to. Alternatively, maybe its crew felt secure that the rest of the fleet was now sufficiently far away from us for them to drop back and join up with them.

Already, a little more than a week after arriving at the ice edge, the strain was starting to affect us all. Endless patrolling up and down imaginary lines, constant mist that seemed to lift only when we were being battered by storms, almost perpetual daylight, freezing temperatures, to say nothing of the uncertainty, the close confinement of a group of twenty-eight people—all were beginning to take their toll. In this respect, we were following a proud tradition of Antarctic explorers and overwinterers, a great many of whom have at some stage or another fallen victim to what is now known as Antarctic Syndrome. In his book *The Last Wilderness*—an account of the maiden voyage of the *Gondwana*—*Guardian* journalist Paul Brown mentions some symptoms experienced by others who had battled against the elements, themselves, and each other in the forbidding Antarctic environment:

> On his first journey to the Pole Shackleton resorted to secret code to record in his diary how much he hated Scott. . . . Two Britons who walked to the Pole in 1986 refused to speak to each other for two years afterwards. The crew of a US ship which rescued seven Argentines from outside their destroyed base on the

Peninsula suspected the base commander of setting fire to it. His strange behaviour with fire extinguishers and his habit of stealing the crew's toothpaste made the Americans believe he was suffering from the syndrome.

We'd been south of the Convergence for only ten days and we weren't experiencing anything that bad, at least not yet. Nonetheless, the early signs were definitely there: little irritations piling up, unimportant details blown out of all proportion. For some reason, I started to feel annoyed at the way Alex, who had the bunk above mine, hung his legs over the edge and near my face before he got out of bed in the morning. Others fumed when assistant engineer Marco de Bruijn insisted on turning off the stereo in the lounge at dinnertime. Some of the watch-keepers started muttering darkly about one of the mates who seemed intent on annoying everybody by boasting about his long experience at sea, playing music in the wheelhouse that everybody else loathed, and pulling attention-seeking stunts such as standing up archly during crew meetings and noisily eating fruit in the middle of the lounge.

Then there were the cravings: for a bath, warm sunshine, a luxurious meal at an expensive restaurant. One morning, while I sat in the wheelhouse imagining myself in front of a steaming plate of enchiladas, Lena Sierakowska, the third mate, announced a sudden and overwhelming desire for liver-and-pickled-gherkin sandwiches.

Alone in the ocean, surrounded by gray sea and sky, with few visual cues outside the ship, and the inside dominated by the pitch and roll of the ship and the rhythmic throbbing of the engines, our minds began creating some more varied stimulations of their own.

"Penguins, penguins!" shouted Ted Hood, one of the deck-hands, as he pointed at a patch of gray, penguinless sea. "At least, I thought I saw penguins. 'Course, I just smelled flowers, too."

Just about the only things we did have to look at—apart from the albatross and petrels, and the occasional whale—were the icebergs. Our starved imaginations went into overtime, turning bergs into snails, trailers, or castles. Some of them were truly spectacular, shining cobalt blue and towering above us, or twisted into extraordinary shapes by the waves. Others had caves hollowed through them; one, old and riddled with fissures, collapsed in front of us.

Icebergs became the defining element of our scenery. The approach of the most beautiful prompted calls from the wheelhouse to the lounge, and the crew would rapidly assemble on deck and stare and take photographs as the *Greenpeace* slipped past the bergs. I pictured them building up slowly over millions and millions of years and then one day, with a violent, ear-shattering crack, breaking away from the ice shelf and setting off on their own. From that moment they were doomed, destined to erode under the steady assault from wind and waves until nothing was left. I stood there and watched these beautiful, ancient witnesses of eons past, and I felt a wrenching sense of loss as they drifted silently past and disappeared from view.

One of a writer's most powerful tools is comparison. Whether directly, through similes, or indirectly, a writer needs to summon a description of the subject that triggers references to things familiar to the readers, so that even if they haven't seen a person or place or experienced an emotion before, they can at least get a feel for what the writer is describing. As I stood on deck on the afternoon of December 15 with Sîan Bennett, the assistant cook, looking out at the water and the dozens of icebergs guarding the ice edge, I was cursing my inadequacies as a writer. How was it possible, I asked myself, to draw comparisons when what you are trying to describe is so unlike anything you've ever witnessed before?

"I've never seen so much calm sea," said Sîan, and it was true: the sea was flat as far as the eye could see. The bow wave of the *Greenpeace* seemed not to disturb it, but to splash gently over its surface. The water, close to freezing, had an oily appearance.

The gentle lapping of the water pushed aside by the *Greenpeace* brought back memories.

"This reminds me of college, watching the tide wash against the shore," I said. "My college was by the sea, and at lunchtime I would go down and walk among the rock pools and just sit on the beach."

"It's like that at home," replied Sîan. "Where my parents live, they have a house near to water, and I can go and sit there, and you see the way the land is shaped and it's exactly the same as on a map. You get the feeling you're at the end of the country."

I was making a mental note about our now being at the end of the world when Alex went running up to the bridge wing, followed by Hidemichi Kano, our deckhand from Japan. The chief engineer strode past with binoculars.

"I wonder what's going on," I remarked casually to nobody in particular.

"Oh God!" gasped Sîan suddenly. "Is that it?"

"Is that what?"

A large red-hulled ship was emerging from behind an iceberg.

"Oh God!" I repeated.

"Is that it?" she repeated.

"It must be," I said.

"It's most peculiar," observed Robin, leaning over the bridge wing. He too had been observing the ship's approach while Sîan and I had been contemplating the universe. "It isn't a whaler."

"It isn't?" I echoed. "What is it?"

"Some sort of resupply vessel, with a load of junk on the back."

"What sort of junk?"

"Looks like old bicycles." He sniffed at Alex, who was standing next to him. "Probably Dutch."

It was the *Akademik Federov*, heading for the Soviet station at Mirny. Ironically, Greenpeace had been involved in an action against this very vessel during the 1989–90 season, preventing it from unloading its supplies as a protest against the level of waste at Bellingshausen station in the Antarctic Peninsula. In the course of the action, one of the *Akademik Federov*'s inflatables had nearly sunk in a squall, causing the Soviets to launch two lifeboats. When these broke down, the *Gondwana* had trawled out lines and brought them on board.

Bob and the skipper of the Soviet ship exchanged greetings. Bob asked if they'd seen a whaling fleet nearby—the *Federov* captain said no, he hadn't—and we continued on our separate ways.

"Jesus, but there can't be more than ten ships in this part of the Antarctic, and five of them are the whalers and us, and when we do see a ship, it's Russian!" exclaimed Grace O'Sullivan, our deckhand from Ireland.

It bordered on the surreal—meeting another ship in a sea that seemed to have almost the consistency of oil, while surrounded by icebergs and bergy bits of the strangest shapes. It was like being in an episode of *The Twilight Zone*. There seemed a certain sense of inevitability about it all.

Convinced the whalers were nearby, Bob grew tense and agitated. A visit to the bridge during one watch, when all the lookouts had been peering ahead, caused him to comment sarcastically that maybe the next watch could be instructed to put people on the wings as well, as a ship could approach from any direction. With so many icebergs around, the radar was of limited benefit, so Bob relegated it to standby and posted lookouts in the crow's nest to scan the horizon.

And it was from the crow's nest, just before 1800 that evening, that Marco, who was volunteering for lookout duty, called down to the wheelhouse. A catcher was dead ahead. Everybody raced up on deck or to the bridge to see for themselves and look for the rest of the fleet. The catcher moved in front of an iceberg and then behind another one. We all scanned the horizon, straining to see something, hoping desperately that if we stared long and hard enough at an iceberg in the distance, it would turn into the *Nisshin Maru*. We had no time now to admire the view, to gaze at the still, clear water or breathe in the fresh air. Eyes were everywhere, searching.

We launched our large, long-range inflatable—which we called the Rock Boat, or Rocky for short, in recognition of the fact that it was once accidentally driven aground on some rocks and survived. Rocky sped up to the catcher, moving along its starboard side to identify it as the *Kyo Maru No. 1*, and prompting the whaling ship, as soon as its crew caught sight of the large inflatable bouncing toward them, to head off at nineteen knots into a patch of brash ice, where the Rock Boat couldn't follow. Athel, driving the Rock Boat, waved at the catcher's crew, who were lined up on deck and staring at the activists through binoculars, and then set off in search of the *Nisshin Maru*.

Spirits were high. This was it. This had to be it. The day had had a strange feel about it, a sense that something was going to happen. And now we were back among the fleet. The *Nisshin Maru* couldn't be far away.

Then again, maybe it could. It didn't take long for disappointment and despair to descend again. After Rocky had searched twenty miles in several directions, Bob—always concerned about letting the boats roam too far from the Black Pig; as he was constantly pointing out, this was the Antarctic, and terrible weather could whip up at any time—called the boat back on board. And after a short period of effortlessly outpacing us, the *Kyo Maru No. 1* was adopting a familiar position off the stern. I summed up the frustration in an update to Greenpeace offices:

> It gradually became clear how agonizingly close we had come to winning the star prize and catching the *NM* herself. In addition, the potentially devastating consequences of running into the *KM1* instead also began to dawn. We reckon that the *NM* can have been little more than fifteen or twenty miles away when we encountered the catcher, but by the time Rocky was in the water it was already speeding away as fast as possible. Rocky covered a

range of 27 miles to the north and 21 to the west, but saw no sign of it.

We had been within striking range of the *NM*, but instead, on virtually the only occasion when we didn't have a convenient iceberg we could hide behind, we bumped into a catcher again. We were back where we had been before—out of range of the *NM*, and a catcher on our tail reporting our every movement. In some ways, our situation was worse even than when we were on 100E; it is becoming clear that a major goal of the fleet is to keep us away from the *Nisshin Maru*, even if that means ignoring or curtailing the scientific program. Unless we are able to see them before they see us, and take them by surprise, there seems little way we can ever get to the *Nisshin Maru* without running into a catcher first. And, most worrying of all, the fleet will shortly be turning north into the much larger Middle Zone of the whaling area, which will give them far better opportunity to lose us altogether.

In some despair, I went to make myself a snack in the pantry. I was swiftly accosted by Grace and Marco, both agitated. While Grace was a veteran of the *Rainbow Warrior*'s final voyage and the expedition to establish World Park Base (Grace Base, the base's informal moniker, was in her honor), Marco, a young, fresh-faced Dutchman, was a relatively recent recruit to Greenpeace. But he shared Grace's powerful enthusiasm and possessed an almost overwhelming determination to see us succeed; with events going against us, he and Grace regularly teamed up and presented the campaign team with ideas in a desperate effort to prompt us into "doing something."

"What's the plan, Kieran?" asked Grace. "What's going on?"

"They're not playing fair, Grace," I said.

"Well, of course they're not playing fair. When has anybody ever played fair with us? So what are we doing?"

"Well, we're moving west still, trying to figure out a good point to launch Rocky. . . ."

"Why just talk about it? Let Rocky go now, send it over to

the catcher, blockade it, and use the Black Pig to look for the *Nisshin Maru*."

I suggested they talk to Athel—hell, he was in charge of actions, not me, and I was more than happy to pass the buck. When I went down to the cabin, they were all talking back and forth and really at cross-purposes, with Grace and Marco insisting that we were not reacting quickly enough, and even if we couldn't block the catcher, at least we could have a conversation with it or test its reaction; and Athel responding that the catcher's brief was to stay with us, and if the *Greenpeace* did somehow manage to move away, the *KM1* would report that fact to the fleet and the *NM* would move even farther away.

"The point is," explained Athel, "they can do what they want, they can go where they want. If we go somewhere, they won't go near us. End of story. We're fucked."

I tried to put a positive spin on things.

"Don't forget," I offered, after doing some quick mental arithmetic, "that they're not putting the pressure on us, we're the ones who are putting pressure on them. We're making them go where they don't want to go, we're messing up their program. By now they should have killed forty or fifty whales; I bet they haven't killed half that many."

I went up to the lounge shortly afterward and said much the same thing to a bunch of folks sitting at the round table. And it was almost certainly true: by diverting two of their three catchers and forcing the *Nisshin Maru* to keep moving away from us, we probably were seriously disrupting their whaling. It was a straw to clutch, but it wasn't really enough to make me happy about the situation, and it certainly didn't convince many of the crew. They were more than prepared to cut us some slack and give us the benefit of the doubt, but patience was beginning to wear thin. Sure, we'd succeeded in finding the whalers twice, but what was the point if they could simply monitor and avoid us? We tried to tell them that, although the situation was not looking good, all was not lost, and we were having some effect. But what reason did they have to believe us? There wasn't a lot of evidence that we knew what to do or how to go about it. Once again we were being followed by a catcher, which was reporting our position to the rest of the fleet and making a mockery of our efforts, and as far as anyone could tell, we weren't doing anything about it.

Unable to sleep, I'd already had a couple of drinks by the time Sîan arrived, and was becoming a little maudlin. She had scrawled a message on the board: *Can we please have a meeting so everyone can find out what's going on?* It was a sentiment shared by most of the crew.

"Sure you can," I muttered, "as soon as we know ourselves."

Constant prodding by Grace and Marco, and the general restlessness of everybody on board, finally convinced us. Whether or not there was any point to it, regardless of whether it would scare the catcher away or have any other discernible effect, we had to do something, if only to find an outlet for everybody's frustration and surplus energy. So on December 16, we decided to launch all four inflatables and send them chasing after the *Kyo Maru No. 1.* I reckoned we would at least be able to get some good photographs out of it, which would give us the opportunity to kick off some media coverage.

The launch went well and, as Thom Looney the radio operator and I played "Flight of the Valkyries" over Channel 16, all four boats descended on the catcher. I described the scene in another update to Greenpeace offices:

> Being on this expedition is a bit like taking your emotions on a three-month roller-coaster ride. After the relative despondency of last night, all was once more upbeat and confident on board the good ship Black Pig earlier this evening.
>
> Frankly, we were growing tired of being followed by whaling ships all the time when we were meant to be following them, so we decided to do something about it. At 1745, we dispatched all our inflatables towards our latest shadow, the *Kyo Maru No. 1.* The *KM1* stopped when we stopped; then, when it saw us

lowering our boats, it turned around and, in a puff of smoke, fled into the wind at about fifteen knots. When the inflatables caught up with it, Hidemichi attempted some conversation with the crew, without success. Two inflatables carried small flag banners that read STOP! and No WHALING They zoomed up and down the *KM1*'s port side for a little while and then came back. It wasn't too dramatic, but it made the *KM1* feel our presence and it put the pressure on them for a little while. It was also good practice for us.

The *KM1* disappeared behind an iceberg and, when it didn't reappear on the other side, Bob decided to take us around to have a look. They saw us coming, began to move away a bit, and then stopped again. They watched as Bob took us slowly in a circle around them at a distance of a couple of hundred yards. We waved at them, and they waved at us.

Robin and I sent out a picture of one of the inflatables in front of the *Kyo Maru No. 1*, together with a press release announcing that we were in the whaling grounds and that the *Greenpeace* and the whalers were, as I put it, "playing cat-and-mouse among the icebergs." It had an immediate effect, and that evening I began fielding calls from radio stations in Australia.

For a while, all in the radio room was chaos, with me talking to Australian media on the phone and Thom maintaining regular radio contact with the Rock Boat, which had gone out on a long search for the *Nisshin Maru*.

As the evening wore on, the radio room grew quieter. My interviews had dried up for the day but also, more worryingly, the Rock Boat had stopped making contact and didn't seem to be responding to our calls. By 2300, as a snowstorm blew up and Rocky had been out of contact for two hours, we had grown very concerned.

By 0230, the mood was quiet and tense. The searchlight pierced the snow flurries and moved across the surface of the water. Thom called repeatedly on the radio and sent blasts of Morse. The *Greenpeace* moved slowly west, the direction in which the Rock Boat was last known to be heading. Thom and I kept trying to convince each other that there was no way they had struck a growler. We could only hope that their radio equipment had given out, but that they were safe.

"Always look on the bright side of life," Bob said out loud to himself, but he didn't feel it. He stared at the silent radio equipment, as if doing so would bring it all to life.

"How can they do this to us?" he whispered. "Where are they?"

At 0315, the radio room was silent. I was lying on a bench, reading; Thom was staring out the window. The stillness was shattered as a loud blast of Morse screamed over the receivers. Thom leaped on the radio.

"Was that you, Rock Boat? We are so worried about you! Please signal again."

More Morse, and then the voice of Jörn Haye, the chief mate: "Black Pig, this is Rock Boat."

Bob flew down the stairs. "Just ask their position!" he shouted.

"Was that you, Rock Boat? Please confirm," repeated Thom.

"Yes, it bloody was them," snapped Bob. "Just ask their bloody position."

The mate called down from the wheelhouse: "We've got them on Channel 67."

Bob rushed back up; Jörn gave their position. Bob gave them our position and course, and told them in which direction to head and to look out for our searchlight.

Despite our fears, there had been nothing wrong except a failure of the old hand-cranked radio equipment in the Rock Boat. They had been sending "OK" messages every fifteen minutes, but we had been unable to hear them.

When the Rocky crew came on board, Athel was upset to discover there had been panic. He felt that everyone had completely overreacted. "We go out for a little spin, and everybody loses control," he complained.

By the time we had finished debriefing each other, it was

0500. Going to bed now was pointless: I had two more radio interviews in an hour with radio stations in New Zealand. Both interviews were live and ten minutes long—a generous amount of time in which to make our points. When I was finished, I collapsed into my bunk.

Even if we succeeded in shaking off our tail, our chances of finding the fleet looked increasingly remote. By our reckoning, they had by now moved into the Middle Zone, and John Frizell had sent us information on how, according to their program, they would cover this area. Simplified, their plan enabled them to pick any one of thirty-one lines of latitude along 70E, the western boundary of the whaling grounds, and from there move up or down to any point on any one of thirty-one lines of longitude from 70E to 85E. Whereas the ice-edge zone we had just been in measured only forty-five miles from north to south, each of the diagonals created by their bounces through the Middle Zone would be about 320 miles. It was a lot more area in which to find them.

Fortunately—for my state of mind, if no one else's—media interest gathered apace. The press release and photograph we had sent out generated more and more interviews, not only for me but also for Patricia, our Swedish deckhand Milo Dahlman, and Sake Bosma, the outboard mechanic from the Netherlands. This allowed me to argue that we were now acting as a catalyst for a wider discussion on Japan's whaling, a public dispute, a media war. Then, on December 20, the Institute of Cetacean Research (ICR), the body that oversaw Japan's "research" whaling program, sent a letter to Greenpeace International in Amsterdam, accusing us of being destructive, calling our little boat action against the *KM1* "dangerous," and demanding our withdrawal from the whaling area. At the same time, the FAJ sent a similar message to the Greenpeace office in Japan. It was something to be encouraged about: however bad we felt our situation to be, we were obviously getting under the whalers' skins.

The following day, we faxed a response directly to the *Nisshin Maru*, agreeing to leave—but only if the *Nisshin Maru* came with us. We proposed a meeting point of 62S 100E, from which we could depart together.

It all proved grist for the media mill; even the Japanese press were beginning to report what was going on—admittedly, with small articles, but they were articles that quoted us as well as the government, and for the whaling issue at least, that was unprecedented.

As far as I was concerned, if we were getting media coverage like this, then we were doing our job. No matter how much time we spent with the fleet, if nobody in the outside world knew about it, our message wouldn't get out. From my point of view, media interest now was laying the groundwork for later on, when we would have more dramatic actions to report.

For the crew, this was all very well, but they had come to the Antarctic to save whales; no matter how many column inches or radio minutes were devoted to covering our exploits, we weren't succeeding in our aim if we weren't actually disrupting the whalers. We had come to the whaling grounds to interfere with the hunt, to place ourselves in front of harpoons, and to save some whales. Instead, we were being shadowed by the whaling fleet, and the factory ship was safely out of range. We weren't doing our job.

Day in and day out, the crew worked long, hard shifts—in the wheelhouse, the engine room, the galley. As far as they could tell, the campaign team did nothing except sit around the ship, write updates to Greenpeace offices repeating that we still hadn't found the factory ship, and, in the case of Athel and me, stay up half the night drinking beer. People started making pointed comments to each other about the campaign and the campaign team, not quite out of our earshot. "It Seems Like Bullshit to Me" read the words on the holder that Sue, the cook, used for her beer cans; a couple of the crew snorted and wondered aloud if it had been designed with the campaign in mind.

On December 22, the *Kyo Maru No. 1* was about seven miles behind us when it slowed down, and soon disappeared off our radar. It was a relief to be rid of it, but it meant we were no longer tying up even one whaling ship. It seemed clear from the way the *KM1* had acted that it was leaving us so it could rejoin the fleet. Obviously we were a long way away. Our best hope was that they believed we were heading for the "meeting point" we had proposed, that we would wait for them there, and that when they didn't show up, we'd go home.

At least Christmas was here to provide something of a diversion. Back in Singapore, Robin had organized a "secret Santa" drawing: each person drew the name of another person on board, for whom they had to get a Christmas present. They could either buy something in Singapore if it cost less than ten dollars, or make something during the voyage. As Christmas approached, everybody busied themselves with putting the finishing touches on their creations or wrapping the gifts they had bought. Decorations went up in the lounge, with Robin and Alex providing several sets of flashing lights from our cabin, and Christmas music playing merrily on the stereo.

On Christmas Day, everybody placed their anonymous presents in a box. Lena dressed up as Santa Claus and handed them all out. For one evening at least, all our problems were forgotten. Bob James, a cynical, salty ex-submariner who was our third engineer, sang a succession of increasingly lewd shanties and engineers' songs. Athel and I sang some blues. Alex played with the toy helicopters he had been given. Everybody else played with the toy helicopters Alex had been given. Bob James fell asleep in a chair, where he was promptly garlanded with some of the Christmas lights.

I took some media calls. One journalist asked why we were at sea, thousands of miles from home, on Christmas Day. I explained about the whaling campaign and our desire to prevent the killing of whales under the guise of science.

"I see," said the journalist. "So will you all be wearing pointed hats?"

The BBC World Service, surprisingly, wasn't much better. To be fair, there isn't much news on Christmas Day, and the person on duty had obviously been informed that we would be good "filler."

"Ah, Kieran," said the producer when he telephoned to arrange the interview, "I understand you're down there policing an international ban on drift nets, is that right?"

"Er, no," I corrected. "You could say we're policing an international ban on commercial whaling, though."

"Well, you're policing an international ban on something, and that's good enough for us."

The next morning we encountered another ship. This meeting, though, was scheduled. Since we had been in the Southern Ocean, Bob had been making contact with the *Aurora Australis*, one of the two resupply ships for the Australian bases in the Antarctic and a ship on which he had been first mate two years previously. Over the past few days it had become clear that our paths were converging, so Bob and the *Aurora* had arranged for us to meet. That morning, hangovers notwithstanding, the Rock Boat was lowered into the water and sent over to the Australian ship, complete with mail to be posted in Hobart, including video of the action against the *Kyo Maru No. 1*. We had no other way of getting mail or video to the outside world, and Alex and I looked forward to the reaction at Greenpeace Communications when his tapes showed up out of the blue. The *Greenpeace* crew, lined up on deck to stare at these new humans, watched Rocky sink lower and lower into the water as the crew of the *Aurora* piled it with supplies of food, drink, and reading material.

The encounter was fun, but brief. The *Aurora* wished us well and went on its way, and soon we were alone again.

We ended the year with a crew meeting to assess the situation so far. Naoko kicked off with a general review, and then Athel said his piece. I spoke about the media scene and how news of our campaign had even been reported in Japan. Then we encouraged those assembled to come out with any constructive ideas and suggestions they might have.

A short silence ensued, and then the floodgates opened.

Someone asked why we were relying on the search methods we had been using when they obviously weren't working and didn't show any signs of ever working. Grace asked about chartering a plane to conduct a search instead. That option had been investigated in the expedition's planning stages, Athel pointed out, but the only possibility had been a long-range aircraft with an extremely high budget that would spend only a couple of hours in the whaling area. Somebody asked if we had a spending limit: would Greenpeace give us extra money to do our job properly, or would we leave? Athel replied that as far as he was concerned we were staying until we were told to leave, and that we were going to do everything we could to find the fleet. We were asked again if Greenpeace had put a limit on how much we could spend, how much of our supporters' money would be spent on chasing shadows. Some people started complaining about, of all things, the cost of the nonexistent plane flight.

"So is it going to happen?" asked Robin about the plane.

"It's a possibility," said Athel.

"So it's *not* going to happen?"

Grace asked why we didn't just go after one of the catchers, and then Jobst Mailander, the doctor, asked how long we would wait until we gave up on finding the *Nisshin Maru*. We might as well hit a catcher, he argued, or give up now because as far as he could work out, the chances of us finding the *NM* were pretty remote: "So we need to get within twenty miles, so we need a snowstorm, so we need them to have some not-so-good officers on the radar, and we need to be very alert. I don't think it's very realistic."

"No," said Bob James, "it's unrealistic. I think we've underestimated them all the way."

It was a total shock. We'd known that the crew was unhappy with the situation, and I'd noticed the occasional snide comment or sarcastic remark. But nobody had ever come out and said it before, and now suddenly the crew had risen up almost as one and showered us with negativity. We had totally missed the extent of the disaffection permeating the ship.

Nonetheless, even as I criticized myself and the others on the team for our failures to communicate and inspire trust, I also felt hurt and let down by the people I had thought were our friends.

"Athel was pleased that everybody started speaking out at last," I said to Sîan as we sat in the lounge in the early hours of the morning, after I had rung in the New Year on the ship's bell, "but, fuck, everyone's giving up. Everyone's *given* up. And you know, I really don't think we've done very much wrong—we've just had the odds against us."

Robin had certainly given up.

"I don't know what this is in aid of, really," he muttered as inflatable crews suited up, at Athel's instigation, for some practice in boat driving the next afternoon.

"It's probably so people can practice for the *NM* action."

"The *NM* action?"

"Well, everyone was complaining last night that they didn't know what to do when we find the *NM*—who's in what boat, and so on—so this is probably to keep them happy."

"I don't see there's much point in practicing for an *NM* action when there isn't going to be one."

"Look, I was getting really pissed off with everybody last night for being so negative."

"Negative? What do you mean?"

"Everybody is basically saying we're doomed, we haven't a hope of getting the *NM*."

"I don't think that's being negative—just expressing the realities of the situation. I mean, you've got to admit it's 99.9 percent unlikely we're going to find them."

The problem, volunteered Thom, as he, Athel, Naoko, and I sat in the radio room, was that we weren't communicating our plans, progress, and news adequately, and the crew's opinions weren't being solicited. We protested that maybe we weren't always good at giving out news, but that was at least partly because it changed so often.

"But until last night," said Thom, "all the crew meetings have been more like debriefings, telling people what's been decided and not really asking them to put forward ideas."

"That's not true," I protested. "What about the meeting we had a while back, to discuss ideas on how to tackle the *Nisshin Maru*? The whole purpose of that was to get people's ideas, but nobody said anything except Abby and Jobst."

"The thing is," continued Thom, "you've got an experienced crew, used to doing Greenpeace actions on things like smoke-stacks or test sites—things that don't move. They're not used to this sort of campaign."

We agreed we needed to redouble our efforts to draw out people's opinions and keep them informed. At the same time, though, we had to make the crew realize that we weren't feeling supported, that we didn't feel the fault was entirely ours. However bad things were right now, we had to maintain focus and energy, and to remain as positive as possible. If we started convincing our-selves that we couldn't possibly win, we wouldn't.

CHAPTER FIVE

Contact

IT'S ALWAYS DARKEST BEFORE THE DAWN. ON JANUARY 4, FORTY-
eight days after leaving Singapore and at a time when morale on
board had reached its lowest ebb, we located the *Nisshin Maru*.
After all our searching, all our plotting, and all our worrying we
finally found it through not ingenuity and calculation, but pure
luck. Bob had altered course slightly to the south overnight on a
whim, and the following morning we sent out the Rock Boat on
a search, just in case there was anything to be seen.

The chances of Rocky finding anything appeared remote.
The ever present mist was closing in again, and it seemed no
more likely that the fleet would be nearby than it had been any
other place we searched. But after the Rock Boat had been out
for a couple of hours, Jörn's voice came over the radio. They'd
finally spotted the *Nisshin Maru* and were following it. Maybe
everything was starting to come together at long last. But there
was still ample opportunity for things to go wrong. Sure
enough, our luck soon took a turn for the worse.

After shadowing the factory ship for almost an hour, the Rock

Boat lost it in the fog. And then, when we reached the coordinates where the boat's crew had said they would be, Rocky was nowhere to be seen. The *Greenpeace*'s gyrocompass had broken; it was off by between thirty and forty degrees, and we'd been going in the wrong direction. Fortunately, the gyrocompass was reparable, and we were able to pick up the Rock Boat safely.

The following morning we were presented with yet another chance, and this time we were able to take full advantage of it. Another storm had begun to build, making the weather too rough for whaling. The fleet would therefore probably heave to close by, we reasoned; if we could find them, then this would be our best chance to steam straight up to them.

Sure enough, that afternoon the *Nisshin Maru* appeared on the radar. We closed to within thirteen miles without any reaction from the factory ship, which was evidently sitting, drifting. Closer and closer we drew. The echo of a catcher appeared behind the *Nisshin Maru*, and then another, and there was no movement from any of them.

Bob was by now able to see them through his binoculars. As we moved closer, so could others, and then we could all see the factory ship with the naked eye.

We drew alongside and pulled just ahead. Now we could not only see the ship but also hear and practically smell and touch it, too. Its huge black hull loomed over us, several stories high and well over twice as long as ours. Water, tinged with red, spilled out over its scuppers in a steady stream. Its cream-colored superstructure was illuminated by bright deck lights. It was perfectly still, with no sign of any life at all, as if everybody had been ordered to hide from view. No such reticence prevailed on the *Greenpeace*. Everybody stood out on deck or in the wheelhouse, staring at the factory ship, the grail for which we had been so painfully searching for so long. And we all wondered: what happens now?

"Maybe they're just waiting until we launch the inflatables," ventured Jörn.

Naoko read out a statement, in Japanese and English, over

VHF Channel 16, informing the *Nisshin Maru* of the reason for our presence, our opposition to their research whaling program, and the fact that Greenpeace is a peaceful organization. "We will do nothing," the statement read, "to endanger your vessels, your equipment or your crews. We will, however, use all peaceful means at our disposal to prevent you from killing whales."

We prepared to launch Rocky to sit under the factory ship's bow, but it seemed that Jörn's hunch was right: as soon as the launch began, the *Nisshin Maru* took off. We put Rocky in the water, and both the Rock Boat and the *Greenpeace* gave chase. "We have located the *Nisshin Maru* and are presently chasing her across the Southern Ocean whaling grounds," I announced triumphantly to Greenpeace offices in an update.

We were flying; Peter Laue, the chief engineer, had the old Pig doing more than thirteen knots, and even though you could almost feel the ship's rivets popping, the speed was exhilarating. We weren't losing ground at all; if anything, we were gaining. Rocky had caught up with the *NM* easily, buzzed around it to get a good look, and was now returning to us. Almost as soon as the boat was back on board, Athel held a briefing in the lounge.

"There is no way we can get close to that ship," he said. "It throws off a wicked bow wave. The only place you can get close is off the starboard quarter, which we figure is where they pull the whales on board. But neither Jörn nor I could figure out how the mechanism works to haul the whales on board. There are all these ropes and things, but something seems to be missing; maybe some sort of loop comes down out of the slipway."

He asked for ideas on what to do next, but it was difficult to have any thoughts at this early stage. Besides, as long as they were doing thirteen knots, they couldn't hunt whales anyway, so we were doing our job. Spirits were high. We felt as though we had the upper hand. By 1800 the *NM* had even started to slow down, and then, after briefly putting on speed and pulling away from us, it stopped.

We wondered if perhaps they had decided it was costing them too much fuel for too little progress to keep on running away from us. But then we realized that we had stopped dead on 60 degrees South. Maybe this was the top of the "bounce"—the zigzag pattern that the whalers follow through the whaling area—and the *Nisshin Maru* would soon go roaring off to the southeast at an opportune moment.

With the factory ship hove to so close, Athel decided it was a perfect opportunity to have another attempt at an inflatable action. If we put the boats in the water early in the morning, he argued, we'd be in position in plenty of time before the fleet started moving. We agreed to launch two boats at 0430. I looked at my watch. It was already half past one.

At 0330, just after Milo woke everyone up, the *Nisshin Maru* took off. François Lamy, the mate on watch, saw the factory ship turn toward the southeast, and we followed suit. After a couple of hours the *NM* turned, slowed down, and stopped. We had both drifted in the night, and now they had steamed back to their original position, perhaps deciding to test our reflexes while they were at it.

Later that morning, we put the Rock Boat and an Avon, one of the smaller inflatables, into the water alongside the *Greenpeace*; the two boats and the Black Pig moved forward slowly and in unison. Fog had descended and visibility was virtually nil. We had the *Nisshin Maru* on the radar, but the fog was so thick we couldn't see the ship from the *Greenpeace*. As we drew closer, Rocky's crew signaled that they'd spotted it, and they were off. Naoko warned the *NM* over Channel 16 that inflatables were under its bow, so the factory vessel should not attempt to move forward. The crew of one of the boats used magnets to fasten a WHALING MUST STOP banner on the starboard quarter of the *NM*. Somebody from the factory ship called down in Japanese for the banner to be removed—it might get caught in the propeller and they wanted to leave soon. Hidemichi, in one of the boats, responded that we didn't want them to go anywhere and that the banner would come down when we were ready.

"I feel better about asking people to stick with us now," said Athel later, after the boats had come back on board. "But that won't last. People will get frustrated and impatient again if this situation lasts or if they start killing whales in front of us."

And killing whales was just what they started doing.

That afternoon, the catchers *Toshi Maru No. 18* and *Toshi Maru No. 25* were both hunting. Shortly before 1700, the *TM18* could be seen heading back to the factory ship to offload a whale, and the Rock Boat was scrambled. Rocky went crashing through the waves toward the *Nisshin Maru*, the *Greenpeace* in pursuit. The visibility was terrible and before long the Rock Boat, the *NM*, and the *TM18* had all disappeared in the fog. From the wheelhouse of the Black Pig, we could see nothing. I moved to the bridge wing, as if being outside would somehow allow my gaze to part the mist. It was ferociously cold, and when I opened my mouth, the wind raced down my throat with such force that I could hardly breathe.

Athel, Lena, Jörn, and the others in the boats kept us updated over the radio. Rocky was sitting off the *NM*'s starboard quarter, trying to keep the *TM18* away. If the catcher couldn't offload the whale, it couldn't start killing any more. But the *TM18* kept on coming, nudging the Rock Boat out of the way. The factory ship threw a line over to the *TM18*, which was now close enough to offload its catch. The heaving line was hauled in and a cable taken down along the side of the catcher and tied to the whale. A command was yelled and the whale was cut free. With a splash it fell into the water and was swiftly hauled up the slipway and into the factory ship.

As we all sat in the lounge after a crew meeting that evening, I looked at Athel. He was beaming. People were in different groups, arguing how best to limit the whalers and block them from unloading their kill. Some were looking at Robin's photographs, while others were drawing diagrams. They were discussing, exchanging ideas. Athel was thrilled: this was what he'd been after all along.

"He won't go to sleep tonight," I thought, and sure enough, he and I stayed up late, talking to Sake.

Sake, a Dutchman in his mid-forties with rapidly thinning hair and a weathered face, was one of the principal boat drivers, and the person charged with ensuring the smooth running of the inflatables' engines. Lively and loud, a practical joker, he liked to hang out at the round table and socialize until the small hours. But when it came down to business, he was incredibly professional, and was in fact one of the most dedicated individuals on board. He had been one of the few people to defend us during the New Year's Eve savaging by the crew, even though, as he admitted, he had had his own doubts about the success of the trip. But now he was fired up with enthusiasm anew.

"I would like to stay here right to the end of the season," he said. "I would give all my money to be able to do that. It upset me so much to see that whale and the way they pulled it up the slipway. Do they think it's a fish?"

It was, ironically, perhaps just as well we hadn't discovered the *Nisshin Maru* at the beginning after all, we agreed. The strain of wandering the ocean in search of the fleet had certainly taken its toll. But it was already evident that actually having the whalers in our sights, battling to stop them from hunting whales, and knowing that however hard we tried to prevent it, they would still be able to shoot at least some whales while we watched helplessly, was not going to be any easier. In addition, the combat's intensity was such that it would prove difficult to maintain for a long period. If we had been fighting the whalers day in and day out for the whole time we'd been in the Antarctic, most people on board would probably have burned out a long time ago.

The following morning, January 7, "research" began at 0800. By 0930, the *Toshi Maru No. 25* had shot its first whale of the day. Shortly before 1100, the *TM25*—which at this stage was only a couple of miles off our port beam—was hunting again, and we put Rocky in the water. The catcher soon killed a second whale and began hunting for more, but by then Rocky had caught up to it. The *TM25* spotted a couple of minkes and chased after them, but the Rock Boat crew repeatedly placed themselves in harm's way, blocking the line of fire until the whales escaped.

The *TM25* tried once more. Our hearts raced as the catcher spotted some more minkes and Jörn announced from the Rock Boat that a man had walked out to the harpoon and was taking aim. Moments later, it was exhilarating to hear Jörn report that the boat had positioned itself between harpoon and whales and that the harpooner was becoming frustrated. Jörn was looking out from the front of the boat, and Sake was standing up in the back, both of them pointing out to Athel, who was steering, where the whales were so he could maneuver the boat into position before the catcher could take a shot. At first the harpooner played with the Greenpeacers, dramatically pointing his gun one way and then the other, but as Rocky blocked his shot time after time, he became irritated and exasperated. Eventually he gave up, stepped back from the harpoon, and stood in a sulk, his arms folded.

Watching the scene unfold from the *Greenpeace*, I looked across at Patricia and we beamed at each other. Naoko was visibly thrilled. So was Hanno.

"They're stopping them from killing whales," I said to Hanno. "They keep getting in the way."

"Ja?" said Hanno, beaming. "This is good. Fucking bastards."

The *Toshi Maru No. 25* turned toward the *Nisshin Maru* to unload the whale it had already caught, and the Avon, which had been dogging the factory ship's stern, sped off to join Rocky in harassing the incoming catcher. Even as it approached the *Nisshin Maru*, the *TM25* continued to hunt, spotting three minkes and giving chase, but again and again the Rock Boat interposed itself, the whales escaped, and the defeated catcher resumed its course for the factory vessel.

The whaler was determined to unload its catch, and Bob was forced to sound the horn in warning and protest as the *TM25* cut across our bow in order to move in behind the factory ship. The two inflatables attempted to block the slipway, the crew in the Avon waving No WHALING banners.

Gradually the two whaling ships drew closer together, shouting instructions through bullhorns. At first I'd thought the shouting was in response to the success of the boat crews in blockading the slipway. Hidemichi, alongside me on the bridge wing of the *Greenpeace*, strained to hear what they were saying, but couldn't make out the words. The heaving line had been thrown skillfully, though, and the cable had been taken down to the whale in no time at all. They were merely waiting for the right moment. Then, swiftly and suddenly, the whale was cut loose from the side of the catcher and hauled through the water. It paused briefly at the bottom of the slipway, and then was pulled up and onto the deck. I winced inwardly at the sound of all the camera shutters on the *Greenpeace*, including my own. As the whale disappeared onto the deck, two gates closed ominously behind it, shielding the view.

Conditions in the inflatables were rough. Even when the swells seemed tame from the bridge of the *Greenpeace*, speeding across them in small boats could be like hurtling from mountaintop to mountaintop. The pounding from the waves shuddered through the boats' hulls and jarred the spines and kidneys of their occupants, lifting their stomachs up toward their ribs. It was hard work, and any lapse of concentration could be disastrous. During the first action against the *Kyo Maru No. 1*, one of the inflatables, caught behind the catcher's bow wave, had been sucked against the hull and almost under the ship. On another occasion, one of the boat crew became distracted and, when her inflatable hit a wave, fell into the water; fortunately, well protected by cold-weather gear, she was unhurt and scrambled back in.

And it was miserably cold out there, too: driving small boats at twenty knots into thirty-knot winds made for a windchill factor of twenty to thirty degrees below already-freezing temperatures. All told, being out in the inflatables was demanding work, and the boat crews were soon hungry. With nobody on the harpoon or in the crow's nest, Bob James allowed himself the luxury of a bite on a Mars bar. There was a crack as the crown came off his front tooth. The candy bar had frozen solid.

I had a radio interview at 0230 the next morning, with *Morning Report* on National Radio, New Zealand. I'd been busy with radio interviews all day: we must have been the most famous people in Australia and New Zealand. I'd had little sleep and was just bone tired. I saw no point in heading down to my bunk, as I'd likely have to come back up soon for another interview, so I decided to crash in the radio room. I'd been asleep for only an hour when the phone rang. It was Cindy Baxter from Greenpeace Communications in London, saying that the update I had sent to Greenpeace offices about the day's events was really exciting and asking if we had any good photos yet. And then she asked where the video had come from. I was still sleepy, so it took me a while to collect my thoughts.

"What video?"

"This video just arrived in the mail. It's footage of these inflatables in front of a whaling boat."

"Aah, *that* video. I can't tell you where that came from, I'm afraid. It's a secret. Let's just say we had visitors for Christmas dinner."

Next morning the *Toshi Maru No. 25* had already shot a whale and was on its way back to the *Nisshin Maru* by the time we launched the boats. It was agonizing to watch as the *TM25* and the inflatables closed on the factory ship. The catcher made it first, but the whalers must have made a mistake with the transfer because the *TM25* was still off the stern of the factory ship, the whale tied to its side, when Rocky and one of the Avons arrived. The catcher let the whale go, and the carcass flew through the water alongside the inflatable. Athel, who was driving the Avon, followed it to the stern and actually went partway up the slipway, to the bemusement of the watching whalers. As the boat fell

back away from the stern, Athel looked up at the whalers and
shrugged; they in turn looked down at him and shrugged back,
as if to say, "Better luck next time."

On January 9, the *Nisshin Maru* had positioned itself within
range of the *Greenpeace* and was moving slowly as the catchers
steamed far out of sight and radar range. Were they trying to
keep the catchers away from us, we wondered? Or were they
preparing their escape, sending the catchers to some
prearranged spot and then, when they were safely elsewhere,
sprinting away from us to meet up with them? This was scheduled to be their last day in the Middle Zone, and we feared they
might lose us on the long sprint south into the ice-edge zone.

Naoko offered an alternative explanation. Much smaller than
the old *Nisshin Maru No. 3*, the new *Nisshin Maru* would not be
able to last the length of the whaling season without refueling at
least once. A converted resupply ship, the *Hiyo Maru*, was
rumored to be in the area, and Naoko wondered if the factory
vessel was preparing for a rendezvous.

Whatever the case, it was now clear that the *NM* could easily
outrun us if it really wanted to. Once the catchers were out of
sight, the factory ship put on speed and took off to the north.
We followed through the evening, the *Nisshin Maru* steadily
pulling away from us as we reached the northern limit of the
whaling grounds.

When the factory ship disappeared from our radar screens,
we turned around and headed south. Naoko figured that if they
were indeed refueling to the north and east of the whaling area,
they would then head around and enter the Southern Zone
from the east in a few days. We decided to stop just north of the
ice edge, lying in wait to ambush the fleet when it returned.

We reached the ice edge two days later. As we hove to, the
weather took a turn for the worse. The wind grew to Force 9,
and great gray walls of foam-flecked water loomed over us,
bearing down on the ship and seeming as if they would tip us over.
The gale had an interesting indirect effect on the atmosphere

on board: the furniture in the lounge slid over to the port side and nestled there, bringing everybody—literally—much closer together. The whole room seemed much cozier. One huge wave brought a crashing sound from the mess room. A beer can rolled into the lounge, paused, and then rolled back, with Hanno in close pursuit. It was followed by a bowl of peas, which spread out across the floor.

"Aha," chuckled Anders Stensson, one of the engineers, "this is a green peas ship."

We wired out a press release, with a photograph of the inflatable at the base of the *Nisshin Maru*'s slipway and the whale being winched up. For a few days there seemed to be no response, and I worried that it had bombed. But then offices began to report the coverage the story had received in their countries. The print media, at least, had picked it up extensively: seven pages from Belgian newspapers, something like twenty articles from Germany. From Britain, a photograph and caption from the *Daily Express*:

> A baby whale is dragged into a Japanese factory ship as Green-peace protesters risk their lives to defy the hunters. The environmentalists have played a deadly game with the whalers in the icy waters of the Antarctic all week. As the harpoonists aim, the protesters try to put their dinghies in the way to stop them firing until the whale can escape. This was one whale they could not save . . . but the game goes on.

A couple of days later, the *Express* ran the photograph again, this time on its letters page. Several readers had written in to praise what we were doing: "I was distressed to see the picture of the baby whale being captured and very impressed by the bravery of the Greenpeace protesters," said one. "They are the real heroes, risking their lives in matters that will not bring them personal glorification. The powers that be should recognise and honour them."

Some of the people on board were uncomfortable with such

accolades, worried that we ran the risk of basking in media glory before we accomplished what we set out to do. They were concerns I didn't share. I was delighted with the reaction. Here we were, on a little ship in the middle of the ocean, thousands of miles from anywhere, and our actions were being read about and discussed by people at the other end of the world, even moving some of them to write letters to their newspapers. Before I joined Greenpeace, I had wondered if anything I did or wrote would ever be noticed by anybody; well, here was the answer. If I wanted to feel that I was accomplishing something, or really making a difference, I couldn't ask for anything better than this.

The place we had chosen to wait for the fleet turned out to be near an enormous swarm of krill—the tiny, shrimplike crustaceans that form the bulk of baleen whales' diet in the Antarctic—and for a couple of days, minke whales arrived in droves to feed on it. One evening, so many were nearby that we even launched the boats just to take people out for a closer look. Even then, the best was yet to come. That night, as Bob, Jörn, Athel, Patricia, and I sat at the lounge table, the number of whales in the vicinity kept growing.

It was calm and also light, despite the late hour, so Athel that we try to get footage of the whales from the Rock Boat. He roused Alex, who was less than keen about being woken up—it was two-thirty in the morning, after all. We launched the boat and Athel, Alex, Jörn, Patricia, and I set out slowly among the feeding frenzy of minkes.

It was incredible. I had seen whales before, of course, but never this close. We were literally surrounded by them—fifty, a hundred, it was difficult to say. We turned off the engine and sat there, the only sounds the lapping of the water against the hull of the boat, and the blowing and surfacing of the whales. Some breached just a few hundred yards in front of us. One surfaced so close that if we'd been quick enough we could have reached out and touched it. It swam slowly past us, dwarfing the little

Rock Boat, and its huge back rolled through the water before disappearing from view beneath the waves. Behind us, we could see Bob and Grace racing from one side of the *Greenpeace* to the other, leaning over the rails to look at the minkes swimming under the ship.

For the past few weeks, we had been so absorbed by the task at hand, so wrapped up in our petty squabbles and in life aboard ship, that we had almost lost sight of the larger picture, the reason for all our work. That experience—the crisp Antarctic morning light, icebergs glistening on the near horizon, whales all around—was a reminder of both where we were and why we were there.

A few days later, the fleet reappeared on our radar. The fog was descending, and the *Nisshin Maru* was apparently drifting as we steamed up to it. But as soon as we launched the boats, the factory ship took off into the mist to meet up with the *Toshi Maru No. 25* and pick up two whales. The fog thickened some more and the whalers stopped for the day.

On January 20, we launched a couple of boats toward the *NM*, which took delivery of two whales from one of the catchers and then steamed into a patch of thick brash ice, where the inflatables couldn't follow. At least while we had been out of sight of the fleet and sitting in an area surrounded by whales, we had felt that there was one patch of ocean we were guarding from the whalers. If they wanted to kill whales there, they'd have to come past us. But that was just what they were now doing.

"We haven't even been able to stop them from coming into our area and killing whales," Athel fumed when the fleet began "research" that morning. "We've got to do something."

It was time, Athel said, to stop messing around and to raise the ante. The next day, we did.

We launched two boats—the Rock Boat, with Sake, Jörn, Jobst, Robin, and Alex; and one of the Avons, carrying Athel, Milo, and Jens Grabner, an assistant engineer from Germany. The two boats had been following the *Nisshin Maru* for a couple of hours when the *Toshi Maru No. 25* approached to unload a whale. The Rock Boat drove in close to the stern of the factory ship, and Jobst started to tie a rope to one of the safety lines that ran down either side of the slipway. Immediately, the crew of the *Nisshin Maru* turned a fire hose on the Rock Boat, but Rocky slid across the slipway and tied off on the other side. The *NM*'s crew lowered a grappling hook, lifted the rope, and cut it in half, but Rocky had held onto part of it and threw one half over to Jens in the Avon, who had seized the other end. The two ends were tied back together and the Avon hooked on.

The *Nisshin Maru* and the *Toshi Maru No. 25* sped up, the *NM* continuing to shoot water at the boats, aiming directly at Robin's and Alex's cameras. Rocky dropped back out of range and the hoses were turned on the smaller inflatable, which by now was being dragged behind the factory ship. The *NM*'s crew lowered a hook a second time, grappling the rope again. This time they appeared to fasten the rope to a winch, and began to pull it in. Athel, Milo, and Jens inflated their lifejackets as the Avon was lifted almost vertically, all the time being drenched by water from the hoses.

At this stage, Alex's camera gave out. The salt water from the hoses had had its desired effect. Though Alex could no longer see through the viewfinder, he continued to point the camera at the action anyway in the hope that it was recording.

Having hauled up the rope, the crew of the *NM* cut it again. The inflatable crashed back into the water and stalled, its engine flooded.

Rocky carried on. As the *TM25* drew closer and the ships slowed down in readiness for transfer of the whale, Jobst stood at the bow of the Rock Boat, rope in hand. As the whale was released from the side of the catcher, Jobst threw the rope over the cable that was pulling in the whale. At the end of the rope was an inner tube with a message from Naoko to the *Nisshin Maru* attached. Jobst's timing was perfect: the rope caught on the cable and the inner tube was pulled up the slipway with the whale.

After both boats had been safely brought back on board, we checked Alex's footage; remarkably, most of it came out fine. The prognosis for the viewfinder was not so good: it was caked with salt, inside and out. Undeterred, Thom set to work, cleaning it as thoroughly as he could, and thanks to his diligence, it was soon almost as good as new.

Within a couple of hours, Alex and his camera were once more out in the Rock Boat, harassing the *Toshi Maru No. 18*. The *TM18* was hunting and, at one stage, chased a whale across the bows of the *Greenpeace*, causing Bob to sound the whistle in warning. The Rock Boat stayed with the catcher for several hours until visibility worsened, at which point, with only forty minutes remaining until the usual end of the whalers' day, Rocky came back on board.

That evening we held a meeting to discuss the day's events and plot our next move. A consensus began to emerge that if a similar action were attempted, the rope used to tie on to the slipway should be replaced by a steel cable that the crew of the factory ship couldn't cut. Naoko had been sitting quietly. Somebody asked her what she thought.

"This was my limit," she said.

Her voice was shaking with emotion; the idea of tying the inflatable to the slipway had not been hers, and she hadn't liked it. Neither, she said, had the crew of the *Nisshin Maru*; from what she could tell, the episode had totally freaked them out.

Certainly, their reaction had been highly irresponsible and dangerous. Dangling three of our crew above freezing Antarctic water was pretty reckless behavior, particularly given that the Institute of Cetacean Research had accused *us* of life-threatening activities when we had simply driven inflatables in front of the *Kyo Maru No. 1* back in the days when the catcher had been following us. The next day, the Fisheries Agency of Japan held a press briefing in Tokyo at which they spoke about the action, and how the crew of the *Nisshin Maru* had driven off our inflatables with fire hoses. No mention was made of the fact that the crew had hoisted one of our boats into an almost vertical position and then dropped it into the frigid, ice-strewn water.

Irresponsible it may have been, but the fact that the *NM*'s crew was prepared to go to such lengths was a demonstration of how much stress our actions were causing them. The situation was becoming increasingly tense and, in the Antarctic, that could easily lead to trouble. As the meeting went on, what had begun as a discussion on how to increase the pressure led to agreement that in the interest of safety, it would be wiser to take the opposite course and henceforth essentially leave the *Nisshin Maru* alone. From now on, we would concentrate our efforts on the catchers.

The next morning the *NM* and the *TM18* seemed to be playing with us, turning and maneuvering sharply and at one stage both following us. After a while we decided to ignore them and, when the *TM18* turned sharply, we assumed they were still teasing us. Then somebody walked out to the harpoon and Ted, watching from the wheelhouse, saw two whales in front of the catcher.

Athel and Marco leapt into one of the inflatables and raced over to the whaling ship. It seemed a forlorn hope: there appeared to be no way the inflatable could make it in time to do anything except watch one of the whales being harpooned.

Incredibly, they made it and positioned themselves between the harpoon and the two fleeing minkes. The catcher chased the inflatable and the whales across the bow of the *Greenpeace*, Bob again having to sound the whistle in warning. But the chase was to no avail, and the whales escaped.

If there remained any doubt that we were having an effect, it disappeared when we received word of a new Reuters story. It reported that, because Greenpeace was based in Amsterdam and the Black Pig was a Dutch-flagged vessel, the government of Japan had formally asked the Netherlands to somehow rein in our activities. The request had been made several weeks earlier, but no reply had been received; the Dutch, we surmised, had contrived to bury it in a pile of paperwork. I was thrilled, and so were the others. Even cynical old Bob James took a photocopy of the story. If the government of Japan was asking the Dutch government to intervene, we must have been causing them serious problems.

On the morning of January 23, the *Greenpeace* was close to the *Toshi Maru No. 25*, so we duly dispatched the Rock Boat toward it while we chased after another catcher, some way in the distance. Rocky radioed that the *TM25* was hunting; but after walking out to the harpoon, the gunner turned around and went back inside.

As the day went on, we all neared the ice edge from different directions: the *Greenpeace*; the catcher we were chasing at the time, the *Toshi Maru No. 18*; the Rock Boat and the *Toshi Maru No. 25*; and the *Nisshin Maru*. Alex was eager to film some statements about the campaign by Naoko and me, ideally with a whaling ship in the background, but neither she nor I nor Athel was prepared to go to the hassle of launching a boat especially for that. Instead, Athel suggested we shoot the pieces from the deck of the Black Pig. A crew change for Rocky was about to take place, so Alex came on board and started to film us making our statements while, in the background, the Rock Boat chased the *TM18*.

A few minutes later, Alex knocked on the radio room window and motioned to the heli-deck. The *Nisshin Maru* was approaching and he wanted to film my statement again, this time with the factory ship in the background. I went outside and whined that it was windy and gray and besides, the *NM* didn't really look all that close, but Alex was insistent that we try it a few more times.

So we carried on and, as we did, a crowd began to gather on the heli-deck, pointing in my direction with fingers and cameras. I turned around and instinctively leapt back from the stern rail in surprise. The *Nisshin Maru* was no more than fifty yards off our port quarter. I did a final take with Alex, and then the *NM* came past along our port side, towering high above the *Green-peace*, its giant black hull dwarfing us, its crew looking down on ours, ours peering up at them.

Athel was growing agitated.

"They're going to come straight past us and cut across our bows," he said. "You've got to get film of this, Alex; we'll need it for evidence."

Alex fetched another tape and, as he put it in, Athel kept telling him to hurry. The *Nisshin Maru* pulled ahead and then cut right across us, Bob sounding the whistle five times in warning.

It was another incredibly stupid and dangerous move. They had left their trackline, altering course to reach us, and had intentionally cut across our path for no apparent reason other than to create a collision, or at least to scare us into thinking they would collide with us.

"I'll have to file a close-quarters report now," said Bob. "They must be really pissed off to do something as bloody stupid as that."

Meanwhile, drama ensued with the Rock Boat and the *Toshi Maru No. 18*. Rocky had stopped to refuel, and as the crew emptied the third fuel can, they noticed that the catcher had reversed course and was heading straight for them. Then it stopped and turned to starboard. The gunner walked along the catwalk to the harpoon, and the ship began to move again. And then a blow appeared in front of the whaler.

Rocky took off in pursuit of the *TM18*, and the race was on to reach the whale before the catcher fired the harpoon. The Rock Boat raced along the whaler's port side. The catcher turned to port. Rocky turned as well and was level with the bow when there was a loud crack, and the harpoon flew through the air and into the water.

There was a long pause. The catcher's crew began to haul in the rope. There was no struggle, no movement in the water.

"They missed," said Ted. "At least, I think they missed."

They had missed. But it had been a close call. Rocky stayed

with the *TM18* until about 1900, at which point the gunner showed them the lock and put it on his harpoon. Whaling was over for the day.

Around dinnertime on the 24th, I was called up to the wheel-house. The *Kyo Maru No. 1* was only a few hundred yards in front of us and was hunting. All was deathly quiet as the *KM1* moved in circles, the gunner at the harpoon.

Breathing quickly and beginning to panic, I ran out onto the bridge wing. The wind cut through my hands as I gripped a pair of binoculars and focused on the unfolding scene. I saw a blow! There *was* a blow! A whale was right in front of the catcher, right in front of the harpoon. But the harpooner didn't shoot; the catcher turned so its stern faced us, and for a moment I thought I heard the crack of a harpoon.

The blow appeared again. But we didn't see it a third time. The gunner stood down, and both ships resumed steaming.

I wondered why nobody had scrambled an inflatable. The reason, it turned out, was that nobody had thought to tell Athel what was happening. Furious, he put a boat crew on standby, but the *KM1* pulled away and the boat crew was stood down.

I couldn't be sure if the *KM1* had genuinely been hunting. Perhaps they had been sighting and had put somebody on the harpoon to freak us out. That whale had been no more than twenty yards in front of the bow; the harpooner could surely have struck it if he'd wanted to. But maybe he hadn't been able to get a clear shot, and we were just lucky. Either way, we'd had some heart-stopping moments, and I'd been afraid I was going to see a whale killed.

The next evening, we became separated from the fleet in the fog, and elected to move ahead of the whalers and lie in wait along their projected route. We were still entombed in mist the following morning when we saw first one catcher, then another, and then a larger target, which we took to be the *Nisshin Maru*, appear on our radar screen. We prepared the Rock Boat for launch and continued to sit still, hoping the whalers would confuse our radar echo with an iceberg, when the second catcher altered course to check us out. It had closed to within a few miles when the fog lifted, the whalers saw us, and the *Nisshin Maru* turned and ran. Rocky raced over to the nearest catcher, which turned out to be the *Toshi Maru No. 18*, in time to see the harpooner at the bow and a whale a few hundred yards ahead. Rocky took position ahead of the catcher, and the whale escaped. It had been another close call. As Athel remarked later, it was getting to the point where we needed to set up a chart so we could mark off the number of whales we'd saved.

Nonetheless, it seemed as if we had lost our edge almost overnight. The fleet's activities had a new consistency: leaving one catcher close enough to keep us occupied, but scattering the rest as far away as possible. They seemed prepared to try to shoot a whale, even in front of us, if they could; but as soon as an inflatable turned up, especially if Robin or Alex was on board to document the action, they promptly stood down. It led to a slight slackening of the tension, and as a result, a certain lassitude began to settle over the *Greenpeace*. The fact that nobody had thought to call Athel, even as the *Kyo Maru No. 1* had seemed on the verge of shooting a whale in front of the *Greenpeace*, was a sign that perhaps we were beginning to let things slip. We were running low on fuel, it was becoming increasingly difficult for Sue and Sîan to make interesting meals from the rapidly dwindling supplies, and someday soon we would have to make a decision. Suddenly, it seemed, it was almost time to leave.

The *Toshi Maru No. 18* headed down to the ice edge, followed by the Rock Boat. Close to the ice, the temperature dropped rapidly and a vicious wind screamed off the water, tearing at the faces of the Rock Boat's crew and frosting their beards. The catcher steamed behind an ice tongue, and Rocky found itself surrounded on all sides by brash ice. Visibility began to fade, and the lookouts on the *TM18* were stood down.

Robin began to whine.

"Is there any point in us being here?" he asked.

"Yes," replied Athel.

"Why?"

"Because there are other considerations apart from yours."

"Like what?"

"Like keeping the campaign alive for the last few days."

"But they're not even looking for whales."

"They will as soon as we go."

"No, they won't."

"Tell you what: we'll drop you off and come back."

So Rocky headed back to the *Greenpeace* to disembark Robin and Alex. When they arrived, they found Bob in a flap. The gyrocompass had gone wobbly again, and Bob was having to resort to basics to figure out which way the *Greenpeace* was headed:

"OK, now the sun should be in the west. . . ."

His blood pressure was beginning to rise, and he was looking quite red. He stood in the wheelhouse, shaking his head and muttering.

"Take me home, Neddy," he said.

Rocky returned to the catcher and, sure enough, found that lookouts had been posted in the crow's nest while the inflatable had been out of sight.

We had completed a full circuit of the whaling area. That day, the *Toshi Maru No. 18* reached 100E, went north a little, and then headed southwest. We went northwest and the *TM18* came with us. It was difficult to know if it was trying to lead us astray or not, so at 2000, we hove to. The catcher stopped at the same time.

There was a certain circularity about it all. We were back where we had begun, slightly west of 100E and being watched by the *Toshi Maru No. 18*. It had been exactly fifty days since we had first made contact, and our time in Antarctic waters was almost up.

We knew we were approaching the final few days: the only thing to decide was the exact cutoff point. In discussions with

Greenpeace Australia, we had tentatively agreed that a suitable departure date would be January 29, for a return date in Fremantle of February 6 or 7. On January 28, Naoko and I had a discussion in her cabin and conceded the obvious: although our fuel supplies could allow us to stretch the length of our journey a little more if we wanted, there was no real point. Besides, yet another storm was brewing, Bob warned us, one that would likely last a few more days, so delaying our departure would achieve nothing. The decision was made: it was time to go.

We announced a crew meeting for shortly after 1300 on the 29th. Everybody knew what it was about. Some people seemed in a good mood about it, more than ready to leave after over two months at sea. Others were less happy, feeling that we were leaving without having done enough to stop the fleet from killing whales or, conversely, disappointed that we had to leave just as we were seriously beginning to have some effect. Sake looked tense, while Anders, one of the engineers, was playing on a Game Boy.

Naoko announced that we were leaving. I explained the media arrangements for our departure and arrival in Australia. Athel said nothing. Sake asked why we hadn't tried more actions against the *Nisshin Maru*. Anders's Game Boy started to beep. Everybody laughed, except Sake. Grace started asking about the prospects for conducting an action against the *Nisshin Maru* when it arrived in port. Naoko explained that that would be difficult because word was never received about the factory ship's return until, at best, the morning of its arrival; and anyway, the ship was berthed in a fisheries wharf, where it was difficult to gain access. Grace looked at me, began to say something else, then stopped and smiled.

"I know," she said. "This isn't the time."

The meeting broke up. Some people sat around, looking tense and unhappy. The voyage had taken a lot of emotional energy, and it was difficult to suddenly let it go. It was scary, also, to think of what lay ahead: for the past three months, our world had been the *Greenpeace*, the whalers, the Antarctic, and each other. Everything each of us had done—from the way we blew our noses or stirred our drinks, to the opinions we expressed—mattered to everybody else; now we'd all be returning to a world in which we would all be largely anonymous and where the experiences that we had shared over the past three months, and that were so important to us, would generate little more than passing interest from anybody else. Adjusting to the real world wouldn't be easy.

Naoko and I sat at the round table, a little dazed, then went down to our cabin, where Athel was already sitting, staring into space, utterly drained. Bob came in, and Thom. We speculated about what we would do first when we arrived in Australia.

"Read a newspaper," I said.

"Pet a dog," ventured Thom.

"Walk in the grass," offered Bob.

Before long we found ourselves imagining another expedition. We'd do it again, and we'd do it well. We'd be better prepared, with better equipment; the whalers wouldn't stand a chance.

After dinner, I was sitting in the lounge when Sîan shouted down from the deck that we should come and look at the view.

Icebergs were all over. The sea was flat and silver-gray. The bright bergs stood out in sharp relief against the dull sky. Above one large iceberg was a strange, almost ethereal patch of light.

"This place is weird," I said.

"I've never seen a sea like that," commented Sîan.

"And that light above the iceberg is just strange."

Ahead of us was a field of brash. Bob took a look at it and smiled to himself. It was loose and light; it wouldn't harm the ship.

"You wait," he said. "There'll be the banging of doors soon."

Sure enough, as the ship echoed to the crashing of the ice against its side, people came rushing out on deck to watch the *Greenpeace* cut a swath through the brash.

We turned north toward Australia and away from Antarctica, and soon we had left the whaling grounds behind us.

CHAPTER SIX

A Brief History of the Mismanagement of Whaling

THE WHALERS, NATURALLY ENOUGH, CONSISTENTLY SOUGHT TO belittle our efforts. A 1993 publication from the Institute of Cetacean Research, the body that oversees Japan's "scientific" whaling program, characterized the *Greenpeace* crew as spending "most of their time speeding pell-mell in their inflatables, emitting black exhaust in the tranquil Antarctic, without being checked by anybody, and unable to take any effective action against the Japanese fleet":

> [F]or most of the 82-day trip to the Antarctic the Greenpeacers' routine alternated between doing nothing and playing around in their boats, interspersed with picnics, cups of coffee and occasionally flying a kite.* It was hard to resist concluding that their true reason for coming to the Antarctic was not the official one, i.e., to save whales, but to enjoy the water sports. . . . All they

---

* At one point we experimented with the idea of flying a kite from an inflatable to try to block the harpooner's vision. Because of the Antarctic winds, that feat proved impossible to execute, and we never got any further than testing it out on the heli-deck. It must have indeed looked odd to the whalers.

needed to do was to send three or four photos of their action to the world's mass media through Reuter [*sic*], AP and AFP to satisfy contributors of funds to Greenpeace and to justify spending a small fortune so a group of youngsters could take a three-month cruise to the Antarctic . . . what a great deal these Greenpeace guys are getting if they can take a three-month cruise, eating and drinking and speeding around in inflatables, and all for nothing—not only for nothing, but actually getting paid for it!

However much our opponents may have mocked our efforts to stymie their fast catchers and giant factory vessel with our rubber boats and thirty-year-old tug, by the time we returned to Fremantle in western Australia, most of us felt we could hold our heads high. Whether we had actually achieved one of our primary initial goals and limited their catch, we couldn't be sure: when the fleet arrived in port in April, it was 42 whales short of its self-assigned quota of 330 whales, and although we saw some Tokyo press reports suggesting that the shortfall had been at least partly due to our efforts, the ICR later claimed that it was entirely due to two weeks of bad weather following our departure from the whaling grounds.

But of course, attempting to limit the number of whales killed by that particular fleet during that particular season was just one element of the expedition's rationale. The broader, more important goal was to help bring all commercial whaling—in the form of "scientific research" or any other guise—to a halt; in the spirit of the first *Phyllis Cormack* voyage, and indeed of Greenpeace activities worldwide ever since, it was just as vital, arguably more so, to use our presence in the Antarctic to highlight the fleet's continued activities, keep the issue in the public eye, and maintain political pressure on nonwhaling governments to encourage Japan to put its whaling fleet quietly out to pasture. Judging by the thick pile of press clippings awaiting us when we reached Australia, the first part of that strategy—attracting public and media attention—had been an unqualified success. What Greenpeace now needed to do was to ride the momentum our expedition had created, to take advantage of the increased media and public awareness of the fact that commercial whaling was being conducted in the Antarctic, to develop some serious political initiatives in order to bring that whaling to an end.

Not only did the Institute of Cetacean Research and its cronies at the Fisheries Agency of Japan dismiss the actions of those on the *Greenpeace* as risible, they questioned our very motivation, and that of everyone who worked for or supported Greenpeace or any other organization committed to ending commercial whaling. In particular, they sought—and continue to seek—to paint the whaling debate as a case of cultural imperialism, of Western nations and environmentalists attempting to impose their ill-considered, anthropomorphic sentimentality about whales onto a society that had hunted whales for centuries and that sought only to continue "harvesting" them in a sustainable manner that posed absolutely no threat to whale populations anywhere.

Such characterizations are dealt with easily enough. Japan does have a long cultural history associated with hunting cetaceans, but such hunting was sporadic at best until, somewhere around the end of the sixteenth century, scattered villages began chasing whales into bays or inlets, closing the entrances with nets, and rowing out to kill the whales with lance thrusts. Later, Yoriharu Wada organized crews in Taiji who rowed out to sea in pursuit of whales rather than waiting until they came close to the village. Wada's initiative, the first truly organized commercial whaling enterprise in Japan, began about 1675, a long time ago indeed. But the tradition of the British and Dutch, who ended commercial whaling in 1963 and 1964 respectively, dates to even earlier: dispatching vast fleets into the Arctic in pursuit of bowhead whales (and dominance over each other) for more than sixty years before Wada's venture got under way. Japan's Antarctic whaling has even less claim to cultural uniqueness, having started in 1934, by which time even such countries as Denmark and Panama had become minor

players on an Antarctic stage that had been dominated by
Norway and Britain since the first South Georgia whaling operation in 1904. It was resumed after World War II only under
instructions from General Douglas MacArthur, who considered it
necessary to provide protein for the defeated nation (and, not
coincidentally, oil for its conqueror).

As for the notion that the campaign against whaling is some
kind of East-versus-West clash of civilizations: that is belied by
the fact that Greenpeace and others have directed their efforts
against Australian, Icelandic, Norwegian, Peruvian, Soviet, and
Spanish whalers as well as Japanese ones; they would most
assuredly have prosecuted campaigns against the British, Dutch,
and Americans too, had not those three nations hung up their
harpoons when they did. The fact that most of the effort to end
commercial whaling in the late twentieth and early twenty-first
centuries is directed at Japan is an accident of history and
economics: whereas the likes of the Norwegian, British, and
Dutch whaling industries relied almost exclusively on whale oil
for their income, the Japanese also marketed the meat, and as a
result were able to continue squeezing profit out of a dying
industry even as vanishing whale populations made it impossible
for the others to continue. The Japanese whaling industry, in
other words (and, to a lesser extent, that of the Norwegians and
perhaps the Icelanders), simply happens to be the last one standing.

But the FAJ and ICR posit such arguments with a purpose,
developing them as smokescreens to obscure the fact that the
primary reason there is currently a moratorium on commercial
whaling, and the primary reason whale-hunting arouses such
opposition worldwide, is that the commercial whaling industry
has driven whale population after whale population, species
after species, into decline, toward or into extirpation, or even
into outright extinction. It has done so consistently and without
exception in the last four hundred years, and when obstacles in
the form of rules, regulations, or restrictions have been placed
in its path, it has typically found a way to hurdle or circumvent

them, ending its relentless pursuit of whale populations only when those populations have been exhausted.

There are few confident estimates of whale population numbers before the whalers did their worst, but where such estimates exist, the scale of the impact is clear. It has been reckoned, for example, that between 300,000 and 650,000 fin whales once lived in the Southern Ocean; today there are believed to be between 12,000 and 24,000. The blue whale has fared even worse, plunging from an estimated pre-exploitation Antarctic population of 250,000 to no more than 1,400 and perhaps as few as 400. Globally, numbers of humpback whales have declined from approximately 150,000 to roughly 35,000 (although most populations seem to be recovering or at least stable); southern right whales, from 70,000 to 7,000; bowheads, from 62,000 to 10,000.

For every piece of good news, there is seemingly at least one cause for pessimism: southern right whales, for example, are increasing steadily, at about 7 to 8 percent annually, and have been for some time; in the western North Atlantic, however, right whales number perhaps 300, and in the North Pacific possibly even fewer, while in the eastern North Atlantic, sightings are so infrequent that there is no certainty whether a population even remains there, or whether the occasional rights seen in that part of the ocean are wanderers from the western North Atlantic population. Bowhead whales in the western Arctic are also increasing by about 3 percent a year, but elsewhere the outlook is not so positive: in the Sea of Okhotsk, the species has plunged from more than 3,000 to 300–400; in the Davis Strait region, from almost 12,000 to approximately 350; in Hudson Bay, from about 580 to 270; and around Spitsbergen, where there once may have been as many as 24,000, the population now numbers, at most, in the tens. In the eastern North Pacific, the gray whales that migrate from Alaska to Baja California and back again, attracting thousands of onlookers along the West Coast, have rebounded to a level that is likely in excess of their pre-exploitation numbers, the only population to have done so; but in the western North Pacific, grays total perhaps 100, and in the Atlantic, the species has been extinct for approximately three hundred years.

Everywhere you look, it is a similar story. In the *Encyclopedia of Marine Mammals*, scientists Phil Clapham and Scott Baker note that

> Humpback and blue whales at South Georgia were commercially extinct by 1915 and 1936, respectively, and are rarely observed there today. Blue whales were wiped out from the coastal waters of Japan by about 1948, and no members of this species have been recorded there in recent years despite an often extensive survey effort. Off Gibraltar, a population of fin whales was extirpated with remarkable speed between 1921 and 1927. The population of humpbacks that used the coastal waters of New Zealand as a migratory route crashed in 1960 as a result of shore whaling and the 1959/1960 Soviet catches of almost 13,000 humpbacks in the feeding grounds to the south.

Not until well into the twentieth century did the whalers, recognizing that their lucrative industry risked extinguishing itself with its own voracity, begin to enact some kind of self-regulation. Norway, the pioneer and at that time the most prominent practitioner of modern industrial whaling, was the first to take steps to bring it under control. In 1929, its parliament passed the Norwegian Whaling Act: a landmark piece of legislation and the first law to control whaling on the high seas, it prohibited the killing of right whales, of calves of any species, and of females with calves in attendance; established minimum lengths for all species below which whales could not be killed; required all factory ships to keep records and carry observers; encouraged the full use of whale carcasses; formed a bureau for the collection of whaling statistics; and created a role for scientists in the formation of whaling policy.

The Norwegian Whaling Act was localized to the North Atlantic region, where that country's whalers had decimated rorqual populations. Two years later, under the aegis of the League of Nations, much of the Norwegian legislation was adapted to form the core of an international treaty, the Geneva Convention for the Regulation of Whaling. Completed and presented for signature in 1931, it did not enter into force until 1934, largely due to tardiness on the part of Britain in ratifying the document. Even then, it was ignored completely by Japan, Nazi Germany, and the Soviet Union. In 1937 another conference convened in London, once again boycotted by Japan and the Soviet Union, but attended this time by Germany as well as delegates from Argentina, Australia, Britain, Ireland, Norway, South Africa, and the United States, with Canada and Portugal sending observers. Intended to strengthen and expand existing regulations, it proved a dismal failure. As noted by Daniel Francis in *A History of World Whaling*:

> Delegates set minimum lengths for blue and fin whales, but these lengths were still high enough to allow the capture of sexually immature animals. They banned pelagic catching of baleen whales, except in the Antarctic, the North Pacific, and from shore stations, where 90 percent of world whaling took place. They established an open season for the Antarctic, December 8 to March 7, that was too long to have any effect. And they refused to limit the number of catchers, a measure that might have at least capped the growing slaughter.

If anything, Francis understates the agreement's shortcomings. Not only was the pelagic season too long to provide any respite for the whales, but it was actually a week longer than it had been prior to the conference—and still not long enough for the Japanese, who, having ignored the conference, also ignored its conclusions and further extended their own season by thirty-six days. Indeed, in the season following the London agreements, whalers killed a recorded 11,519 more baleen whales, and produced 683,815 more barrels of oil, than in the year before.

Following World War II the whaling nations tried again, this time with greater success. Whereas previous efforts had had little opportunity to gain traction, and anyway were spurned from the outset by some of the most important players, the International

Convention for the Regulation of Whaling, which was signed in
Washington, D.C., on December 2, 1946, remains the driving
force behind whaling management almost sixty years later,
making it among the most enduring of international agreements.

The ICRW started well. Its preamble recognized that "the
history of whaling has seen over-fishing of one area after another
to such a degree that it is essential to protect all species of whales
from future over-fishing." Article III established a standing body
to implement the convention, the International Whaling
Commission (IWC), which has met every year since 1949.

But there was a conflict at the heart of the ICRW and thus
the IWC from their very inception. The convention was, as
reflected in the language quoted above, essentially a fisheries
agreement (although whales are not, of course, fish), geared
toward regulating the hunting of whales rather than protecting
them for conservation's sake; the preamble noted that the
convention's purpose was to "provide for the proper conservation
of whale stocks and thus make possible the orderly development
of the whaling industry."

Given commercial whaling's history to that point, it might
seem that those twin goals would be irreconcilable, and so it
proved. In fact, for the first three decades of the IWC's
existence, neither whale populations nor the long-term
sustainability of the whaling industry was particularly well
served by the actions of the commission's member states. During
much of that period, the IWC was dominated by nations that
were actively practicing commercial whaling, and the theoretical
need to limit whaling for long-term sustainability almost always
lost out to the short-term desire to extract as much profit as
possible and let the future take care of itself.

From the outset, the Schedule to the convention (the ICRW
rule book, governing such issues as catch limits, restrictions, and
prohibitions) contained a set of guidelines taken from and built
upon the Geneva and London agreements: bans on the hunting
of right and gray whales anywhere in the world; establishment
of minimum-size limits; restrictions on factory ship operations;

and a prohibition on the hunting of humpback whales in the Antarctic. In most cases, these restrictions were no more rigorous than they had been under the ICRW's predecessors, but even then a few were too strong for the commission's founding member states. At the first IWC meeting, members promptly removed total protection of humpbacks in the Antarctic; it would not be reinstated until 1963. On those occasions when, instead of loosening standards, the commission imposed stricter limits, any countries that took exception could simply lodge objections within ninety days and be exempt until or unless they later chose not to be. France was the first to take advantage of this provision, objecting at the IWC's founding meeting to a decision to restrict the use elsewhere of factory ships that were primarily deployed in national waters; but others soon followed. Australia protested a 1951 decision to restrict sperm whaling from land stations; Iceland and Denmark exempted themselves from a ban on blue whaling in the North Atlantic. When the Netherlands lodged an objection to reduced Antarctic catch limits following the 1958 meeting, Japan, Norway, the United Kingdom, and the USSR—which had all voted for the catch limits during the meeting—followed suit to prevent the Dutch from gaining an unfair advantage; as a result, the restrictions were not binding on any of the countries that operated Antarctic whaling fleets.

Member states could also go one step further and threaten to leave the commission altogether. Japan, the Netherlands, and Norway announced their decision to withdraw in 1959; in response, notes the chairman's report of that year's meeting, "the Commission showed a willingness to consider making some increase in the Antarctic catch if thereby the loss of those member countries which had given notice of withdrawal could be averted." Japan did not, in the end, leave; Norway did, but rejoined in 1960. In an ultimately successful attempt to woo the remaining prodigal nation, the commission decided to set no Antarctic catch limits at all for the 1960–61 and 1961–62 whaling seasons.

But the gravest and most costly of the commission's failings in its formative years was that, with the exception of Southern Ocean humpbacks (and right whales and gray whales worldwide, catch limits for which were set at zero), the IWC did not regulate catches by limiting the number of individuals of particular species that could be killed in a given year. Instead, it maintained a system the whalers themselves had established in their pre-war efforts at self-regulation, based on the concept of the Blue Whale Unit (BWU).

The BWU was meant to represent the amount of oil that could theoretically be extracted from an individual of a particular species. Predictably and logically, if you killed one blue whale, you had one Blue Whale Unit. You could also reach one BWU by killing two fin whales, two and a half humpbacks, or six seis. (The BWU applied to baleen whales only in the Antarctic. Initially, the IWC did not overly concern itself with regulating North Pacific whaling, which was at this point very limited; nor, until the late 1960s, did it set catch limits for sperm whales anywhere.)

Until 1962—and the signing of a belated, formalized agreement to divide the BWU catch limit into national quotas—the operation was a free-for-all: on the opening day of the season, Antarctic whaling fleets immediately began chasing and catching whatever they could find and kill, reporting their catches at the end of each week to the International Bureau of Whaling Statistics in Norway. The bureau tallied the totals, guesstimated the point at which the limit would be reached, and declared that that day would be the end of the whaling season. The announcement sparked an even greater frenzy of all-out hunting: every whaling ship would work feverishly, twenty-four hours a day, seven days a week, to catch as many whales as possible before the deadline, in a concentrated slaughter known as the "Whaling Olympics."

No consideration was given to the abundance of different species, or of populations within those species. No distinction was made between male and female, adult and juvenile, pregnant and lactating. The whalers sought simply to extract as many BWU as swiftly and easily as possible—and that led to a pattern in which, one by one, the three largest rorquals were systematically driven close to oblivion. The logic was simple: harpooning one blue whale yielded the same number of BWUs as chasing down and hunting six seis, and was considerably less labor-intensive. When the blues were no longer plentiful enough to be found in any great numbers, the hunt switched to the fin whale and then the sei. In the 1930–31 Antarctic season, for example, whalers took a reported 29,410 blue whales (the highest total ever) and 10,017 fins; five years later, the figures were, respectively, 17,731 and 9,697. That was the last year the number of blue whales hunted by whalers exceeded that of fin whales; the following year, the take was 14,304 blues to 14,381 fins, and the year after that, the fin whale catch soared, to 28,009. In the 1935–36 season, Antarctic whalers killed just two sei whales; twenty-one years later, the sei catch overtook that of blues for the first time: 1,697 to 1,512. Blue whales were in a rapid downward spiral, and the sei whale catch started to increase; but throughout the 1950s, it was still the fin whale that bore the brunt of the Blue Whale Unit. From the 1953–54 season until 1961–62, the fin whale catch in the Antarctic never once dropped below 27,000, and then suddenly it crashed: from 1962–63 to 1965–66, reported catches fell from 18,668 to 2,536. Sei whale catches increased to take the fin whale's place— leaping from 8,695 in 1963–64 to 20,380 in 1964–65—and then also started to take a nosedive. One by one, the rorquals of the Southern Ocean had been systematically wiped out, leaving only the hitherto largely ignored minke whale in anything close to its original numbers.

The IWC finally abandoned the Blue Whale Unit in 1972, but by then the damage had been done. The same year, the U.N. Conference on the Human Environment called for a ten-year moratorium on commercial whaling, and a similar proposal was put before the IWC. That proposal failed, however, with just four countries (Argentina, Mexico, the United Kingdom, and the United States) voting in favor, six (Iceland, Japan, Norway, Panama, South Africa, and the USSR) voting against, and four (Australia, Canada, Denmark, and France) abstaining. In 1973 the moratorium's supporters tried again: Australia, Canada, and France shifted from abstaining to favoring the proposal, and Panama's no vote became a yes. For the first time, a majority of the IWC now favored shutting down commercial whaling altogether, at least for a while, but the margin of victory (8 votes to 5 with one abstention) was well short of the required three-quarters majority.

In 1974 the U.S. delegation tabled a moratorium resolution for a third time, but the commission instead adopted an Australian compromise proposing that, whenever the IWC's Scientific Committee determined that a population had fallen below a particular level, that population should automatically be declared off-limits to commercial whaling. Coming into effect in 1975, this New Management Procedure (NMP) divided whale populations into three levels, of which the lowest—Protected Stock—conferred automatic protection (subject, of course, to the usual use of the objection clause and other avoidance devices). A vast improvement over the IWC's mismanagement of whales and whaling up to that point, the NMP, it soon became clear, was nonetheless far from a panacea. It proved highly effective in preventing further commercial whaling on already severely depleted populations, but for others it required a level of scientific knowledge—both of current numbers and of estimated pre-exploitation population sizes—that simply didn't exist. Members of the Scientific Committee were rarely able to reach agreement on whether a stock should be protected, and while they squabbled, the commission continued to assign quotas that were all too frequently higher than the population could withstand.

By the time I stood up to discuss Greenpeace's recent Antarctic adventures at a press conference to open the 1992 IWC meeting in Glasgow, Scotland, the NMP had long been abandoned, although it was officially still on the books. Unable to iron out the kinks, the commission had in 1982 finally adopted a global moratorium on commercial whaling, and the Scientific Committee was dedicating itself to developing a more reliable management program to take the NMP's place. At the Glasgow meeting, the commission adopted in principle a mathematical algorithm for calculating catch limits of baleen whales, agreeing that it would form the core of what was being referred to as the Revised Management Procedure, or RMP.

One media outlet mistakenly reported, following the adoption of the catch-limit algorithm, that the IWC had agreed to overturn the moratorium. That wasn't the case at all. What it had done was to agree in principle to a particular method of calculating catch limits that could be used as part of a future management program. It was far short of a green light to an immediate, or even imminent, resumption of commercial whaling; even if it adopted the RMP in principle, the IWC would still be under no obligation to lift the moratorium. Nonetheless, it was a definite sign that the IWC was taking the first, positive steps toward adopting a new, hopefully safer means of managing commercial whaling.

Whether that was a good thing or not was far from a matter of unanimity, but support for and opposition to the RMP sometimes came from different quarters than might have been expected. Some of the countries whose governments ostensibly stood resolutely opposed to all commercial whaling were actually quietly keen on the RMP, feeling that it provided an excellent opportunity to slam the door on the whalers' plans while simultaneously giving them the chance to wash their hands of an issue that wouldn't go away.

To its most optimistic supporters, the RMP would, once adopted, prove so conservative and limiting that the whalers' hopes of returning to full-fledged, large-scale commercial whaling would be dashed. Much more conservative than previous management programs, it would automatically prohibit whaling on stocks for which there was insufficient information or which had achieved Protected Stock status under the NMP—two considerations that immediately placed the vast majority of whale populations under automatic protection—and seemed likely to set extremely low catch limits on the rest.

Privately, some of the pro-whaling nations were concerned that the RMP as it was being developed was actually a little too conservative for their tastes; and so, as much as they lamented the unfairness of the moratorium and their desire to have a new management system in place as soon as possible, some were quite happy to play for time and hope that delays in the procedure's formal adoption would give them opportunities to weaken it until it was to their liking. The RMP process was thus the center of a delicate dance, with some of those who proclaimed most loudly and publicly that they wanted it implemented, and the moratorium overturned, as swiftly as possible, in fact being the most keen to maintain the status quo; and some governments that officially were strictly opposed to the resumption of commercial whaling on scientific grounds fairly keen to see the RMP come to fruition.

But if the RMP looked likely to be extremely hard on at least some whaling interests, it was far from universally welcomed by whaling's opponents. For one thing, the majority of environmental organizations, and governments of countries such as Australia and New Zealand, rejected the notion of "management" of commercial whaling, however it was done; they felt that the world had simply moved away from needing to kill whales for money. It was time, they argued, to learn the lessons of the past, to look at the world's whales as something other than a "resource" to be exploited for profit.

Even among those IWC member countries that felt unable to adopt a blanket statement of opposition to commercial whaling, there were some concerns about the consequences of adopting a new management program. By every indication, the RMP was more conservative, more foolproof, almost watertight. But hadn't similar assurances been given about the NMP as well? The RMP was based on computer models that necessitated inputting estimated data on such things as the reproduction rates of whale populations; what if those estimates were wrong, and the RMP also accidentally led to declines in whale numbers? Those responsible for devising the RMP were scientists whose concern for whale conservation was well known, and who insisted that no such mistakes could happen with this new program, that safeguards were built in to ensure its safety and security. But still, it was difficult to be sure.

There was another issue, and a very specific one. The RMP's catch-limit algorithm included a "tuning level" of 72 percent: in other words, among its aims was to manage whale stocks at, or close to, 72 percent of their pre-exploitation levels. For the vast majority of whale populations, massively reduced by decades and even centuries of hunting, that was way above present levels. But there was one population that, it was believed at the time, remained way above 72 percent of pre-exploitation numbers because it had been the last to be targeted in significant numbers; according to most estimates, even after some depletion as a result of recent whaling, it was closer to 90 percent. This population was the one that those of us on board the *Greenpeace* had recently devoted three months to protecting: the minke whales of the Southern Ocean. The Antarctic minkes were the most vulnerable to renewed large-scale hunting if the moratorium were overturned; now, under the rules being proposed, the RMP, if adopted, might actually *require* their numbers to be severely reduced.

What was needed was a safety net—something that, while not compromising the scientific effort that had led to the RMP, protected the Southern Ocean minkes from depletion. The safety net arrived, just prior to the Glasgow meeting, courtesy of the government of France.

In fact, it went further than merely providing a safeguard for Southern Hemisphere minkes. The proposal was to "designate all the waters of the Southern Hemisphere south of 40 degrees South latitude as a sanctuary." In other words, if adopted, it would make the Antarctic off-limits to commercial whaling irrespective of whether a management system existed. To quote from the text of the proposal:

[T]he RMP will be implemented on a species by species, stock by stock basis, whereas a sanctuary for all species of whales would have as its focus the restoration, as a whole, of a complex of species and populations. Such complexes have been much damaged and distorted by industrial whaling, and nowhere more so than in the Southern Hemisphere. It might be thought that humans could manipulate and thus assist restoration while continuing to kill some whale species in commercial numbers. It has even been suggested that a resumption of minke whaling is needed in order to assist the recovery of the Blue whale. But scientists do not agree about whether there is evidence—as distinct from mere speculation—for substantial interactions between these species, and between them and other species. Furthermore, even if some evidence were to appear, we certainly are far from being able to calculate the consequences of continued selective whaling or of assessing objectively the consequences of such intervention. So, if the Southern Ocean is, as a matter of long-term policy, to be restored—as far as the whales are concerned—close to its state before the most destructive whaling began in the 1930s, then we have no option but to protect all whales there and monitor the changes in that ecosystem as best we can.

The area the proposed sanctuary would cover included the main feeding grounds of the sperm whale and all the baleen whales except the tropical Bryde's whale. Its northern boundary—40 degrees South—marked roughly the northern limit of distribution of most of the species on which the whales feed. Added to an existing ban on pelagic whaling worldwide for all species except minkes, and an Indian Ocean Sanctuary that had been established in 1979, the Southern Ocean Sanctuary had the potential to become the cornerstone of a package that would effectively protect close to 100 percent of the world's whales, even if the moratorium were lifted at some point in the future—particularly if, when and if the moratorium were ultimately lifted, it were replaced with a highly conservative RMP.

Evidently the whalers saw it the same way, because immediately after the proposal was made, they paid it the greatest possible compliment by attacking it. Iceland and Japan wrote to the IWC Secretariat arguing that the proposal was "inappropriate," even though no details had at that stage been distributed.

But there had always been a provision within the ICRW for the establishment of whale sanctuaries, most notably, as previously mentioned, in the Indian Ocean. There was even a precedent for a sanctuary in the Antarctic: following the London Agreement of 1937, all southern waters between 160 degrees West and 70 degrees West were set aside as "the Sanctuary," ostensibly to protect part of the Antarctic feeding grounds that had not yet been subject to commercial whaling. But in 1955, under pressure from some of its members (led by Japan), the IWC opened "the Sanctuary" to commercial whaling.

It was clear that the prospect of a sanctuary covering the entire Antarctic, and then some, filled Japan with dread. Its adoption would prohibit the Scientific Committee from even calculating catch limits for any Southern Ocean populations, as well as prevent the commission itself from ever setting any limits. It would, in other words, bring down the curtain on any hopes of a resumption of large-scale, and profitable, commercial whaling in the Southern Ocean.

Unfortunately, because of the vagaries of IWC rules, the sanctuary would only affect openly commercial whaling; it would not prohibit Japan's "scientific research." But it was no secret that the purpose of the "scientific" whaling program was to keep equipment operational, crews trained and experienced, and a whale meat market open, until such time as full-scale commercial whaling could be resumed. If the sanctuary could remove the prospect of such a resumption, then perhaps, over time, it would diminish and eliminate the incentive to maintain the research facade.

The Japanese government sent teams of diplomats fanning out across the world in an effort to persuade other IWC members not to support the sanctuary proposal. This "persuasion" took different forms depending on the country concerned, although Japan continued to insist that any confluence between a nation's voting pattern at the IWC and the amount of Japanese fisheries development aid it received was entirely coincidental.

Unfortunately for the sanctuary, barely had the proposal been announced than the French government collapsed and Brice Lalonde, the environment minister and prime architect of the proposal, resigned. With nobody in Paris to push the sanctuary with anything like the same fervor that Tokyo was trashing it, the fight was lost from the opening bell, at least for that year. But the proposal was circulated at the Glasgow IWC meeting, and it was agreed to return to the subject the following year, in Kyoto, Japan.

At Greenpeace, the sanctuary became the centerpiece of the anti-whaling campaign; a couple of months before the Glasgow meeting, shortly after the French announced their intention to table the proposal, we began publicizing it, and lobbying for its adoption, with vigor. Its failure in Glasgow only encouraged us to redouble our efforts; we would have a lot more time to prepare for the Kyoto meeting than we had had for Glasgow, but even so, we were concerned by the apparent lack of enthusiasm for the idea even among many of the more ardently conservationist nations in the IWC. We realized that to give ourselves the greatest possible chance of making an impact, we'd have to deploy the biggest guns we had at our disposal, and in recent years nothing Greenpeace had done had been as successful at drawing attention to the issue of whaling in the Antarctic as the previous year's expedition. If we launched another expedition, and if that voyage could match or even exceed what we had achieved before in terms of confronting the whalers and generating media coverage and public support, and if that coverage and support could be directed not just at the general notion of protecting whales in the Antarctic but at supporting the sanctuary, then maybe we might start winning the hearts and minds of enough governments to set the proposal on the path to success.

Fremantle, Australia, November 8, 1992
"Welcome aboard," said Arne, extending his hand as I appeared, trailing bags, in the mess room of the *Greenpeace*. Then he stopped and corrected himself. "Welcome *back*, I should say."

Arne Sørensen was slim, with a thin beard skirting his chin and jaw. Less expansive and outgoing than Bob Graham, our captain on the previous voyage, he had bright eyes that revealed a fierce intelligence hidden behind an apparently quiet and self-effacing exterior. He was quick-witted, logical, and possessed of a virtually unrivaled knowledge of the natural and human history of Antarctica.

Among Antarctic skippers and ice pilots, Arne was something of a legend. He had been the master of the *Nella Dan*, the Australian government resupply and research vessel that had been stuck in the ice for seven weeks during the infamous 1985–86 season—the same season that had thwarted the Black Pig's initial attempt to establish World Park Base at the southern end of the Ross Sea. Shortly thereafter, he had joined Greenpeace and had been at the helm of the *Gondwana* on all its voyages to the Greenpeace base. Now, with the *Gondwana*'s mission over and Bob Graham unavailable for this campaign because of family commitments, it was Arne's turn to take us south.

His experience and ability in and around the ice would be essential on this voyage. The previous year the whalers had been operating in what the IWC refers to as Whaling Area IV; this time they would be in Area V, farther to the east—south of New Zealand and eastern Australia, as opposed to south and south-west of Australia. Area V included the Ross Sea, which is accessible to non-icebreaking vessels such as the *Greenpeace* for only a few weeks each year, and which extends as far south as it is possible to go in a ship. There would be plenty of ice here, and after several seasons taking the *Gondwana* to McMurdo Sound and Ross Island, in the south of the sea, to resupply World Park Base, Arne knew the area as well as anyone.

The previous season's expedition had been put together with no thought of it becoming a regular event. It was too big, too complicated, and too demanding, and its chances of success too uncertain, for it to be considered anything but a one-off campaign. Even after we had returned, and the verdict was rendered that, despite all the difficulties and doubts we had experienced, the trip had been an overwhelming success, nobody began making any concrete plans for a follow-up. But the *Greenpeace* was laid up in Fremantle, we conducted lots of "what if" discussions (Bob Graham, Walt Simpson, John Frizell, Naoko Funahashi, and I had a meeting in Glasgow to put together a possible crew; and Paul Bogart, the Antarctic campaign coordinator, asked me what I thought of combining a whaling campaign with some base visits), and before long we had in some sense drifted into the inevitable.

There's only one way to follow up a once-in-a-lifetime experience, after all, and that's to do it all over again.

There was more than a touch of déjà vu about it all. Once more, the decisive step was taken after my boss, Anne Dingwall, and I talked it over in a bar in Amsterdam one night. We agreed we had to try it a second time; with the ship in Australia and a sanctuary proposal on the table, it was too good an opportunity to miss. Days later, we had drafted a prospectus—digging through the files for the previous year's version, shortening it, upping the cost estimates a little—and presented it for approval to the Greenpeace board.

This time, we argued, little would be left to chance. We would review the mistakes and shortcomings from the first trip and see where we could improve our planning and execution. We would be better organized, better prepared, better equipped. We would be altogether more professional. The first time around, we had caused the fleet undoubted grief. If we were going to justify a second trip, this time we would have to do more than that: we would have to be able to keep up with them, stick with them, follow them everywhere and, as much as possible, shut them down.

The main cast of characters was essentially the same: Naoko, Athel, and I would be leading the campaign on the ship, with the slight difference that, in an attempt to improve information flow, I would be promoted to joint expedition coordinator; John Frizell would be guiding us from land; and Walt Simpson would be the person in Amsterdam putting it all together. The crew would be mostly different: some of the past year's crew were currently serving on other ships in the fleet; some had left Greenpeace; and we searched for replacements with as much experience as we could find. By the time the final crew list was drawn up, its outline fit that bill pretty well indeed. Of thirty people—campaigners and crew alike—making the trip south, eighteen had been to the Antarctic at least once before, most of them with Greenpeace. Eight were first-class navigators, holding mate's or master's tickets. And although a few were making only their first or second voyage with Greenpeace, most had been around for several years and some for over a decade. It was a crew that would, it seemed, be able to keep its head when things weren't going well, but would give their all when the heat was on.

This second time around, our equipment would be substantially upgraded as well. There would be an extra long-range inflatable, the Hurricane, with the same speed and range as the Rock Boat, making it easier to cover two out of three catchers at any one time in all but the worst weather. And while the whalers' fastest ships were still some seven knots faster than the *Greenpeace*, this time we'd be taking a helicopter, which was more than eighty knots faster than any of them. A helicopter would expand our search capabilities and, we hoped, make the fleet less inclined to run away when they saw us come over the horizon. It would give us an extra weapon to cover any of the vessels in the fleet: the idea of using a helicopter to hang in front of a harpoon was more dramatic—and doubtless more intimidating—even than the tried, tested, and already successful technique of placing inflatables between whales and whalers. And the helicopter would also provide a new and more versatile platform from which to gather the all-important documentation of the fleet's activities and our efforts to stop them.

Distributing that documentation to the rest of the world would also be easier. On the first voyage we had been able to wire out still photographs virtually at will, but releasing video footage had been limited to mailing some tapes home via the *Aurora Australis* and handing them to the media when we arrived in Fremantle. Since then, Greenpeace had bought a new machine, generally referred to as a "squisher," which would allow us to save snippets of video to a computer and send them via satellite phone to Greenpeace Communications, where they could be disseminated to the world's television news desks.

There was one other major difference from the previous trip. This time around, our duties would extend beyond chasing after the whaling fleet. On the previous expedition, we had not even seen land for almost eighty days; this time we would actually be going ashore on Antarctica. Built into the voyage was a week to visit the Italian and German stations, Terra Nova and Gondwana, in Terra Nova Bay on the western edge of the Ross Sea, as well as the U.S. base of McMurdo and New Zealand's Scott Base, both in McMurdo Sound. And while we were down in McMurdo Sound, we'd pay a visit to the site of World Park Base.

The year before, in October 1991, the member states of the Antarctic Treaty had agreed on an Environmental Protocol, which imposed tough new standards on countries operating on the continent and declared Antarctica off-limits to mining for at least fifty years. Although environmental standards in the Antarctic weren't going to clear up overnight—or even necessarily in the foreseeable future—Greenpeace felt that its permanent presence on the continent had achieved what it could and that, with the mining ban, the main justification for the base had gone. And so, while we had been enjoying the company of the whalers, the crew of the *Gondwana* had been quietly dismantling World Park Base and taking it back to New Zealand.

Now, one year later, we would be going back to check up on the site, conduct an environmental impact assessment, and remove any litter or debris, however small, that may have remained. One of Greenpeace's strongest criticisms of countries with bases on Antarctica was that, when the bases were no longer needed, they were simply abandoned, usually with no effort made to clean up the site afterward. In contrast, Greenpeace was determined that, its work on the continent having been completed, World Park Base would be removed and all traces of its presence there taken away also.

In charge of the work onshore would be Dana Harmon. Making her third trip south with Greenpeace in as many years, Dana had been in charge of the *Gondwana*'s last voyage the year before, and was well known to many of the old Antarctic hands we would be taking with us as crew this time around. I'd known her for years, pretty much from the time when I first joined the organization and she was helping edit the Greenpeace magazine in Washington, D.C. Dana was quiet, studious, and efficient, but she was also a lot of fun to have around, and I was looking forward to her being on the trip.

Everything was set. It would be the same as before, but better. We had a more experienced crew, better and bigger inflatables, even a helicopter. We had a political objective—the proposed sanctuary—to support. We had made our mistakes, seen the fleet in action, noticed their strengths and weaknesses, and tried to build them into our game plan.

The problem, of course, was that the whalers would be better prepared as well. The first time around, we hadn't appreciated exactly what they would be able to throw at us, and had been caught totally off-guard when they replaced the old factory ship with the new *Nisshin Maru*. But at the same time, we did at least have the element of surprise. Perhaps we hadn't known quite what to expect, but they had had no idea we were coming at all.

One year later, that was no longer the case. And if we had basically thrown this trip together over the course of a few weeks, there seemed little doubt that the folks at the ICR had been plotting and planning a lot longer, and in much more depth. And no matter how much extra or upgraded equipment we carried, we would still be heavily overmatched: four fast ships against one slow tug.

No one will ever know, of course, if we could have done anything that would have substantially changed the way things went, that would have produced a different outcome. As it was, as Australia receded into the distance and we plunged once more into the Antarctic, as the temperature dropped and we became enveloped in the now-familiar shroud of fog and ice, as each morning passed without the company of the whaling fleet, as the little breaks that might have fallen in our favor instead turned firmly against us, as each setback magnified the one that came after it, and as the uncertainty and dismay at losing the initiative gnawed at us and caused us to turn on each other, it grew increasingly apparent that, slowly but surely, we were steaming into a disaster.

CHAPTER SEVEN

Chronicle of a Voyage from Hell ·

IT WASN'T UNTIL CHRISTMAS, AFTER WE'D BEEN AT SEA A LITTLE more than two weeks, that the voyage began to unravel. Until then, even as the weather turned against us, even as the days slipped by with no sign of the whalers or any certainty where they might really be, there was no obvious sense of despair.

We developed all kinds of excuses to explain why we hadn't yet found the fleet. We'd only just arrived in the whaling grounds. They were probably just over the horizon and we would have spotted them with the helicopter if the mist hadn't rolled in when it did. We had been incredibly close, but they had been just outside radar range and had slipped past us in the night.

So many reasons, all of them credible, and all of them good enough that we were almost able to convince ourselves of their veracity. But with every new reason for failure, each additional missed opportunity, our faith in a positive outcome steadily diminished.

The expedition had been plagued with problems since

Australia. Groupies and hangers-on constantly pestered us, inviting friends onto the ship for parties we hadn't arranged and appointing themselves our intermediaries with the press. Mechanical problems cropped up constantly: the propeller shaft broke; a small oil leak threatened to put us out of action for weeks; a part for the freshwater-maker was missing and its replacement, ordered from Denmark, languished in a crate at the airport because of a baggage-handlers' strike. During boat practice shortly after leaving port, one of the crew was struck full in the face by the crane hook and knocked almost unconscious. And all the while, we battled an underlying, omnipresent yet somehow indefinable feeling that this time around, it just wasn't going to work out right.

Yet there was initially no shipwide sense of frustration or panic. The crew was remarkably patient and relaxed, content to wait for action and willing to cut us campaigners some slack, happy to believe we knew what we were doing. And for the first few days at the ice edge, the overall feeling was largely one of cautious optimism. The weather was clear and bright; inflatables and helicopter were dispatched on searches, hopeful of finding the fleet just behind the next iceberg.

A few days after we had reached the ice edge, the weather closed in. Day after day, the fog seemed ever present, swirling around us continuously, cutting us off from the rest of the world and sealing us inside our own cold, gray cocoon. Not only did the fog make it more difficult to search for the fleet—at times it burned off just long enough for Paula Huckleberry, the helicopter pilot, to suit up and for her mechanic to fuel the helicopter for takeoff, only to watch helplessly as it rolled back in—it also had a strange effect on life on board. It added to the sense of isolation, weighing down on us, dulling the senses, and dampening sound as well as limiting vision. Everything appeared colder, quieter. Optimism began to seep away, and we all steadily slipped into monotonous routine. The ocean tapped diffidently at the *Greenpeace*'s hull as we drifted idly or steamed into the murk, as most of us on board went through the motions of doing our watches, whiling away the hours in our cabins, or lounging in the mess. From time to time, those of us on the campaign team reckoned we'd worked out the fleet's movements and, for a day or two, there would be a slight surge of encouragement as we steamed in a new direction or hatched a new plan. But as the disappointments grew more numerous, the level of excitement diminished with each new turn as we cushioned ourselves for the inevitable letdown.

By December 26, as the ship idled quietly in the mist and the crew recovered slowly from Christmas Day, we had been searching without success for two weeks. We had assumed from the very beginning, long before setting sail again, that this time around, the fleet would adopt a more flexible strategy for its movements through the whaling grounds. From information we received in Australia, we knew the whalers' revised plan allowed them to steam through the night, for one thing: ostensibly a development for the betterment of science, it presumably was also motivated by a desire to flee from Greenpeace for long periods, if and when necessary.

The new plan also included time in what was referred to as a Special Monitoring Zone, or SMZ. This was an area of the whaling grounds on which the fleet would concentrate special attention, visiting it for fifteen days at a time before, during, and after the rest of the regular survey. Unfortunately for us, we had no indication as to the SMZ's size or location; and if we couldn't figure out where it was, we wouldn't have a clue where the whalers would start, or where they would be headed next. At a stroke, the whalers had turned our strategy upside down: if we couldn't find them within the first fifteen days, the odds were suddenly that much greater that we wouldn't find them at all.

After two weeks of fruitless searching, we were already staring failure in the face, and frustration was building up in all of us. The more helpless each of us on the campaign team felt, the more we lashed out at the others, as if the problems we faced were their fault. As a result, campaign meetings became not only unhelpful but hostile and unpleasant. We each began to dread them more, to hate the prospect of undergoing the ordeal yet again, having to stumble around tiptoeing through the minefield of collected egos and sensitivities, and trying to solicit information and ideas without offending anybody. On occasion, our efforts to avoid conflict went so far that we did little except sit around the table in Arne's cabin, staring at a chart as if the whalers might suddenly appear on it, mumbling a little, and agreeing to continue steaming up and down or drifting for half a day at a time.

As teamwork in these circumstances became progressively less productive, we splintered into different cliques. Athel's hours changed: he would wake up in the middle of the night and spend the 0400–0800 watch plotting with David Iggulden, the first mate. Sometimes, after they'd hatched some plan, he'd wake me up and try to get me to make a decision on the spot. Or he would sit in the cabin, quietly fuming and then, every so often, exploding in a fit of frustration, trying to force Naoko into more meetings, or lecturing the two of us that nobody knew what was going on and it was all our fault. I sought out the companionship and support of my closest friends on board: Dana, Paula, Thom, and Martin Freimuller and Sarah Macnab the cooks. Arne and Naoko mostly sat alone in their respective cabins.

With the whalers by now presumably finished in the SMZ, we truly had absolutely no idea where the fleet might be. Even if the fog did roll back enough to allow us to launch the helicopter, that was of only minimal help without a rough idea of the fleet's location. For fuel and safety reasons, the helicopter could fly no more than about a hundred miles away from the *Greenpeace*, but the whaling area was thousands of miles from end to end and over a million square miles in area. Paula could help us refine our search, but she couldn't work miracles.

Among "management"—Athel, Naoko, Arne, David, and me—the sense of despair and frustration grew ever more palpable. And it was only made worse by the knowledge that there was no escaping it, that each morning brought another day of floundering in the mist and trying to patch together a plan without promoting yet more internal fissures.

The Ballenys are a group of five volcanic islands located a few hundred miles north of Victoria Land, west of the Ross Sea. Even in summer, the path between the islands and the mainland is frequently blocked by ice; some years the ice extends far and thick, well to the north and impenetrable to all but the sturdiest ships. Until the age of giant icebreakers ferrying tourists on cruises with strict itineraries, the Balleny Islands had been seen by very few, even among those who had sailed to and explored the Antarctic at length. There have been hardly any landings; some islands appear to have no area where a human could ever hope to gain a foothold. In a time when even the frozen continent has slowly yielded its secrets to human exploration, the Balleny Islands stand out as one of the few remaining bastions of resistance to our species' urge to conquer.

As we struggled to salvage something from the expedition, we encountered the Balleny Islands twice. We should have felt proud and excited—and indeed, for a while at least, most of us did. But there is a reason why the Ballenys are so rarely sighted or even approached: they sit in one of the stormiest, iciest, most treacherous areas of water in an ocean renowned for being the stormiest, iciest, most treacherous in the world. Those two encounters, bookending a couple of weeks in which the search for the whalers reached both its peak of excitement and its debilitating trough of defeat, saw those conditions at their most extreme. In a sense, at least looking back on them a few years later, they were the defining moments of the whaling campaign, a double body blow that pretty much finished off any hope we had of doing anything except getting back alive.

However grim our situation seemed, we couldn't simply roll over and play dead. A lot was riding on our shoulders, and we had to keep trying. There was no telling whether the fleet might have been behind the next iceberg, or whaling just out of range. As long as we could muster enough dialogue between us to agree to move on when it was clear that we had exhausted our prospects in a particular place, we would at least be able to maintain a sense of positive action.

On about the fortieth day at sea, we were approaching one of those moments when a rapid decision was vital. For a few days, we had been crashing about the mouth of the Ross Sea, charging from one side to the other, probing the steadily retreating ice edge and then steaming back in the direction from which we had just come; it was in the whalers' plans to enter the Ross Sea at some point during their voyage, and we hoped that maybe, as they did so, we would come across them during one of our mad dashes along the entrance.

Enthusiasm was flagging; we needed to either find the whalers soon or start thinking about trying something else. Following the requisite combination of goading, prodding, teeth-pulling, demands for action, temper tantrums, and reluctant acceptance of the inevitable, we decided to try our luck else-where, on the assumption that if they weren't entering the Ross Sea, the whalers were still working the ice edge to the west. We headed around Cape Adare, the promontory that marks the unofficial boundary of the Ross Sea, and steamed toward the Balleny Islands, beyond which we reasoned the fleet might lie.

The journey was dangerous. The ice was thicker than any we had encountered so far on either voyage, and for several days as we made our transit, life below decks was dominated by sounds of crashing and rumbling as the ice ground against the hull, reluctantly giving way to the Black Pig's urgent pushing. Occasionally the ship would slam into particularly hard pieces, knocking unlashed belongings off shelves in cabins down below.

At times the ice grew too thick to risk tackling it head on with a ship as old and relatively fragile as the *Greenpeace*. When that happened, we had no option but to yield and steer around it in hopes of finding a way through. In places it was so thick that we even had to steer east-southeast as the safest and surest way to eventually head west.

And all the while the seemingly omnipresent fog toyed with us, clearing away long enough to lull us into a false sense of security before appearing suddenly once more and blanketing us in its cold, gray shroud. When that happened, the view from the bridge was eerie: the ship moving slowly, cautiously, nosing its way through the brash, and the lookouts in the wheelhouse peering almost desperately through the windows, watching for the huge lumps of ice that suddenly loomed out of the mist, forcing the mate to change direction. More than once, visibility became so poor that Arne deemed it too treacherous to risk going any farther and ordered the ship stopped. So we sat in the fog, ice swarming around us, and watched and waited for the chance to move on.

On the morning of January 18, Athel woke me up at 0630. We were ahead of schedule, he said, and practically on top of the Ballenys. We were on course to head east and then north of the islands, he said, so if the whalers passed south of the islands on their way to the Ross Sea, we'd miss them. And Thom had told him that if the islands were between us and the whalers, we'd miss the opportunity to hear any radio transmissions they might make.

I got up, had a shower, made a cup of tea, and went to the bridge. David Iggulden pointed to the course that Arne had plotted—which, indeed, would take us up the eastern side of the Ballenys, then north of the islands. I assumed that was because there was no passage south of the islands due to ice, but David reckoned that no, according to the latest ice charts, it didn't look as if that route was blocked. Why I imagined that any decision concerning Antarctic navigation that I could make at seven o'clock in the morning would in any way be superior to one that Arne had reached after due consideration the night before, I don't know. But I listened to David and I listened to Athel and I shrugged and I said OK. Then I woke Naoko and asked her what she thought; she, in no better state to work these things out than I, agreed. And so we changed course to head south of the Ballenys.

Later I went into Arne's cabin to say hello. He asked if the purpose of going south had been purely to check the ice edge and I said that was part of it, but also relayed what I had been told by Athel and David earlier that morning. He mumbled that that was all very well, but heading south of the islands was pretty pointless if we couldn't then get through. For some reason, he didn't press the point and I didn't follow it up. It was a measure of the state into which we were all falling that I let it glide over me and we continued heading south of the Ballenys.

We sat there for a while, and spoke about how clueless we all were, and how we were really just groping in the dark. Arne looked at the apple he was holding and began slowly juggling it from one hand to the other.

"To be honest," he said, "I don't think this is working very well," and I could only agree. "It certainly isn't teamwork," he added, and I nodded some more. "Right now," he continued, still juggling his apple and looking out the window, "it isn't very challenging, very worthwhile, very interesting, very—anything."

Arne was one of the most experienced and highly respected Antarctic pilots in the world, and here he was being jerked around by the ineptitude and attitude of the campaign team. I really felt bad for him, and hated that I was at least partly responsible for the depth of his despair.

I looked outside. The fog, which had begun lifting earlier, was closing in again. It was starting to snow. We both snorted a laugh of sorts.

"Well, there is one thing to be pleased about," offered Arne. "They certainly won't be whaling in this."

It was small consolation.

As the day went on, the weather deteriorated. Fog was continuing to close in, and a Force 8 wind was whipping up rolling, whitecapped swells. Ice was everywhere. At about 1400, Arne gave up trying to go due west, which would have taken us south of the islands. Did he want to turn back and resume the course north of the islands that he had plotted earlier? No, he'd try to find a passage to the leeward side of the islands that was ice-free.

It was a miserable afternoon, and I started to get pissed off. It was gray, it was horrible, the ship was taking a battering, it was rough up in the wheelhouse, and we weren't getting anywhere. The visibility was so poor that even though charts and radar showed we were within two and a half miles of Sturge Island, the largest and southernmost Balleny, we couldn't see it.

Within fifteen minutes, everything had changed. People were beginning to wander up on deck with their cameras. One of the crew came by the cabin and said we could see land.

"What, with the naked eye?" I asked, surprised. Sure, he said, and Arne was getting closer, too. I wrapped up, grabbed my camera, and went up to take a look.

When I got up on deck, the sight was truly breathtaking. Sturge Island, wrapped in an ethereal cloud, rose out of the frozen water like an ancient, imposing fort guarded by a moat of pack ice. As if moving to defend the island, the pack headed toward us, wave after wave of thick floes of ice coming to meet and repel us as Arne tried to steer a way through. It was devastatingly beautiful. Here we were, in the middle of nowhere and suddenly face to face with a dramatic, silent sentinel, black volcanic rock partially covered with ice and shrouded in mist, standing guard over this otherwise empty patch of ocean as we struggled to get past.

Grant Harper came and stood next to me. Our resident scientist, on board to head up the shore work at the site of World Park Base, Grant could hardly contain himself. "Do you realize that probably only a couple of thousand people have ever seen these islands?" he pointed out, beaming. "Most people just sail right by them and never see them, because of fog."

The pack was closing in now, and Arne, instead of trying to wind a way through, had resorted to trying to nudge it out of the way. We would approach a piece of pack, Arne giving orders to go half ahead, half astern, or stop, and David frantically working the telegraph. As everybody else gazed open-mouthed at the sight before them, poor Dave Caister, one of the assistant engineers, was left alone in the engine room, trying to respond to all the telegraph signals and wondering what the hell was going on.

There was quiet as a piece of pack disappeared beneath the bow and then a thud as we hit it, either nudging it aside or breaking it in half. The ship was crawling along, and somehow, from where I stood, the slowness and quiet only added to the majesty, the mystique of it all. Snow petrels were everywhere, and an Adélie penguin leaped out of the water and onto a piece of pack. It could have come straight from central casting: "Go out there and act like a penguin." It jumped on the ice, shook itself down, flapped its wings a couple of times to hoots of delight from those on board, then stood and silently watched us go by.

When I peered into the wheelhouse and saw the anxious faces on Athel, Arne, David, and the rest, I suddenly realized that we were not in the best possible situation. It may have made for great sightseeing, but the ship was surrounded by some extremely thick pieces of ice. It was pretty clear that any possible path south of the Ballenys was blocked. Now that we were here, we somehow had to get out.

We ate dinner quickly, and quietly. As we ate, the ship periodically jarred and groaned as it struck an ice floe with a jolt.

"I hope," I said softly to Dana, who was sitting next to me, "that we won't have ended up wasting a day."

But we had. And I knew it when I went back up to the wheelhouse after eating. Arne was there, peering ahead, nudging his way through the ice. David appeared concerned, flustered even. Sophie Piette, the second mate, stood guard by the telegraph. Arne had managed to steer us around so that we were on our way back out of the dead end into which we had sailed. Most of the ice had cleared from our path, and just one large piece—several hundred yards in area and weighing probably tens of thousands of tons—lay ahead. Arne ordered the ship to stop, and Sophie pulled the telegraph. We drifted slowly forward.

The MV *Arctic Sunrise* in the Antarctic ice.

TOP: (l. to r.): Captain Andy Troia, the author, and first mate Waldemar Wichmann pore over charts in an attempt to locate the whaling fleet.

BOTTOM: The crew of the *Arctic Sunrise*.

TOP: The sight of penguins, such as these chinstraps, frequently brought the crew rushing out on deck.

BOTTOM: The visual relief of a spectacular iceberg contrasts with the monotony of a gray Southern Ocean day.

TOP: The *Nisshin Maru*, factory ship of the Antarctic "research" whaling fleet.

BOTTOM: The *Tòshi Maru No.25*, one of the fleet's catcher ships.

We're
measuring
body proportion

TOP: Campaigner Yuko Hirono attempts to communicate
with the whaling fleet by radio.

BOTTOM: The crew of the *Nisshin Maru* trying to convince
the world of the importance of their "scientific research."

TOP: Jesse Reid attempts to steer an inflatable from the *Arctic Sunrise* in front of the *Kyo Maru No. 1*, to prevent the catcher from shooting a fleeing minke whale.

LEFT: The *Arctic Sunrise* gives chase as crew members place their inflatable in the line of fire of the *Kyo Maru No. 1*.

TOP: The whalers
train fire hoses on
Greenpeace crews in
an attempt to keep
them at bay.

BOTTOM: Despite
the best efforts of
their crews to protect
them, drivers of the
inflatable boats fre-
quently took direct
hits of freezing-cold
water from the
whalers' fire hoses.

A whale is winched up the stern ramp of the *Nisshin Maru*, as the factory ship's crew deploys water cannons to beat back Greenpeace inflatables.

Arne wrenched the port telegraph to full astern, catching Sophie, whose hand was on the starboard telegraph, by surprise. Slowly we moved toward the ice. With a bump and a crash we hit it, and the ship shuddered. David and I looked at each other and took a deep breath. Arne moved the telegraph to Dead Slow. The telephone rang, and Sophie rushed to answer it.

"That was the engine room," she reported. "They have one engine on full ahead and one on full astern."

Arne nodded his acknowledgment and went outside onto the wings to check the pack. He moved the telegraph again and again, sawing his way through, until eventually we were clear. He clicked the controls back to auto and swept a lock of hair away from his forehead.

"I'm going to find some dinner," he said to David, and pointed straight ahead. "That way."

I went down to the radio room, furious that I had allowed myself to be persuaded to change course. I sat with Thom, looking glum. He tried to cheer me up and asked me what was wrong. I said I was pissed off because we had wasted a day, we had almost put ourselves in an extremely dangerous situation, and I shouldn't have let myself get bounced into making a course change. He tried to say no, the day wasn't wasted: we had established that the whalers couldn't pass south of the Balleny Islands and, perhaps most importantly, crew morale had gone through the roof, at least for a while, at the sight of land and snow and ice and penguins. I remained unconvinced. Thom tried again to cheer me up.

"No," I insisted, "I'm going to have a sulk. And a beer. I'm going to have a beer and a sulk."

So I went below, fetched myself a Cooper's, and decided to inflict myself on Dana. She was very comforting, as Thom had been, insisting that it was impossible to predict these things: there *could* have been a channel to the south, or had we gone along the east coast of the islands, the weather could have been terrible there, too.

Grant came in. He had been totally transformed by seeing

the islands, he said. Having felt down in the dumps early in the morning, he was now full of enthusiasm.

"Cheer up, old bean," he tried. "We'll find them."

It didn't have any effect.

"It's my fault," I said to Arne later. "I shouldn't have let myself get bounced into a decision at six-thirty in the morning. I should have waited another thirty minutes; then you'd have been awake and none of this would have happened."

Arne smiled and said yes, it was better not to make such decisions first thing. He seemed in much better humor than I had expected, and certainly much better than me.

We were silent for a short while.

"Still," I sighed. "These things happen."

Yes, he agreed, they certainly do.

In the evening, Thom and I stood out on the poop deck with Chris Robinson, the bosun. Forty years old, powerfully built, and with a full beard, Chris looked every inch the sailor and had been crewing with Greenpeace for years: on the *Gondwana* and the original *Rainbow Warrior*, but mostly as captain of the *Vega*. Thom had been talking about a trip he had made to Russia earlier in the year on the new *Rainbow Warrior*: it had been difficult and tiring, he said, but nothing compared to this. I asked Chris if he'd ever been to Russia in his Greenpeace travels. No, he said; Moruroa, Antarctica, and Iceland, that was his gig. And Spain. Spain had been the site of his greatest moment, the time he, Athel, David McTaggart, and a few others on the original *RW* escaped from the Spanish authorities after being arrested for whaling protests.

"Man," I said, "I still can't believe how you guys escaped. How did they miss you?"

Mostly, he offered, it had been incredibly bad luck on the authorities' part.

"We'd been there for five months, and every day there'd been somebody watching the ship, twenty-four hours a day. Occasionally some of them had to go off and quell riots or something, but generally we were always being watched. But on this one day they had just one guy, a new guy, watching us, and he just up and decided to go for a walk. McTaggart had been watching, and he suddenly came down and said, 'Shit, this is it. We've got to go now.' And within a couple of hours we'd slipped our lines and were gone."

So what happened then?

"Well, they all reckoned that we didn't have much fuel. It wasn't news we'd actually put about on purpose; it had just accidentally got out, that we didn't have much fuel. So they sent out these fast patrol boats to go around all the bays and inlets, looking for places where we could be meeting another boat and refueling. Meanwhile, when they didn't find us there, they reckoned we must be heading out to sea at top speed, but we had all this seaweed and shit on our hull after all those months in dock and we couldn't go that fast, only five or six knots, so they were looking along the line they reckoned we'd be following, but they were just too far ahead. It was just really bad luck."

It felt kind of comforting, knowing that the Spanish navy could miss a ship that was steaming out of their harbor. I thought about the authorities, and I reckoned I knew how they must have felt. Most of all, I thought about the poor guy who'd let them escape.

We'd been at sea about fifty days. I was lying in bed, trying to collect my thoughts, preparing myself to face whatever horrors the day was going to throw at us this time, when Thom burst into the cabin.

"*Iniquity*'s just six miles away, man," he panted. "You can see it off the port side. Hey, man, we should stop and pick them up, bring them on board and give them a shower and stuff."

Soon after we had left Australia, I had been chatting with David Iggulden about how small the Antarctic community is. There are still, even now, relatively few who have made the trip south, so that the chances of paths crossing repeatedly are pretty good. David, for example, had been on the *Southern Quest*, the ship of the ill-fated "In the Footsteps of Scott" expedition, which had been trapped between ice floes and sunk in 1986. Also on board what David now cheerfully referred to as the "Sunken Pest," although not at the time it went down, was our doctor on this voyage, Earl Dorney. On board the *Quest* had been a team of Austrian climbers, aiming to be the first to scale the peaks of an Antarctic mountain called Mount Minto; one of them, Bruno Klausbruckner, went on to become base leader at World Park Base during the 1989–90 season. Two years after the *Quest* sank, the Australian team that did become the first to climb Mount Minto was retrieved from the slopes on its way back by helicopters from the MV *Greenpeace*. One of the crew on the boat from which the climbers were operating was a guy named Peter Gill. That same Peter Gill later joined Greenpeace Australia, and I had spent some time with him in Sydney while the Black Pig had been pounding from Fremantle to Hobart to provide a better starting position before leaving on this expedition. While we had been looking for whalers, Pete had been part of a team on board a small yacht called the *Iniquity*, which was sailing around the Antarctic to study humpback whales. Now Pete, his colleagues, and the *Iniquity* were just a couple of miles away. It wasn't the vessel we were looking for, but it was afloat, it was close, and it contained people—including someone I knew and people David knew—and that was far more interesting and exciting than just about anything else that had happened to us over the past month and a half.

I raced into the wheelhouse and there it was, its sails plain for us to see in the near distance. We'd known the *Iniquity* was in the Southern Ocean, but still, the odds of finding it had been pretty remote. We'd been going slowly nuts for six weeks looking for four steel ships, and instead we had stumbled across a tiny little yacht full of scientists.

Instead of calling the *Iniquity* over the HF radio—the last thing we wanted to risk was alerting the whalers to our presence by blasting a signal over HF, should they actually be nearby—we just steamed toward the yacht. As we drew alongside, David shouted through a bullhorn, giving them a VHF channel to tune into. He asked if they all wanted to come aboard, whether they wanted to be tied alongside or drop anchor, whether they wanted somebody from the Black Pig to come on board. The captain wanted some of his own crew on board at all times, so they agreed to come onto the *Greenpeace* in two sets of three. David offered to launch an inflatable and get there in ten minutes. Some of us raised an eyebrow and suppressed a snicker. We hadn't actually had a lot of practice at launching inflatables lately, after all. The effort of organizing people and starting the outboard was greater than the mate had anticipated, but eventually the boat was launched and came back with the first three of the *Iniquity*'s crew, including Pete Gill.

"Here's a sight for sore eyes," I said as I saw him come down the stairs. "What's a nice boy like you doing on a ship like this?" We shook hands and hugged. "Last time I saw you, we were sitting on a park bench in Balmain."

The poor guys looked totally bewildered and shell-shocked, overcome by the relative hustle and bustle and size of our ship. With so many places to go compared with their tiny craft, they didn't know what to do or where to put themselves. It must have been totally disorienting. For all that we moaned about being at sea for so long, our ship was a sprawling paradise compared to what they were used to. We had room to move, stretch, and walk upright. We had a VCR and a stereo. The smell of freshly baked bread wafted from the pantry. The floor didn't even move much. It must have felt like the Sheraton Antarctica.

We showed them the way to the hot showers and invited them to help themselves to lunch. As we all sat down to eat together, someone remarked that Ted Hood, one of our deckhands, was still asleep. One of us suggested that we go wake him up and tell him that new people were on board; somebody else reckoned that we should ask one of the *Iniquity*'s crew to wake him, and see what happened. When you're on a ship with a fixed number of people for a long period of time, the sight of somebody new is a shock to the system. It's like waking up in your home and finding a bunch of strangers sitting at the breakfast table.

While we were plotting the possibilities, Ted walked in, and we all cracked up.

"Somebody told me," he admitted. "Pity though, 'cos it would've been fun. I went into the bathroom and somebody came out of the shower who wasn't on the crew list."

The *Greenpeace* crew reveled in the presence of the newcomers; with this infusion of new personalities, and the experience at the Ballenys a few days previously, the expedition had taken an interesting and unpredictable turn. For a while at least, the atmosphere on board seemed different, more lively. But as fun as it was, there was work to be done and whalers to be found. The weather, for once, was clear enough for a helicopter flight and, as Paula began to get ready, I asked her if she wanted anybody in particular to go with her as her lookout. Anybody I knew who wanted to go up, she offered, and I said I knew someone, all right: "Me. I'm desperate to get off." Selfish, perhaps, but I didn't care. So Thom and I clambered into the helicopter, and we took off.

Paula always liked to entertain the troops before setting off on a scouting mission, so we buzzed the *Iniquity*, circled low and away, and then screamed over the *Greenpeace* at around a hundred knots, banked, and flew off in search of the whalers. If the rationale behind our heading west had been correct, and the whalers hadn't somehow passed us over the last week, then the chances were that they were around here somewhere. If we didn't find them soon, we'd have to accept that they were either behind us, heading into the Ross Sea, or whaling somewhere in the Middle Zone. We were approaching our last roll of the dice.

We left the *Greenpeace* behind us, first of all traveling east to make sure the whalers hadn't just slipped past us, and flying close enough to the mainland that we could see the coast. After all this time—the two months in the Southern Ocean on the first voyage, the fifty days during this expedition—I was finally actually looking at Antarctica. We flew over Commonwealth

Bay, widely regarded as the windiest place on Earth. I thought of the explorers and scientists who had struggled mightily against the conditions, and those who had died a few thousand feet below us, and yet, from here on a summer's day, it looked calm and peaceful. We saw tiny black specks on some of the icebergs and rocks; when I trained my binoculars on them, they turned into penguins, waddling and squawking and apparently oblivious to the distant aerial intruder.

It felt strange, actually, to be looking down on the continent. It was as if, all the time I had been at sea, the place had been some mythical grail that I could only aspire to find. But there it was, white and icebound but for the occasional area of bare rock to break it all up. It was extraordinarily beautiful in its starkness, yet none of us said anything about it. But I was glowing inside, and wondered if the others were doing the same.

All along the coast, the view was stunning. We saw no thick ice edge, just lots of brash, breaking up the blue sea and reflecting the sunlight back up at us. All the signs were right: the *Iniquity*, the beautiful weather, the sight of Antarctica . . . this had to be the day. Even when we ran into some weather and had to turn back, I wasn't discouraged, nor was Paula. What the hell—it was a beautiful day, so we'd just get gassed up and fly off in the opposite direction. On the way back to the ship, I started writing out loud to Paula and Thom: "Dear Diary: Today I met a friend of mine in the middle of the Southern Ocean, then went for a flight over Antarctica, and in the late afternoon found some whaling ships."

As we reached the *Greenpeace*, Paula hovered off the starboard bridge wing, and we could look into the wheelhouse and see folks waving at us. It was a hoot for everybody on board when she did that, and it was good practice for her, too, for when she would have to position herself next to a harpoon. That was one of my ambitions for this trip: to hang next to a harpoon and look the gunner straight in the eye as we blocked his aim and stopped him from shooting a whale.

First, of course, we had to find the fleet. We hovered off the wheelhouse long enough for everyone to get some pictures, then settled back down on the deck. The *Iniquity* crowd had left during our absence, after being loaded up with water, apples, and beer and relieved of their garbage; we had a few cups of tea, I listened to some music to get myself cranked up some more, and we took off again, way to the west.

We flew on and on, leaving the *Greenpeace* far behind us, flying almost a hundred miles west, banking up to skim along the ice edge. But we saw nothing, and ahead of us was snow.

"We'll play around here for about ten minutes," said Paula, changing course to skirt the weather, "and then we're going back."

Then, just as she began to turn toward the ship, Paula seemed to flinch. She had pointed her radar detector out the window, and now it looked as though she might have something, as though she was looking at the instrument and double-checking.

"I don't know how to tell you guys this," she began, "but I'm getting some radar."

We turned and headed toward the signal. It was coming from a northerly direction and was within twenty-five miles. As we closed in on it, we began to pick up another signal. Thom started laughing in the back, and I was smiling too, even though I couldn't quite believe it. Our hearts were thumping and I was practically leaning out the front of the helicopter, as if pushing my binoculars an extra few inches toward the window would somehow allow me to see something sooner. Damn, damn, where were they?

Icebergs were everywhere now, and Paula dipped lower, skirting the tops of them, a huge number of tabular bergs, each of them plenty big enough to hide a ship behind. It was like flying through Manhattan, the icebergs like tall buildings reaching for the sky and the clear water between them, Fifth Avenue. With each turn we made, I expected to see a whaler emerge from behind one of the blocks of ice. They were here; they had to be here.

Paula looked again at the radar detector. They were dead

ahead; they had to be close. Any moment now, we'd see them. We looked up and there, right ahead of us, in the middle of the patch of icebergs, was a great bank of fog.

"The fuckers are hiding in the fog," cursed Paula. Of all the places for there to be fog, it had to be right here.

We flew in low, still checking around as many icebergs as we could, hoping against hope that a catcher would emerge from the mist. Still the signals were coming, but there was no doubt about it: they were in the fog. We informed the *Greenpeace* that we were getting some radar, and headed back.

Once we touched down, I grabbed the binoculars and raced up to the bridge. Arne was standing in the chart room.

"Well, Arne, we got some radar out there!"

"So I heard," he observed, calmly. "Of course," he cautioned, "it might well have been the *Astrolabe*."

As well it might: we had been close to the French base of Dumont d'Urville, and their resupply ship was scheduled to arrive at any time. In addition to the *Iniquity*, another yacht, the *Buttercup*, was nearby. The multiple signals we had been receiving could have been one radar reflecting off all the icebergs. It could have been one of any number of possibilities, but it was the best sign we had had all through the trip and we couldn't let it go. Anyway, *I* reckoned it was the whalers, and we agreed there was no point in standing around discussing whether it might have been them or not. We had nothing else to go on, so we steamed over there.

It took the *Greenpeace* five hours to get there, by which time it was dark, making it impossible to launch the helicopter for another search. Athel, Naoko, and I had a row about whether to launch boats ahead of the Black Pig to dart around and through the icebergs, looking for the whalers. Naoko argued that it wasn't necessary, that launching boats would slow us down, that if the whalers saw the boats they'd take off in a flash, and that anyway, the mates on watch were trained to distinguish between ships and icebergs. Athel countered that it was next to impossible to tell an iceberg from a ship on radar unless the ship was moving, and that if we didn't do something, we ran the risk of letting a golden opportunity slip through our fingers. I probably took some kind of safe middle ground. In the end, we agreed that if we were to do anything, it would be first thing in the morning, as soon as it began to get light and before the fleet started hunting.

But the next day dawned misty and stormy, unsuitable for flying or using boats. When it finally began to clear up, another day had passed and we had missed our chance. If that had been the whalers, and I was certain it had been, they had escaped us again.

Only four days later did the weather improve enough for us to go flying, and by then our moment had passed. Again, Thom, Paula, and I made the trip early in the morning, before many of the crew were up and about. This really was it; if we didn't find them now, they had gone. We flew to the north and west, away from the coast with not even the sight of Antarctica to cheer and inspire us, just miles and miles and miles of empty, gray, whaler-less ocean. It was a quiet flight out: it was early, we were tired, I was despondent, Thom was falling asleep.

After we turned around to head back to the ship, conversation began to pick up, as if the thought of being back on board, eating breakfast, and returning to our bunks somehow lifted our spirits.

"Boy, Kieran," offered Paula, "you guys have a tough job. I wouldn't want your job for a million dollars."

"That's good," chimed Thom, "because that's not what they're paying him."

When we got back, I pronounced myself officially depressed. It was over. The whalers weren't here. Not only had we not seen them, I couldn't smell them anymore, either. We had had our chance, and we'd blown it.

We sputtered on for a few more days after that, but I couldn't motivate myself anymore. Naoko was still able to concoct scenarios to explain how the whalers could have been just over the hill but able to avoid detection by the helicopter flight. I was quite happy to go along with the notion, willing to be convinced, but deep down I knew they weren't there. If they had been around when Paula had picked up those radar signals, then they were long gone now. I guess everybody else pretty much saw it that way too, because when we sat down for one of our rare campaign meetings a few days later, there was no argument from anybody as to what we had to do next. Even if, by some fluke, the whalers were still around, we hadn't provided any evidence that we'd be able to find them, let alone do anything with them. It was time to face up to the facts of the situation and accept defeat.

We had been at sea fifty-six days without a sign of the whaling fleet, and we still had no clue where they were. We were tired and bereft of ideas, and the weather continued to mock us. At the same time, Dana was eager for us to make tracks for Ross Island as soon as possible, so we could put in a decent period at Cape Evans and McMurdo Sound before the area began icing up.

In a sense, it was almost a relief to make the decision that was staring us in the face. We were doing the humane thing, putting ourselves out of our misery. For well over a week, every morning when I woke up, I had wanted so badly for that to be our last day. It had become increasingly obvious that we were getting nowhere, and all we were doing was prolonging the agony. It had to end. If we later had any idea of the whalers' whereabouts, we could always return to looking for the fleet when we were in the Ross Sea. But now it was time to give Dana a chance to ensure that at least some aspect of the expedition would be a success.

The morning of February 2, we held a crew meeting. It was the most difficult ten minutes I had ever experienced. Had it really come to this? Even in our darkest hours, during both this voyage and the first, even when it had seemed impossible that we would ever find the fleet, even when I had all but given up, I had never actually been able to picture what it would be like to stand up and accept failure. Now here I was, doing just that. I didn't really know what to say. All I could think of was to apologize to everyone. The crew had done exactly what we asked, and then some. Time after time, we had told them we thought the whalers were close, and they believed it. We believed it. I believed it. It just never happened.

That night, we held a wake in our cabin for the whaling campaign. A bunch of us drowned our sorrows and got outrageously, mind-numbingly drunk. At least it seemed that the nightmare was finally over. But the Antarctic hadn't finished with us yet.

CHAPTER EIGHT

"Great God! This Is an Awful Place...."

WITHIN DAYS OF SUSPENDING OUR SEARCH FOR THE WHALERS, we closed in once more on the Balleny Islands. This time we had no discussion of seeing them up close, of spending a day gazing at them in awe. We no longer had any incentive to search for obscure routes through the ice, or to push south and attempt penetrating the impenetrable. Our only interest now was in rounding Cape Adare and heading into the Ross Sea as soon as possible, and most of all in reaching McMurdo Sound before the onset of winter put our shore work at Cape Evans beyond reach. But we had reckoned without the unpredictable Southern Ocean.

Barely had that final, difficult, and dismal crew meeting finished than the wind began steadily picking up. Mean, white-flecked swells soon menaced the ship, and the barometer began a downward slide. The ship started to pitch and roll, forcing everyone to check their lashing and secure their drawers, shelves, and equipment. Furniture slid across the lounge, chairs and couches pinning each other and their occupants to one side of the ship.

Initially, we had no idea of the severity of the storm that was bearing down on us. It began as little more than a mild annoyance. After a period of gray but relatively calm weather, we soon had to rapidly reacquaint ourselves with the art of spooning food onto our plate with one hand and holding onto the plate with the other. Moving around the ship became an exercise in intermittent weightlessness: more than once, as I was heading up to the bridge, the ship plunged over the crest of a wave and into a deep trough and the floor seemed to give way beneath me. With one bound, I flew up the length of the stairs, touching down just as the ship climbed another wave and the floor moved up to meet me again.

To tell the truth, I initially looked on the approaching storm as something of a godsend. Instead of having a week to focus on the failures of the past two months, everybody was now preoccupied with standing up, holding onto their drinks, and staying in their bunks. Three or four days of reasonably bad weather would be foremost in everybody's minds, after which we all would focus on the upcoming base visits and the work at World Park Base.

But the following day the barometer kept dropping, the wind blew stronger, and the waves grew higher and higher. It began to feel as if the *Greenpeace* were being batted from wave to wave. Looking out the windows of the radio room as the ship rolled to starboard, Thom and I blanched at the sight of the horizon disappearing behind a barrier of dark, forbidding ocean. The waves blocked out everything else; all we could see were walls of ocean, gray and menacing, rising higher and higher, falling toward us as we tipped, then lifting us back upright again as they crashed against the sides and sprayed the windows with their foam. The wind was screaming now, pounding into us from the side and sending the ship lurching with each wave that hurtled into the hull.

As the storm grew in ferocity, Arne turned us head on into it. The wind now was so powerful that even as we steamed into it at full speed, we could do little more than tread water. The hourly progress marks on the chart drew closer and closer together until, by nightfall, we were making at best one knot and the dots on the chart seemed to blur into one.

That evening, Dana came up to me as I stumbled toward the sanctuary of the cabin.

"The *Astrolabe*'s sunk," she gasped.

I looked at her in disbelief.

"The *Astrolabe*'s sunk," she repeated. "At least it's sinking, or it's in trouble."

En route from Dumont d'Urville to Hobart, the French resupply ship had evidently hit the same storm as we had. There had been no radio communication from the ship for seventy-two hours, and now it was transmitting signals from its Emergency Position Indicating Radio Beacons. The Marine Rescue Center in Australia had transmitted a mayday to all ships in the area, and Arne had responded with a telex, stating our position and offering to help.

Thanks, responded Sydney Radio, but another vessel—the Russian cruise ship *Kapitan Khlebnikov*—was closer and already on its way. A spotter plane would be under way out of Hobart at first light.

"Say," asked Thom, "did any of the whalers come back to you at all?"

Nah, said the guy from Sydney Radio, the Marine Rescue Center knew the whalers were down there and had tried to contact them, but hadn't received any response.

"Man," clucked Thom, "just goes to show what kind of guys we're dealing with down here, if they won't even answer a mayday call."*

---

* We later heard that, after initially ignoring the call, the *Nisshin Maru*, perhaps unaware of the unwritten rules of the sea—to say nothing of common decency—had responded that they were in the middle of extremely important research and were too busy to assist. Upon reflection they evidently thought better of their decision, and woke an English journalist on board to insist that he contact Australia, apologize on their behalf, and offer any assistance needed. By then, of course, the *Khlebnikov* was on its way. The story came to us from the journalist; I have never confirmed it with any of the whalers.

We sat in the radio room, Dana, Thom, and me, looking out at the waves, which were beating against the hull and emptying across the deck. The thought of being adrift in life rafts in weather like this was terrifying.

"I'm getting a weird feeling about this whole trip," observed Dana. "It gives me the creeps when there's a run of bad luck like this. I want us to get out of here."

"We shouldn't even be down here," I muttered. "Humans don't belong here."

The following morning, February 4, I lay in my bunk for a long time, snug and cozy and in no hurry to test the environment outside. Around lunchtime, Dana came in to see where I was.

"What's the news?" I asked her.

"The *Astrolabe*'s safe. The Orion from Hobart spotted it immediately and was able to make contact. The ship had had an electrical failure of some sort because of all the water it had been taking on board. But it's making its way to Hobart under its own power."

"Thank God for that. What's it doing outside?"

"Still picking up. Force 11."

I got out of bed and snuffled around. The *Greenpeace* had moved only about eight miles overnight. Even steaming into the storm, we were still taking a fearful battering. It was an effort now to even stand up, and everyone was growing fed up with being thrown into bulkheads with each wave that crashed into us.

Out on the poop deck, the lids were knocked off the barrels of organic waste, and garbage began to float around the deck. Chris Robinson and one of the engineers, Anders Stensson, went out to try to clear it up, wrapped up in flotation suits for insulation and protection from the waves. Anders came in at just after 1600, late for watch; he hadn't wanted to leave Chris alone, but the bosun had insisted he'd be fine.

Marc Defourneaux, one of the assistant engineers, found Chris shortly afterward, staggering, dazed, with a gashed, bleeding forehead. He had been knocked down by a wave powering its way over the side, and had woken up face down in the scuppers, water gushing around his head. He claimed to be all right but obviously wasn't, and Marc rushed in to find Earl, the doctor. As Marc helped Chris into the lounge and onto a couch, Thom and Dana sprang into action, fetching towels and a blanket. Friends gathered around Chris to comfort him as Earl tended to his head wound.

"That's three people we've nearly lost on this trip," said Dana. "First Pat with the crane hook, then that time when the helicopter slid across the deck and nearly pushed TC [Ted Cassidy, our helicopter mechanic] overboard, and now Chris. Jesus."

Thom moaned, head in his hands, as the ship shuddered with the force of another wave. "This trip has been a nightmare from beginning to end."

In the early-morning hours of February 5, as the storm reached its peak and gusts measured a hundred knots, we suffered our most devastating blow. Nobody saw exactly what happened, but as best as anyone could figure out, the ship was hit broadside by an enormous freak wave. The wave was so powerful that it lifted the two-and-a-half-ton Hurricane up in its cradle, snapping the straps that secured it in place. Only the stanchion next to the boat cradle prevented the boat from flying across the deck, although the pole itself buckled with the strain. Thwarted in its efforts to rip the Hurricane free of its shackles, the wave threw itself across the deck and slammed into the helicopter.

Athel, Paula, and TC were sitting at the round table when the wave hit. They clung to their seats as two enormous jolts shook the ship; when the crashing of airborne furniture and crew members subsided, Paula said she could hear a door banging. Athel and TC went up on deck and found the door to the air-conditioning room crashing back and forth. After they secured it and turned to go inside, Athel glanced at the helicopter. It had somehow moved over and was skewed across the deck. Athel shouted to TC that one of the straps had come loose, but it was worse than that. Struggling back toward the heli-deck as waves crashed over them, they could see that the right rear leg strut was broken. The wave had snapped it clean in two.

Come daybreak, the helicopter was tragically splayed across the deck. But there was nothing anyone could do. The storm was still raging, sending chairs and people flying. Heading out to the heli-deck for anything but an instant was too dangerous: another freak wave could wash across the ship, taking out anybody in its path.

Assuming the tempest would eventually subside, thoughts turned to finding spare parts. Remarkably, given that we were in a storm in the middle of the Southern Ocean, it seemed that we might have a chance. A cruise ship called the *Frontier Spirit* would be leaving New Zealand in a couple of days and heading down to McMurdo. If we could arrange to have the necessary parts sent in time, Greenpeace in Auckland could contact the *Spirit* and ask if they would carry them down and maybe meet us at McMurdo. Paula and TC made a couple of calls to find the new set of skids that were needed. Dana called Maj de Poorter of Greenpeace New Zealand, who agreed to call the cruise ship.

But by the time Maj called back to say that the *Spirit* was more than willing to carry the parts for us, things had taken a turn for the worse. Taking the risk to check and resecure the helicopter, TC and Paula had managed a more complete look at it. What they saw was devastating. Damage to the helicopter had been more extensive than was first realized. The front landing gear was broken, and parts of the main air frame had buckled.

We stood outside the campaign office—Thom, Dana, Naoko, Arne, Paula, TC, and me. TC, exhausted after twenty-six hours without sleep and distraught over the state of the helicopter, had tears in his eyes as he told us about the situation. There would be little point in ordering spare parts now, Paula added, until we had the chance to pull into shelter and get a handle on the full extent of the damage.

That, Arne commented, was highly unlikely anytime soon. We were still 120 miles from Cape Adare and, even though the storm had begun to abate, we were making only four knots at best. By the time we reached shelter, it might be too late to order the parts and get them to the *Spirit*. In other words, asked Arne, would we be better off ordering the skids anyway, in the hope that the damage was not as extensive as was feared, and that the helicopter could be mended?

All eyes turned to Paula and TC.

"To be honest," began TC, "no, there isn't any point. From an engineering point of view, I'd have to say no."

My head sagged and came to rest against the door frame. It was over. The helicopter had been wiped out.

"At this stage," continued Paula, "if we manage to get away without further damage to the machine, I'd regard it as a major victory."

There seemed precious little danger of that. If the storm was subsiding, it was doing so only very slowly. The ship was still being thrown around. People were tired, uncomfortable, and irritable. We had missed the whalers, we had lost the helicopter, we had almost lost Chris, and if we didn't soon start making better progress, we might not even be able to do much shore work. It was a nightmare, all right. As I had said to Dana, when it was her turn to take over: "Welcome to the Voyage from Hell."

CELEBRATION DAY, somebody had written on the blackboard, and rightly so. On the morning of February 6, we finally escaped the storm and made shelter. We were drifting in Robertson Bay, near Cape Adare, and it was beautiful. Jagged, dramatic cliffs crowded in all around us, mountains and glaciers looking down on our battered little ship. All of a sudden, after so many weeks and months of seeing Antarctica only from a distance, if at all, it was right there in front of us, almost close enough to touch. The glaciers rumbled, moving slowly forward. Pieces of ice that had broken off were floating in the bay, drifting slowly past the ship.

It was calm at last, and quiet. The only sound was the constant chipping, as everyone tried to break the ice from the ship. All around was evidence of the previous few days, the spray and waves from the storm having frozen up and left a thick, icy coat all over the *Greenpeace*. The Black Pig was now white, the windlass entombed in ice, the port door frozen shut, the view from the foredeck cabins completely obscured. After little sleep and the effort involved in moving around during the storm, everyone was tired, but relieved to be in shelter. Chris was on the mend: his ribs hurt and he couldn't breathe too deeply or laugh, but at least he was still with us.

I was standing on the port bow when Athel appeared.

"I feel like I've organized a fucking disaster," he said quietly, looking down at the water. He paused.

"We've got to save something from this, man."

"Maybe, if we had eight or nine days onshore in Antarctica, then perhaps five or six with the whalers, that would be at least something on which to end," I replied.

"We've got to get them, man," he insisted. "If there's even a chance."

Even as we recovered our breath in Robertson Bay, the storm continued to rage, and the moment we poked our heads outside to take a look, it came screaming after us once more. We hoped that entering the Ross Sea would provide some element of respite, but if anything, the storm picked up in intensity, pounding the ship with wave after wave and caking the decks and hull in layers of ice. The wind-speed gauge registered gusts soaring above a hundred knots, until finally the winds grew so strong they just tore the gauge apart. As we battered our way south through the Ross Sea and toward McMurdo Sound, there was little letup.

Eventually, we reached the relative shelter of the sound and stood out on deck as the imposing features of Erebus and Terror, Ross Island's twin volcanoes, loomed ahead. Even then, it seemed, there was no guarantee that we would finally be given the chance to do anything we had set out to do. As we closed in on Cape Evans, the wind rose again, driving us back out of the bay and raising once more the specter that we might have come all this way for nothing. Finally, the wind died down enough that we could steam back into the sound and anchor off Cape Evans. Within a matter of hours, the first shore party would begin making initial inspections of the site of World Park Base; over the next couple of days, most people would have the chance to go ashore—as part of the teams reporting on the environmental impacts of the U.S. McMurdo Station or New Zealand's Scott Base, or purely to take advantage of the opportunity to feel land beneath their feet and take in the splendor of the Antarctic. At long last, after almost seventy days of failure, frustration, and missed opportunity, it seemed something good was finally to come of this miserable experience.

In the annals of Antarctic exploration, the Ross Sea region holds a special and celebrated place. Only the more northerly and clement Antarctic Peninsula rivals the number of expeditions it has hosted or the extent of the human presence it still boasts. The first party to intentionally overwinter on mainland Antarctica, the members of the British Southern Cross Expedition of 1898–1900 led by Norwegian Carsten Borchgrevink, settled near Cape Adare—in Robertson Bay, in fact, the same inlet where we had earlier sought shelter from the storm; as we steamed back out to confront the tempest that awaited us, we saw the expedition's hut still standing defiantly on the beach. But the great majority of human interest in the region was, and is, concentrated farther south. The Ross Sea slices deep into the continent, granting easier access to the heart of Antarctica. Its southernmost extent is the farthest south it is possible to travel by sea, allowing ship-based expeditions to shave hundreds of miles off the distance across the ice to the South Pole. And parts of Ross Island, the guardian of those southernmost reaches, are among the few places on the continent that are regularly free of ice and snow, making them ideal locations to set up base.

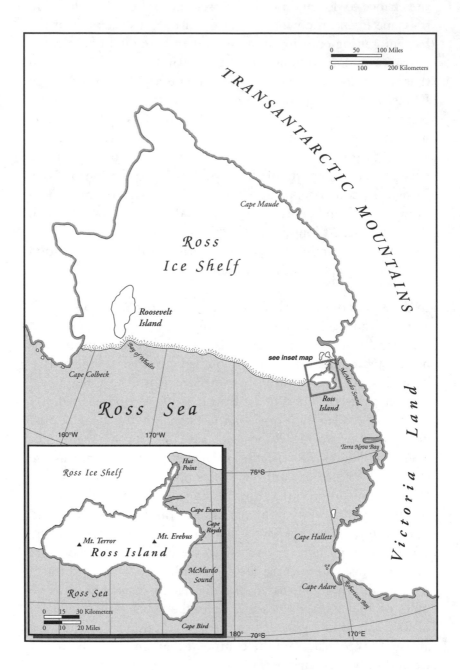

see inset map

Robert Falcon Scott was the first to lead an expedition to land on, and be based out of, Ross Island, arriving in February 1901 and using what became known as Hut Point, almost immediately adjacent to the Ross Ice Shelf, as the base for the National Antarctic Expedition. Among the expedition members was Dr. Reginald Koettlitz, Athel's great-great-uncle; one of the few, brief pleasures Athel derived from our own voyage was the opportunity to spy, on the west side of McMurdo Sound, the glacier named after his forebear. Also part of Scott's crew was a young officer in the Royal Navy Reserve, Ernest Shackleton, who accompanied Scott and Edward Wilson on an arduous three-month sledging journey that saw the three men attain, by some distance, the farthest south yet achieved by humans (although Shackleton did not travel as far as his companions; suffering from scurvy, he was ordered by Scott to set up camp and await his and Wilson's return). In 1908, Shackleton returned to lead an expedition of his own based out of Cape Royds, twenty miles to the north of Hut Point, the highlight of which was an epic journey in which he, Jameson B. Adams, Dr. Eric Marshall, and Frank Wild closed within 97 miles of the South Pole before Shackleton—recognizing that were they to continue, they would not have enough resources to make it back alive, and later explaining to his wife that he would rather be a "live donkey than a dead hero"—elected to turn back.

On January 17, 1912, almost exactly three years after Shackleton made that decision, Scott bested him, reaching the Pole itself with Henry "Birdie" Bowers, Edgar Evans, Lawrence "Titus" Oates, and Edward Wilson. What should, however, have been a celebration turned to despair. A Norwegian flag awaited them: a team led by rival explorer Roald Amundsen had beaten them by a month. Surrounded by the desolate, featureless polar plateau, Scott could scarcely contain his feelings of devastation. "Great God!" he wrote in his diary; "This is an awful place, and terrible enough for us to have laboured to it without the reward of priority." They tarried less than a day before girding themselves for the hard journey back to Cape

Evans—"we have turned our back now on the goal of our ambitions and must face our 800 miles of solid dragging," Scott wrote; but the burden of defeat weighed heavily upon them and added to the challenges of a naturally hazardous journey made yet more treacherous by appalling conditions that, in addition to their inherent hostility, magnified manifold errors in the expedition's planning that ultimately proved fatal to them all.

Now twice beaten to the Pole, Shackleton set his sights on another goal: to be the first to traverse Antarctica. That expedition was to be both dismal failure and glorious achievement: dismal failure in that the expedition ship, *Endurance*, became trapped and crushed in the ice of the Weddell Sea, and none of those on board even set foot on the Antarctic continent, let alone walked across it; glorious achievement in that, despite being marooned in the most hostile of environments, every one of the crew made it home alive. The remarkable details of the *Endurance* story—the crew living for six months on ice floes before striking out in the lifeboats for isolated Elephant Island; the harrowing eight-hundred-mile boat journey Shackleton and others made to South Georgia, culminating in an astonishing traverse of the island, across mountains and glaciers, to the whaling station at Grytviken; the failure of three relief ships to reach Elephant Island before a fourth attempt succeeded—are famed and justly celebrated; less well known, however, is that as Shackleton and his men underwent their extraordinary ordeal, ten members of the expedition were on the other side of the continent and likewise fighting for their survival.

On March 14, 1915, three weeks after the *Endurance* became firmly entrapped in the ice of the Weddell Sea, the *Aurora* anchored itself to Home Beach on Cape Evans, close to the hut that Scott's last expedition had used as its base, and prepared to settle in for the winter. The *Aurora* carried depot supplies for Shackleton's expedition; some men had already been set ashore to lay the more northerly provisions, and others would work their way steadily south with the return of summer. But on May 6, a furious blizzard ripped the *Aurora* away from its anchors;

entombed in pack ice, the ship and its crew drifted helplessly north for ten months and 1,100 miles, leaving ten men marooned at Cape Evans. For eighteen months the castaways remained, dutifully continuing to lay depots and waiting for the Trans-Antarctic Expedition, which never arrived, and a rescue ship, which eventually did. Three of the ten died during the wait and today a large, imposing cross, erected in their memory, looks down on Cape Evans from a mount known as Wind Vane Hill.

More than seventy-five years later, I stood on the poop deck of the *Greenpeace*, staring transfixed at the cross as it stood guard, silhouetted against the evening twilight, over the hut used first by Scott and then by the men left behind by the *Aurora*.

Off our port side, Mount Erebus stood tall, white, and majestic, smoldering away quietly and venting steam from its peak, dominating the landscape and looking, in the clear, Antarctic air, so close that I felt I could lean over the side and touch it. But its peak was twenty miles distant and when later a thin mist descended, the volcano disappeared entirely from view. Nearer to us, the magnificent, rugged Barne Glacier moved imperceptibly toward the water. Farther away, off our starboard side, bathed in beautiful orange and gold by the evening light, lay the rugged and imposing Transantarctic Mountains. The way light played on them made them look somehow unreal: they had no depth, as if they were all part of a painted backdrop. They stood fifty miles distant, maybe more, but again, through some strange trick of light, seemed for all the world as if I could strike out across the bay and reach them in a matter of minutes.

It was bitterly cold. We were much farther south now than I had ever been, and the temperature had dropped to about zero degrees Fahrenheit. With a sharp, biting wind driving off the glacier, the windchill was probably closer to forty below. I tried to take some video of the scene, but the wind buffeted the camera and tore at my exposed fingers. Perhaps, I shrugged, some things should not be filmed. It would be too easy to relegate the surroundings to a few square centimeters in a viewfinder. Far better to take the time to drink it all in, to look, smell, and feel the air, to allow my eyes to wander over the scenery.

As I stood on the poop deck enjoying the quiet, I wanted to feel excited that we were here, that something was coming right at last after two months of hell. And I was, really: I was thrilled to actually be in deepest Antarctica, looking at mountains and glaciers and sites of legendary human endeavor. I was relieved to be away from the conflict and torture of the whale campaign. I was happy to see the change in expression and demeanor in everybody on board, to feel the sense of excitement that we were actually really going to *do* something. But I couldn't help feeling a little empty and out of place.

The shore work was Dana's baby, and it wasn't easy to stand back, watch her organize schedules and make plans for boat launches with Arne and Athel, and know that I didn't fit into it at all except where Dana wanted to toss me a bone. And I guess I was a little jealous that something on this God-forsaken trip was finally about to work out, that everybody on board was feeling enthused, and that it was all down to Dana and not me. I watched her pull everything together and arrange teams for heading ashore; where I pictured myself as having dithered and messed up, Dana seemed efficient and organized, totally on top of her game. My admiration was mixed with a little resentment, though; her targets were "easy," all attached to the shore and not steaming across thousands of miles of open ocean.

I was scheduled to go ashore. The *Kapitan Khlebnikov* was due to arrive and to visit Scott's hut. The representatives of New Zealand's Scott Base, who would be opening the hut for them, had advised Dana that if Greenpeace wanted to go inside also, we should tag along at the end of the *Khlebnikov*'s visit. I could think of a hundred things I would rather have done than shuffle around the beach and peer into a hut with fifty or sixty others. It seemed too touristy, the kind of activity to which we were supposed to be opposed. But Dana asked me if I would go ashore with Alex de Waal, the cameraman, and Marty Lueders, the photographer, walk around with them, watch the tourists, look for evidence of any impact their presence might have, and document their activities, and I had agreed. She would do it herself, she explained, but she wanted to take the opportunity to go on board the *Khlebnikov* and talk to the tour organizers.

I dressed in my gear and clambered into an inflatable for the short ride to Home Beach. Some of the other Greenpeacers were already there, scouring the site of World Park Base for even the smallest debris—such as screws and wood chips—that might have been left when the base was removed, and a couple of them glanced at me as I hopped ashore. I had decided to bring my own video camera, and as I stepped out of the inflatable, it suddenly felt very large and obvious in my hand and I stood awkwardly for a moment, feeling like a tourist.

Here I was, actually standing on Antarctica. After a combined total of something like four or five months sailing Antarctic seas, I was finally walking on the continent itself. I had always assumed that if or when that moment arrived, it would be in some way thrilling. But instead I stood there, feeling self-conscious and out of place, before deciding to wander along the beach.

Cape Evans was like a shrine, untouched and unchanging. The extreme cold and dryness of the Antarctic had prevented decay, preserving moments in time from decades past. A mummified seal lay on the beach, desiccated but otherwise intact; farther along, a husky, still chained outside Scott's hut in the very spot where it had died, bared its teeth in a permanent snarl. The human artifacts also were unmoved from the spot where they had fallen or been built: cans, pieces of wood, and even row upon row of dead penguins, presumably killed for food, fuel, or scientific research, were scattered around the hut. The anchor of the *Aurora* was still buried in the shore, firmly secured in the spot where it had lain when the wind snapped the lines and sent the ship drifting out of the channel nearly eighty years previously.

I walked by the hut, tiptoeing past a sleeping seal, up to Wind Vane Hill, where the cross had been erected. I looked at the monument and turned around, taking in the surroundings. I could see mountains far in the distance, separated from where I stood by ice overflown by skuas and by the crystal-clear water of Skua Lake. It was perfect, picture-postcard Antarctica. The wind rose and fell, biting at the few exposed parts of my face.

The *Kapitan Khlebnikov* was rounding the corner and steaming into the bay. Its ugly bulk jarred in contrast to the natural beauty of McMurdo Sound. What was it about those old Soviet designers that apparently compelled them to make everything as hideous as possible? The *Khlebnikov* looked barely seaworthy, a gigantic boxy superstructure perched on a hull that seemed far too small. It dwarfed the *Greenpeace* as it sailed past, attempted to stop in one spot, and then, belching smoke, moved on a little before settling on another anchorage.

After a brief pause, the *Khlebnikov* began disgorging inflatables to ferry passengers ashore.

"Is it my imagination?" whispered Marty to me, nodding toward some of the passengers, "or are these guys acting paranoid, like they've been told, 'Greenpeace is here, don't do anything stupid'? Some of them are looking at us a little like you look at the heavy bouncers at rock concerts."

Many of them did seem to be regarding us with suspicion. One man made a point of issuing barbed comments every time a Greenpeacer was in earshot: "Oh, of course, we're on *their* territory, you know. They *own* this place."

One woman nearly wandered onto the site of World Park Base. Martin, one of our cooks, was there and asked if she could keep out because it was a scientific study area. She responded that she was pleased the base had gone; it had been an eyesore next to such an historic monument. Martin pointed out that the historic monument was a wooden hut with trash all around it, and that the Antarctic surroundings were infinitely more historic and, indeed, monumental. She would have none of it. Yes, the hut might be surrounded by broken bottles, wood chips, wire, dead animals, food cans, and the kind of garbage that it is now illegal to even think of leaving on Antarctica, but it was *historic* garbage.

To be fair, though, our presence was awkward. Granted, we were in the area for a reason; but the bulk of Greenpeacers ashore just then were there for recreational purposes, and while nobody could rightly deny them that after everything we all had been through, it still made me feel a little uncomfortable to see us contributing to the relative mass of humanity now here.

Some of the *Khlebnikov* passengers were friendlier than others. Some were revisiting a continent of which they had fond memories after overwintering at scientific bases decades earlier. Others had spent the bulk of their savings on the holiday of a lifetime and were loving every moment. We also met an Australian crew filming a documentary inspired by the 1929 expedition of Douglas Mawson, that country's pioneer Antarctic explorer. Bernie Eddie, the man in charge of the film crew, asked what our plans were likely to be, and I said that in a few days we would be going to McMurdo Station and Scott Base, and after that we might spend a few final days looking for the whaling fleet. He stared intently at me, and then told me he knew where they were.

"Yes," he nodded, a light seeming to come on over his head, "the last I heard, I think about ten days ago—and where are we now, February 11, so ten days ago was February 1—so on February 1 they were at, now let me think. . . ."

Oh my God, I thought, eyes bulging and breath quickening.

"Now let me see," he continued, "Sydney Radio told the *Buttercup*, which was down around Commonwealth Bay at the time, that the whalers were on the Indian Ocean side, off, what was it, Queen Maud Land."

I sighed a little inside. He meant the two research vessels from the IWC's Second International Decade of Cetacean Research program—the *Shonan Maru* and the *Shonan Maru No. 2*. They were indeed whaling vessels, but long ago donated by Japan for purely nonlethal research.

"Yes," I said, "there are two over there, but they're not killing whales. And there are also four around here, and they *are* killing whales."

"Well, they're certainly keeping their bloody heads down."

"Yes," I agreed, "they certainly are."

"Well," he offered, "we'll keep a look out."

I suggested that if we had any indications that they were near the *Khlebnikov* at any stage, perhaps we could give him a call. "Yeah," he said, "and we'll make sure our chopper gets up. We can go film any action," he went on, the glint of a story in his eye.

Over the next couple of days, we paid visits to McMurdo Station and Scott Base. At Mactown (the name by which McMurdo is commonly and colloquially known), we held an "open boat," and more than seventy summer and winter personnel came on board and drank beer in the lounge. More than a few noted that our ship was covered in ice and asked what on earth had happened to it. It was an historic and unprecedented occasion, the first time Mactown base personnel had been allowed to fraternize with Greenpeace: the National Science Foundation, which oversees the McMurdo base, had long maintained a policy of strict noncooperation with nongovernmental organizations in the Antarctic. Mactown residents had supposedly been prohibited from visiting the Greenpeace overwinterers in the days of World Park Base, and even during our visit this time around, a "spy" was assigned to follow our every movement.

At Scott Base we held a small demonstration protesting the New Zealand government's decision to allow flights out of Christchurch to the recently completed airstrip at Dumont d'Urville, the construction of which had displaced more than eight thousand birds of different species and killed unknown numbers of penguins. Between Scott and McMurdo, Thom and I made a slightly surreal courtesy call to the cruise ship *Frontier Spirit*—the same ship that had offered to carry the spare helicopter parts for us had we not decided the machine was damaged beyond immediate repair. On the *Spirit*, we looked through huge windows at the Barne Glacier drifting silently past and peered down on the tiny *Greenpeace* far below us.

Our work done in McMurdo Sound, Dana had one more call to make, to Terra Nova Bay on the western coast of the Ross Sea to visit the eponymous Italian station and the German base, Gondwana. But before we got there, at a moment when we were least prepared for them, we found the whalers.

Paula, serving as a bridge lookout, saw a target on the radar and alerted David, who began to plot it. It was fifteen miles away at that stage, and before long the radar plotter confirmed that it was traveling at thirteen knots. This was no iceberg, and soon one of the lookouts saw it on the horizon.

"Ship in sight," said Naoko, running down from the wheel-house.

"What is it?" I asked. "Catcher?"

She shook her head.

"*Nisshin Maru.*"

I raced down to the mess.

"*Nisshin Maru!*" I shouted. "Dead ahead. In visual range." Everybody immediately began suiting up, except for those who raced to the wheelhouse to take a look. Pandemonium reigned. We were flying at the *NM* with both engines now, and at seven miles out it still hadn't seen us.

Naoko contacted the *Nisshin Maru* on Channel 16, reading them a statement in Japanese that I repeated in English. The Rock Boat was launched, ready to be sent out toward the ship. Everything was going according to plan. And then, right on cue, it all fell apart.

As soon as Naoko called them up, the *Nisshin Maru* turned and fled. The *Greenpeace* was steaming at full speed, but it couldn't keep up. The Rock Boat revved up, ready to give chase. It emitted a puff of smoke, then a spluttering roar, and finally the engine gave up the ghost. The cooling water had frozen again. One of the engineers leapt into Rocky to try to fix the problem, and we launched the Hurricane to take the Rock Boat's place.

Rocky's crew climbed into the Hurricane, and the Hurricane crew came back on board. It was total chaos. In the middle of it all, the radios on the Hurricane stopped working. We had a boat with working engines and sporadically functioning radios, and a boat with functional radios and nonworking engines.

Arne was fuming in the wheelhouse, throwing his radio to the deck and screaming that it was "fucking useless." People were shouting into their radios as if that would help them work. Athel was punching the radio on the boat. And the *Nisshin Maru* was roaring away from us.

By the time we had finished launching one boat and then the other, taking the first boat back on board, slowing down to launch it again and then deciding not to bother after all, we were nineteen miles behind the *Nisshin Maru* and about to lose it completely. All we could do was hang in there as best we could. And the Black Pig was giving its all, crashing valiantly through the water in pursuit of her fleeing prey. Athel said it was a fantastic sight.

Athel had been in the Hurricane a couple of miles off our port bow, watching us pound through the waves. We had been trying to call them almost as soon as they had set off after the *Nisshin Maru*; when we heard nothing in response, we assumed that they were in hot pursuit and too busy to take time to respond. It was a surprise to find out that they were off our bow, and not the factory ship's.

But the inflatable had chased after the whaler up to the first way point that we had set. They had called in for further instructions on where to go next, but didn't hear anything back. Partly this was because the Hurricane's radios worked only intermittently; but mostly it was because Thom had programmed in one channel and David had told the boat crews to use another. We were monitoring totally different frequencies. We asked the Hurricane to see if they could try to make up the lost ground, but it was a futile task. The factory ship was out of sight, off the radar and over the horizon. After two and a half months of painful searching, our only encounter with the *Nisshin Maru* had lasted a couple of hours.

Ironically, after more than two months of putting up with us and sympathizing with our inability to find the whalers, it was now, when we had actually flirted with some tiny element of success, that the crew finally snapped. However dispirited and disappointed everyone had been at the thought that we had failed to find the fleet, they had at least been able to comfort themselves with the idea that, once we had finished with our shore work, we would be going home and putting the whole awful experience behind us. Now all that had been put on hold as Naoko, in particular, sought to wring one final push out of all of us. When she announced her intention to keep at it for a little while longer, the crew, which for ten weeks had shown support above and beyond the call of duty, acted as if they were all but ready to throw her overboard, and me with her.

In effect, the crew gave us a deadline. We had two days to finish the whaling campaign. After that, it would be all over; we would complete Dana's work at Terra Nova and then go home. Two days weren't much better than none: even if we found the whalers again, we wouldn't be able to achieve anything in such a short time. But we had had the best part of eighty days already to make something happen, and had been spectacular in our failure. Two days more were about as much as we deserved, and the plan did hold out a slim hope that we would be able to finish with some kind of token gesture.

But fortune and the Antarctic decided to rub our noses in failure one last time. It was growing late in the season by now, and we were encountering thick ice seemingly everywhere we looked. The ice frustrated us at every turn: if we needed to head west, we had to go north to avoid the ice first; if we wanted to head north, we were forced to steam west. Arne asked Naoko and me to his cabin, where he articulated his feelings. He thought it was pretty ridiculous, attempting to plow on through the ice. It was time to accept that we were not having any luck, that we had never had any luck, and frankly we were not going to start having luck now.

I turned to Naoko and said I agreed with Arne. I had gone along with the idea of those extra few days of pursuit, but once we started encountering this ice, it seemed hopeless. Antarctica had beaten us. It was a good time to concede defeat.

True, said Naoko. But it could be argued that we had been wasting our time for the past two months, so what difference would one more day make? She had given up a long time back, but had recently recovered her belief, and we had duly found the whalers. If we didn't stick it out until the end, she wouldn't feel that she had given her all and done everything she could have.

I said I would support her. But I had my reservations and, sitting in the radio room that night as the ice scraped past the hull and the wind once more began to tear at us through the dark, I doubted we would find the fleet again. I wished we had simply called an end to the campaign after the relative high of finding the *Nisshin Maru*. I was also upset that, after everything we had been through, the crew had felt forced to push a deadline on us to make us accept the inevitable. More than anything else, the one thing I reckoned we could feel good about was the way in which, even with the hellish experience we had all been through for the past two and a half months, there had been none of the rancor and discord between campaigners and crew that had sometimes surfaced during the first voyage. Now even that ray of sunshine had disappeared behind a cloud, and the mood on board had changed, right at the last minute, from one in which we were all in it together to one in which an enormous chasm existed between crew and campaign staff. For me, it was the final blow. All I wanted now was for the nightmare to be over. If we were going to find the whalers again, I wanted us to find them instantly, so we could bring the whole thing to a close as soon as possible.

The phone rang. It was the bridge. There were lights on the horizon. I raced up to the wheelhouse, and through binoculars saw the lights a couple of points to port. An echo was on the radar, about thirteen miles away and heading straight for us. Sophie said she had stopped the ship. We turned off the deck lights, and Grant and I raced down to close the deadlights below, bumping into Naoko on the way.

The ship was coming at us at about eleven knots. Athel suggested we could send out one of the small boats, as that would be easier to launch, requiring fewer people and no deck lights. He and Ted said they'd prepare one and warm it up, ready for when we gave the word.

The ship continued to head toward us. I had assumed it was the *Nisshin Maru* because of the distance at which the echo had appeared on the radar, but as it came closer it became apparent that it was a catcher. I went around to wake up some of the people I knew would be most keen to see this before it all ended.

We put both engines on standby, ready to give chase. The catcher was coming from the northwest. We assumed that it had seen us and that it intended to lead us to the south, away from the rest of the fleet. But we didn't have much choice: once the catcher had us, there was nothing we could do, no way we could go chasing after the rest of them. This was endgame now, and we had few options but to stick with the catcher, wait until it was light enough to get some decent stills and footage, harass it a bit, and then be on our way.

When the ship was within a couple of miles, we threw on the deck lights and turned about to follow it. Athel and Ted had launched an Avon as promised, and were now pounding their way through the sea toward the catcher. But it was tough going: winter was fast approaching, and an angry wind was howling and throwing up a fierce swell. To make matters worse, the water was coated with ice, throwing freezing spray over the two of them.

Athel said the bridge crew of the *Toshi Maru No. 25* almost visibly leapt back in shock when, peering out of the windows into the windy, icy dark, they saw a small orange inflatable off their bow. Not that that inflatable was likely to do them any harm: it was two o'clock in the morning, after all, and pitch dark. They weren't about to start hunting whales. But we had made a point, of sorts.

After sticking with the catcher for a while, the Avon came back. Half of Ted's beard was coated with a thick layer of ice, and even as the deck crew was hauling the inflatable back on board, they were practically ordering him to stand under a warm shower.

We turned the *Greenpeace* north again, thinking the *Toshi Maru No. 25* would follow. It didn't, but we didn't want to turn around and start chasing it again, either. It was time to call an end to our efforts and go home. Almost as soon as we had found each other, we were off each other's radar screens once more, and the whaling campaign was over.

I hadn't particularly wanted to go ashore at Terra Nova. But I had promised Dana that I would help if she needed me to, and so I joined the shore party to check out the Italian station. What once had been a small and exemplary base was now beginning to grow out of control. Evidence of construction was everywhere: oil dripped from fuel tanks, skuas pecked at pieces of plastic left lying around in open skips. On top of everything else we had gone through, this was a disheartening experience, and all the more so knowing that Greenpeace planned to sell the *Gondwana*, so there probably would never be another Antarctic expedition. If we weren't going to be around to check up on the way countries were treating the Antarctic, then who would?

Grant was keen to get me away from the rest. He had been incredibly supportive all the way through the expedition, and now he wanted me to go with him to explore a small scientific field station that had been established a couple of miles away. It would be a nice thing to do on our final day in Antarctica, he said. Of course, I hadn't counted on the fact that he was an energetic climber of Kiwi mountains, and as he started springing up what seemed to me to be sheer cliffs, I wished I'd just stayed in my bunk. Weighed down with heavy clothing, out of shape after three months of being unable to walk more than forty yards at a stretch, and breathing heavily in Antarctica's rarefied atmosphere, I clung to the cliff face and looked below me. Dana and the rest moved around like little specks in the distance.

Great, I thought. I've come through everything that the past few months could throw at me, and now I'm going to fall off a cliff and die.

I didn't, of course. And once I was over the ridge, panting and trying to catch up with Grant, I realized it truly had been worth the effort. We sat on a rock at the top of the hill and gazed down at the scenery around us. Beneath us stretched Terra Nova Bay. To the left and in the distance was the striking beauty of Mount Melbourne. Down to the right, floating on the still, blue water, was our little ship. For three months it had been our home, a self-enclosed world for thirty people. Now, dwarfed by the surrounding hills and mountains, it looked tiny and more vulnerable than ever.

We could have been on another world. Nothing was alive, and nothing moved. The only sounds were the wind, beating my face and biting my fingers with cold, ignoring the protection the gloves were meant to offer; and my own breath, magnified inside the scarves and hoods that cloaked my head, as I tried to recover from climbing the hill.

The wind gusted once more and then, suddenly, died down. For a moment, there was silence. And then the silence was drowned out by the ringing that filled my ears. After months of being surrounded by generator noise, engine noise, and the noise of ice against the hull and people walking around a ship, it was as if my ears were protesting at being deprived of any sound at all. It was absolute, total silence, and it was fantastic. I broke into a huge grin and looked across at Grant. He was beaming back at me. We didn't say anything to each other. We didn't need to.

We stood up to leave. It was time to go home. My body was

weary, my emotions spent. I sighed with relief that I was about to escape, but the thought of leaving was tearing me apart. Would I ever see Antarctica again? The snow crunched beneath our feet. We took one last look behind us and headed down the hillside.

CHAPTER NINE

Sanctuary

ADDED TO THE BURDEN OF THE EXPEDITION'S FAILURE WAS
the realization that, in our absence, the campaign to establish a
Southern Ocean Sanctuary had been floundering. Most of the
governments we had expected to side with us were instead
sitting on the fence or even quietly expressing outright opposition. Part of the reason was undoubtedly the nervousness and
aversion to controversy that is inherent in every country's
diplomatic corps. Partly, also, we suspected some nations were
mildly petulant over the fact that France had submitted the
proposal without first consulting the likes of the United States
and the United Kingdom, which generally insisted on taking the
lead on such issues.

At the same time, many countries simply weren't convinced
of the sanctuary's efficacy. The situation was under control, they
argued: even though the International Whaling Commission's
Scientific Committee was developing a Revised Management
Procedure for commercial whaling, the commission was under
no timetable to accept it. The pressure remained on the whalers

to overturn the moratorium and not on the rest of the IWC to allow whaling's resumption. The adoption of the sanctuary, particularly given that its proponents claimed that it would protect more than 90 percent of the world's whales even in the event of the RMP's adoption and implementation, could only lessen the incentive to retain the moratorium. Such concerns were enthusiastically stoked by a cabal of skeptical environmental groups, who for reasons best known to themselves believed that the fix was in, that the sanctuary was just the first stage in a Machiavellian plan to discard the moratorium, embrace the RMP, and usher in a return to full-scale commercial whaling.

Those of us who supported the sanctuary had no disagreement with the argument that the moratorium needed to remain in place, despite the claims by some of the aforementioned groups to the contrary. It made perfect sense to ensure that all the different elements of the RMP were as conservative as possible; given their history, the onus was on the whalers to prove that they wouldn't break whatever rules and regulations were developed. Where we differed was that first, a number of us (including me) didn't share the rabid opposition to the RMP of some of the more "fundamentalist" crowd; frankly, we felt it was a little disingenuous to argue against commercial whaling on scientific grounds—the devastation it had caused to whale populations around the world—while simultaneously dismissing and denigrating a legitimate scientific effort to correct those past flaws. Second, a lot of us took issue with the stance that the only strategy required to protect whales from future whaling was to remain firm, yield no quarter, and maintain the moratorium.

A hard core of countries within the IWC—notably Australia, Germany, the Netherlands, New Zealand, the United Kingdom, and the United States—remained firmly and resolutely opposed to commercial whaling; but much of their opposition was based as much on ethical as on scientific grounds, which were principles that not everyone else necessarily shared. Other countries (typified by Ireland and Sweden, among others) that opposed commercial whaling on the basis of the damage it had consistently inflicted on whale populations—rather than a sense that whales deserved immunity from future predation because of their inherent magnificence—looked at the draft RMP that was nearing completion and felt that it truly did appear to be, as its authors had promised, extraordinarily conservative and infinitely more likely to protect whale populations than any previous management regime. As a result, the RMP looked likely to be formally adopted, at least in principle, by the 1994 IWC meeting at the latest, with or without the sanctuary. Meanwhile, there were signs that the Fisheries Agency of Japan, the Japanese government body that was the driving force for that country's whaling policy, was using fisheries aid to change the votes of some of the poorer IWC nations, and perhaps to bring in some more members to vote on its side. In other words, a few years from now, the situation within the IWC might not be as beneficial to the anti-whalers as it was right here in 1993; far better to take some action now, to make a preemptive strike against the threat of expanded whaling.

The sanctuary would not, it was true, have much if any immediate impact. If adopted, it would ban commercial whaling in the Antarctic. Because Japan's fleet claimed to be conducting "scientific research," and because the International Convention for the Regulation of Whaling states that the "scientific research" provision "shall be exempt from the operation of this Convention," it would not be able to stop Japan's "research whaling." That might make the sanctuary seem like an empty victory; but the research whaling was being operated solely to keep crew members employed and trained, equipment in good order, and markets for whale meat open, until such time as the moratorium could eventually be overturned and full-scale commercial whaling resumed. The idea behind the proposal was not just to look at today or even tomorrow, but to reach beyond that: to stay ahead of the whalers, anticipate what it was they wanted most (which was undeniably the opportunity to kill several thousand whales in the Antarctic each year), and prevent them from getting it.

We were hopeful that, given enough time and the opportunity to explain our position fully, we would ultimately be able to persuade the requisite three-quarters majority of the IWC of the sanctuary's merits. But both time and opportunities were slipping by, and the proposal had come under an assault—from pro-whalers and anti-sanctuary environmentalists—that was more vigorous and sustained than the counterpunches we were trying to land. Indeed, as I sat in temporary self-imposed exile in Auckland for the first couple of months after returning from the Antarctic in March 1993, hiding from Amsterdam and the inevitable parade of condolences and criticism that I knew would greet me on my return from our failed expedition, staring morosely into the near distance as images of the previous few months replayed themselves endlessly in my mind, the sanctuary looked in danger of drowning, with no obvious life ring in sight.

Already engulfed by feelings of inadequacy, I found it impossible not to be further affected by the sanctuary's sagging fortunes. Not that I considered our expedition's failure to engage the fleet and thus highlight the sanctuary proposal the cause of the proposal's difficulties: even at my lowest ebb, I was able to appreciate that a great many other factors were at play. Nonetheless, the developments added to an overall sense of humiliation and despair that the situation was slipping from our grasp. The whalers had beaten us on the front lines, had laughed at us as we chased phantoms across the Southern Ocean; now they were succeeding in tying our big political weapon in knots.

By the time of the IWC meeting in Kyoto in May 1993, the sanctuary idea seemed poised for oblivion. In order to be adopted into the commission's rule book, or Schedule, the proposal needed to attract a three-quarters majority of those voting either yes or no, and as the commissioners gathered in Kyoto, the likelihood of that happening appeared remote. Not that many whaling nations were in the IWC: Iceland, raging against the allegedly glacial progress toward implementing a new management regime, had waltzed theatrically out of the commission during the Glasgow meeting the previous year, leaving Japan and Norway as the only active commercial whaling countries among the member states. But the Fisheries Agency of Japan had, as feared, bought itself some friends, conducting a "vote-consolidation program" targeted primarily at Caribbean island nations that, after receiving fisheries aid from the FAJ, suddenly and coincidentally developed an overwhelming interest in defending the inalienable right of a sovereign state to hunt whales in the waters surrounding Antarctica. In Kyoto, the number of Caribbean members in the "whalers' bloc" stood at four, Dominica and Grenada having joined St. Lucia and St. Vincent & the Grenadines as commission members the previous year. Between these four, plus Norway and Japan, the whalers had an effective blocking vote.

Six votes would not necessarily have been an insurmountable obstacle were it not for the continued skepticism of normally friendly countries. Although most of those countries would be highly unlikely to vote against a proposal that sought to increase whale protection and limit whaling, many of them seemed disposed toward abstaining. We urged the sanctuary's supporters to put the proposal to a vote anyway; even if it wasn't adopted this time, we argued, a vote would smoke out the countries that didn't support it, and give us the opportunity to bring pressure to bear, so the results would be better next time. The response we were getting from our allies, however, was that support for the sanctuary was so shallow at this stage that if it went to the floor and failed, there might not *be* a next time.

It looked as if the sanctuary proposal was at an impasse. One possibility, however, was to bring the proposal before the Technical Committee. This isn't, in fact, a separate committee as such; it is generally the same people who constitute the commission proper, except that, for part of the time, they call themselves the Technical Committee, speak off the record (and consequently more candidly), and occasionally bring issues to a nonbinding vote. While the commissioners are calling themselves the Technical Committee, they can't actually make any substantive decisions; they can, however, vote to give their opinion to the commission (which is themselves) or to refer a matter for the commission's later consideration (in other words, they can ask themselves to consider in more detail matters that they themselves have been unable, or do not have the authority, to resolve). It's archaic, but it works well enough.

Raising an issue in the Technical Committee enables commissioners to gauge the level of support for it, without risking an official IWC vote on it that might not succeed. That, in the end, is what happened in Kyoto with the sanctuary proposal: it was brought before the Technical Committee, which, by a slim majority, voted in favor of its adoption, which basically meant that the commissioners were recommending to themselves that they should adopt it.

The Technical Committee vote served several functions. It made the more conservationist countries happy, because it allowed them to say they had supported and voted for the sanctuary, without forcing them to commit to backing what was still a losing horse. It put a majority of the commission on record as supporting a sanctuary in the Southern Ocean, at least in principle. And it satisfied our immediate goal of identifying the countries we needed to target, to try to move them from opposing, or abstaining on, the sanctuary to backing it at the next meeting, to be held in Puerto Vallarta, Mexico, in May 1994.

The sanctuary's proponents had also devised another plan to help give the proposal some momentum between Kyoto and Mexico. Australia had sponsored a resolution calling on the commission to endorse the concept of a sanctuary in the Southern Ocean and proposing that a special intersessional meeting be held to discuss a number of outstanding issues and report back its findings to the Puerto Vallarta meeting.

Because the Australian resolution did not actually seek to adopt the sanctuary then and there, it required only a simple majority to pass, which it achieved with votes to spare. Eight months later, in February 1994, the IWC convened the special meeting Australia had called for, on tiny Norfolk Island in the Tasman Sea.

This decision proved to be perhaps the most significant for the sanctuary's fortunes. The meeting accorded the sanctuary a certain positive stature; it satisfied some of the countries that had been offended by France's solo act, assuring them that they were now involved in the proposal's development; and it gave us an additional opportunity to lobby for the proposal's adoption and focus our efforts on those nations that had shown some reluctance in Kyoto. For the sanctuary's supporters, the interim meeting was a resounding success: several months of concentrated work on the countries that had wavered in Kyoto were bearing fruit, and a significant pro-sanctuary movement was building up steam. By a large majority, the meeting adopted a resolution stating that the IWC member states present saw "no insurmountable objection" to the sanctuary's adoption. At the same time, France was able to pick up nine cosponsors: Australia, Brazil, Ireland, Monaco, the Netherlands, New Zealand, Spain, the United Kingdom, and the United States would join the French in proposing that the sanctuary be adopted in Puerto Vallarta.

Puerto Vallarta, Mexico, May 23, 1994

I looked out of my hotel room window and down onto the beach below. A mile offshore, where before there had been only windsurfers and swimmers, there now drifted a warship. Maybe it was coincidence, but somehow it seemed unlikely. Security around the meeting room was as tight as it had ever been for a commission meeting, and in a turbulent presidential election year that had seen two leading political figures assassinated, the government was taking no chances. The meeting marked the final appearance of the Mexican commissioner, Dr. Luis Fleischer, as IWC chairman, and the authorities were determined that it would be a trouble-free and momentous week.

Momentous it certainly looked to be. The people of Puerto

Vallarta, grasping the significance of the meeting, gathered on the beach by the thousands the weekend beforehand, joining hands to form the shape of a giant whale; hundreds more signed their names in support of the sanctuary. A small group of dedicated British supporters stood outside the conference hotel in the blazing heat, brandishing a pro-sanctuary sign. One evening, a crowd of Vallartanese schoolchildren held a candle-light vigil beneath the balcony of a room where the Japanese government was hosting a reception.

Building on the momentum of the Norfolk Island meeting, the sanctuary idea was now on a roll. Nonetheless, despite the new determination on the part of many countries to push the proposal, there was no guarantee of its passage. And even as some form of sanctuary began to look more likely, there was uncertainty as to its boundaries.

Four countries lay partly south of the 40 degrees South line: Argentina, Australia, Chile, and New Zealand. And while New Zealand and Australia had no problem with that, the other two were concerned that an international convention deciding what could and could not take place in their waters would be a serious infringement on their sovereignty. With the voting situation uncertain, the sanctuary's supporters were concerned that losing Chile and Argentina—and, possibly, sympathetic nations such as Mexico and maybe Spain—would consign the proposal to defeat. As a result, momentum began developing for a proposal to head off any possible conflict by adopting a sanctuary with a northern boundary that would skirt all territorial waters. The boundary that was suggested was one matching that of the Convention for the Conservation of Antarctic Marine Living Resources, or CCAMLR: namely, a line that roughly followed the Antarctic Convergence and was mostly set at around 60 degrees South.

The Antarctic Convergence is the boundary that separates the Antarctic from more temperate climes, as if sealing it and pro-tecting it from the rest of the world. It is where cold polar water clashes with more temperate seas; south of the Convergence, the scenery, the climate, and the wildlife are very different than those to its north. Its basic track remains the same year after year, molded by ocean currents and continental landmasses, keeping it far south of Australia and New Zealand, and giving a wide berth to the waters off South America until it slices the Drake Passage, the stretch of water that separates the southern-most tip of the Americas from the most northerly reaches of the Antarctic Peninsula.

Biologically and ecologically, little functional difference existed between the CCAMLR idea and the original French proposal. All but a handful of the whales caught in Japan's scientific program, after all, were killed south of 60S; a sanctuary with that boundary would still provide essentially the same amount of protection for the species concerned.

The CCAMLR proposal still left an enormous amount of ocean, between 40S and 60S, relatively unprotected, but the likelihood of there being much whaling in that area was remote, given that almost all whales in the Antarctic region gather in the nutrient-rich waters south of the Convergence. Even so, the compromise was too much for some. The Irish commissioner, Michael Canny, made it clear that he could not accept such a watering-down of the French proposal. Ireland, he said, would rather see no sanctuary at all than a compromise solution such as this; accordingly, he would vote against the CCAMLR proposal. His stance was echoed by his government's environment minister, Noel Dempsey, who was on the delegation and able to convey Dublin's direct support. The United States, which by now was determined to see some form of sanctuary passed, urged Ireland to reconsider and allow the revised proposal to succeed, but even a phone call from Vice President Al Gore wasn't enough to budge the Irish from their position. Rumors began to float that Monaco was supporting Ireland's stance. The "safe compromise" was plainly nothing of the sort.

The solution was "Super CCAMLR." In essence, this proposed returning the northern boundary to 40 degrees South—except around South America, where it would drop to 60S and thus skirt the continent entirely (and where newly agreed regional sanctuaries would fill in the gaps), and in the Indian Ocean, where the boundary would be 55S, making it contiguous with the existing Indian Ocean Sanctuary and effectively extending its northern boundary in that region to the equator. It rapidly became clear that this version was going to attract the most widespread support. France withdrew its original proposal and combined forces with Mexico and Chile to formally propose the revision. By close of business Wednesday, sixteen additional countries, including the United States, had signed on as cosponsors.

A vote count that evening put total support for the sanctuary at twenty-three, but that still wasn't necessarily enough to adopt it into the Schedule. Its opponents needed to muster only a third of that number to block its adoption. Japan could presumably count on Norway and its four Caribbean stooges, for a total of six. With thirty-two nations attending, that left China and South Korea, whose positions were rarely predictable, and the Solomon Islands, regularly subjected to—but this year so far resisting—Japan's "vote-consolidation program." If two of those supported Japan, and one abstained, the sanctuary was sunk.

By Thursday morning, the cracks were appearing. The commissioner for St. Lucia took an early flight home. The United States began applying heavy pressure on the Norwegian delegation to take a walk on the beach during the vote.

Japan tried to employ stalling tactics, tabling a proposal to delay a vote on the sanctuary until further advice had been received from the Scientific Committee. Australia, seconded by France, proposed an amendment to the resolution, which asked the Scientific Committee to provide scientific advice but which didn't make the sanctuary conditional on its receipt. The commission agreed to vote on the Australian amendment, not the original Japanese proposal, and the amended resolution was passed.

Japan tried again. In collaboration with Norway and the remaining Caribbean islands, the Japanese delegation proposed a sanctuary that would have the Antarctic Convergence as a northern boundary and would provide complete protection for different periods for different species, ranging from fifty years for right, sei, and humpback whales, through eighty years for the fin whale, up to 125 years for the blue whale. The proposal would, however, leave the minke whale unprotected and open to exploitation. It went down, by twenty-three votes to six. The stage was set.

Norway didn't take that walk on the beach, but the delegation did exempt itself from the vote, claiming that it was in some way a violation of the IWC convention. With St. Lucia already gone, the game was effectively up. Japan cut loose its remaining Caribbean allies and prepared to stand alone. China, Korea, and the Solomon Islands joined Dominica, Grenada, and St. Vincent & the Grenadines in abstaining. In the end, the final call wasn't even close. The predicted twenty-three countries voted for the sanctuary; only Japan voted against. It was the largest majority in favor of a Schedule amendment in IWC history.

I was sitting next to John Frizell. As soon as the result of the vote was declared, we turned toward each other, beamed, and hugged. I stood up, walked to the door of the meeting room, took a deep breath, and stepped outside into the waiting media scrum. I launched into interviews with print, radio, and television journalists from the United States, Britain, Australia, and South Africa. As the meeting inside was gaveled to a close and everyone else came spilling through the doors, footage of me triumphantly embracing our press officer, Desley Mather, was broadcast worldwide on CNN. Congratulatory messages began flooding in from Greenpeace offices around the world. That night, as fireworks exploded in the background, we all unwound at a reception by the hotel pool. Almost all the government delegations turned up, including some of the Caribbean representatives. All the environmental organizations were there, even those who had opposed the sanctuary and who now stood a little awkwardly off to one side. For now, two years of tensions and disagreements were all forgotten, and festivity was the order of the evening. For one night at least, it was time to celebrate and relax.

As long as the Southern Ocean Sanctuary remained on the books, commercial whaling in the Antarctic was finished. Japan, naturally enough, lodged an objection, but it was to no avail: the sanctuary's existence meant that, even were the moratorium to be lifted and a new management regime installed in its place, the Scientific Committee would not be allowed to even calculate catch limits in the Antarctic, and the commission itself would not be allowed to set any. And given that the Institute of Cetacean Research claimed that its scientific whaling program was designed to provide information for future management of minke whales in the Antarctic, the fact that the prospect of such "management" had been ended meant that the justification for the program had been removed at a stroke.

Even so, as important as the sanctuary was, and as hard as so many had worked to bring it to fruition, it was hardly the end of the story; the whaling industry wasn't going to roll over and die just like that. After all, it had been twelve years since the IWC had passed the moratorium, and although the number of whales being killed in the Antarctic each year was considerably smaller than before the moratorium took effect—330 minke whales in 1993–94, compared to 6,655 ten years earlier—the whalers had worked relentlessly to enlarge the IWC's loopholes as much as they could, and the industry was still very much in business. Although Japan's Foreign Ministry, long embarrassed by the way that whaling stained its country's image abroad, stated after the sanctuary vote that Japan would now have to find nonlethal means of conducting whale research in the Antarctic, and the country's IWC commissioner responded by protesting that if Japan couldn't conduct lethal research, then it might not conduct any research at all, there was no way the ICR was going to meekly surrender its scientific whaling program just yet. With the sanctuary, we had established an important roadblock, but we knew that the FAJ would almost immediately begin looking for alternative routes to its goal, and in the meantime the whaling industry in Japan was going to do exactly what it had been doing since 1987: dispatch its fleet to the Antarctic to kill three hundred or more minke whales in the name of "science."

That such a move was all too predictable didn't make it any easier to deal with. After all the work we had put into the sanctuary's adoption, it was frustrating to then have to stand by and watch the whaling fleet head back to the Antarctic. But we could do nothing about it, politically or diplomatically, beyond that which we had already been doing for years: like it or not, the sanctuary couldn't prohibit scientific whaling.

It didn't even look as if there was any practical way we would be able to confront the fleet directly, to highlight the fact that, at the very least, the whaling fleet was continuing to violate the spirit of the IWC—and even more so now that an overwhelming majority of the commission had made it crystal clear that they didn't want to see any form of commercial whaling in the Antarctic ever again. All the Greenpeace ships, it seemed, were already assigned to other tasks, with none apparently able to make it to the Ross Sea region in time—and there was nobody, it seemed, with the campaign experience to take charge of an expedition anyway: Athel had retired to Belgium; Naoko had left Greenpeace; and with the sanctuary in place and my feeling a growing urge to venture into alternative pursuits, I was giving serious thought to leaving the organization myself. Besides, I had spent most of the previous year busily telling people that, after what had happened last time, there was no way I was ever going back to the Antarctic.

And then, one by one, the pieces started falling into place.

It was Walt Simpson who began putting them together. One late summer afternoon in Amsterdam, several months after the excitement from Puerto Vallarta had died down, he called me over to his office and quietly showed me the schedules of the various members of the Greenpeace fleet. In December, he pointed out, the *Greenpeace* was scheduled to end a tour of South America in Ushuaia, Argentina, the most southerly port in the

world and a well-known spot for hopping on and off, and pro-
visioning, ships—including, in the past, the *Greenpeace* and the
Gondwana—making trips to the Antarctic Peninsula. Walt, an
early participant in the *Gondwana* voyages to World Park Base
and always eager for Greenpeace to take every opportunity to
return to Antarctica, urged me to try to put together a proposal
that might include, say, base visits in the peninsula area and
documentation of fisheries activities in the region. I threw out a
few feelers with the fisheries folks and ran the idea past the
Antarctic campaign, but although there was some interest,
nobody really bit.

For Greenpeace, a decade of unprecedented growth—
stimulated by, among other things, the publicity, outrage, and
sympathy generated by the French government's bombing of
the *Rainbow Warrior* in 1985; the disaster at the Chernobyl
nuclear plant in 1986; the fall of the Berlin Wall in 1989 and the
desperate need to address the environmental devastation
inflicted by communist policies; and a surge of interest in environmental issues particularly in western Europe, reflected in the
growing prominence of Green parties in many of the countries
of that region—was slowing down. Having expanded rapidly
during that time, geographically and in the issues it addressed,
Greenpeace was now being forced to scale back; as a result, the
organization was convulsing through a period of restructuring
and downsizing, and most people felt too uncertain about the
future of their jobs or their campaigns to make any kind of
medium-term plans for ship use. Under those circumstances, it
was hardly surprising that enthusiasm and vision were a little
difficult to drum up.

Nonetheless, the discussions did at least fire the first sputtering
of a spark inside my own head. They started me thinking about
Antarctica again, and although I was not expressly picturing
myself as the person to lead any expedition that could be put
together, I wasn't exactly dismissing the possibility, either.
Gradually, the thought began to take root in my imagination,
and as it blossomed, it actually looked and smelled pretty good.

After a year of denying the prospect of it ever happening again, I could see myself in the Antarctic with Greenpeace once more; it wouldn't be on a whaling campaign, it seemed, but despite that—or perhaps because of it—the prospect was attractive.

Indeed, the notion that we could use the *Greenpeace* to chase the whalers had barely occurred to me. John Frizell had asked me about it, and I had replied that the timing looked wrong, that Ushuaia was on the other side of the continent from the whaling grounds, and that getting from one side to the other would require spending two weeks or more pounding through wind and waves. Disappointing and frustrating as it would be, given that the fleet would be, at least in spirit, violating a sanctuary that had been adopted only a few months earlier, it nonetheless seemed as if an anti-whaling voyage this year just wasn't in the cards.

But when nothing else came up, and neither the Antarctic nor the fisheries campaign seemed likely to seize on the prospect of using the ship, John and I spoke about it some more, and he offered to draft a proposal. His proposal turned all the apparent disadvantages of the plan to advantages. The whalers would have long since started their season by the time the *Greenpeace* left Ushuaia, but the fact that the Black Pig would still be making port visits in Argentina while they were hunting whales several thousand miles away might lull them into a false sense of security. In addition, John suggested, the long transit to the whaling grounds could be put to productive use, enabling us to conduct our own studies on the region's whales and the Antarctic ecosystem.

Unfortunately, as with the other ideas for the ship's use that I had floated, the proposal seemed to die a quick death once it permeated into the larger organization. Since March 1994 I had been working out of the offices of Greenpeace U.S. in Washington, D.C., away from the Amsterdam power center; my earlier conversation with Walt about the possibility of using the Black Pig in the Antarctic had come during one of my periodic visits to the organization's international headquarters. From my new location, I couldn't see or hear whether the proposal was going anywhere, and wasn't in a position to do anything with it myself. I shrugged my shoulders, assumed it had come to naught, and focused my attention again on planning a life outside of Greenpeace. But Walt had been quietly pushing the plan around Amsterdam at every opportunity, and when the campaigns director suddenly went for the idea, planning rapidly shifted into overdrive. At the end of September, my morning e-mail download revealed a message from John. Headlined PRIVATE, it read:

> Dear Kieran,
>   If current information is correct we will be going to the Antarctic with the MVGP after all.
>   Whatever your plans to depart Greenpeace might be, I suggest you arrange them in a way that you can take in this little gem.

News of the campaign was not universally welcomed. In fact, some parts of the organization expressed outright hostility, and mockery of the notion that we would be prepared to repeat such a spectacular failure. The *Greenpeace* was much slower than the whalers, people reminded us; the only sight we would ever get of the whaling fleet would be of the slipway of the *Nisshin Maru* as the factory ship disappeared over the horizon.

The criticism was understandable. Few knew the full circumstances surrounding the previous expedition, and a number of the critics had not been around when, or had forgotten that, our first voyage had overcome doubters and heavy odds to end up widely praised as a great success. Nonetheless, predictable and reasonable as such griping was, it rankled. I objected to the notion that I, of all people, needed to be told of the failings of the previous expedition or informed of the limitations of a new one. I was the one who had been through it all the last time, and I was leery of putting myself through it all again. I had spent eighteen months trying to piece myself back together after the experiences of the previous expedition. I knew the odds better than anybody; if I was prepared to put myself through it one more time, I figured, then I deserved the benefit of the doubt.

The irony was that the criticism was being directed at an expedition that, for all its risks of failure, had been thought through more thoroughly than either of the previous two anti-whaling voyages. Although success could by no means be guaranteed, it was, for a number of reasons, more likely.

For one thing, the whaling campaign was just one component—although undeniably the largest—in a three-part expedition.

The first stage would take place in the Antarctic Peninsula region. It didn't take long to agree that it made sense to kick off the voyage with a series of base visits. The peninsula, and in particular King George Island, was the site of by far the greatest concentration of research stations on the continent, and visits by Greenpeace over the years had consistently shown that standards there were among the lowest. The 1991 Environmental Protocol to the Antarctic Treaty, which had banned mining and which had prompted Greenpeace to declare victory and dismantle World Park Base, also imposed a series of strict regulations on countries operating in Antarctica, but most of the countries with bases in the area had yet to ratify the agreement. It would have been irresponsible to be so close to the peninsula and steam past it without doing anything, especially as there was no guarantee that Greenpeace would be able to return in the near future.

Besides, kicking off the expedition at King George Island would provide a big boost for those on board the *Greenpeace*. Unlike the previous two expeditions, there would be no waiting around for weeks on end, marking time until the first whiff of action. Three days out from Ushuaia, we would be in the Antarctic, and a couple of days after that, we'd be at work. Then, when our base visits were completed, everybody would still be busy during the long transit to the whaling grounds, involving themselves in the second phase of the expedition, the science program.

This was more John's baby than mine, and one he had drawn up in response to ICR criticisms that the sanctuary would be a "black hole" for scientific research. Any program we could throw together with our limited resources and timeline would of necessity have to be modest, but the important thing was to show that it could be done: with the sanctuary scheduled to come into effect on December 7—as mandated by IWC rules, ninety days after the filing of Japan's objection—it meant that within three weeks of the sanctuary being in place, Greenpeace would be setting out on the first nongovernmental research expedition to be conducted inside its boundaries.

After consultation with various experts, John drew up a series of research projects. We would make photographic studies of humpback whales, and underwater recordings of blues, sperms, humpbacks, and others. We would conduct surveys of floating oceanic debris, both natural and artificial. And we would carry out a baseline study of plankton communities to determine if they were being affected by increased ultraviolet radiation as a result of ozone depletion.

It was ambitious. But if we managed to come back with anything at all from these different projects, if we were able to demonstrate clearly that, even with limited resources and last-minute preparations, it was possible to learn about the whales and ecosystem of the Southern Ocean through a variety of nonlethal methods, then the trip would be a resounding success—whether or not we found the whalers.

Our plan for intercepting the whaling fleet would be different as well. This time around, we would not be heading down at the beginning of the season and groping around blindly, chugging through the whole whaling area on a desperate search for a needle in a haystack. By the time we reached the whaling area, the whalers would be nearer the end of their season and would, more specifically, be preparing to enter the Ross Sea. We knew roughly when the fleet would do that, partly on the basis of previous years, but also because of simple physical and climatic considerations: the Ross Sea is ice-free for only a certain period each year, and during that time the fleet has to go in, take the whales they want, and leave again. We knew the fleet would be entering the Ross Sea: they always had when hunting in this particular whaling area, and the proposal they had presented to the IWC in Puerto Vallarta said as much. The Ross Sea was still an enormous area to search—a little larger than Texas and Wyoming combined—but it was smaller by far than the whaling area as a whole, and at least it had three physical boundaries. Even on the second voyage, we had found the whalers there twice, however accidentally.

And by the time the fleet went in, they would have finished with the rest of the whaling area, so there would be nowhere else—apart from the Special Monitoring Zone, which they had this year announced would be north of the Ross Sea—to which they could run. Sure, they would probably flee once; and if we found them a second time, chances were that they would run then as well. After that, I reckoned, time would be running short, and if they wanted to reach their quota they wouldn't have any choice other than to deal with our presence.

Whether or not we would actually be able to find them three times was a different matter. And even if we did, it was far from certain we'd be able to engage them in the kind of actions we had on the first expedition. But as far as I was concerned, this time around it just felt different. The plan was good, and my own cold sweats notwithstanding, the karma seemed right.

There was another consideration. Greenpeace had made establishment of the Southern Ocean Sanctuary an organizational priority only a few months previously. Having put so much effort into, and been more than happy to accrue some of the prestige from, its adoption, how could we now justify standing back and allowing the whalers to violate it within a few days of its coming into effect? Even if success was not a certainty, we had to try.

CHAPTER TEN

A Place Called Paradise

NO OFFICIAL POLITICAL BOUNDARY DIVIDES ANTARCTICA FROM the rest of the world, but an ocean voyage south toward the frozen continent leaves no doubt where the temperate regions end and the polar realm begins. North of the Antarctic Convergence, there is little sign of the change that is approaching; over the course of just a few hours, however, the temperature begins to drop rapidly, the ship becomes engulfed in a misty blanket caused by the collision between warmer waters from the north and frigid seas from the south, and then, as if having passed through some unseen portal to Antarctica, everything changes. It is colder. The bird life is different. Soon the first signs of ice appear on the water, and old, weathered icebergs drift silently by.

Milo had laughed at me when I asked her to wake me at 0400, when we were scheduled to close in on the Convergence. After all, it wasn't as if there would be a penguin dressed as a border guard or a bright neon sign flashing WELCOME TO ANTARCTICA. But I had been in the wheelhouse and on deck for my previous two crossings, and I didn't want to miss it this time either, even if it did mean getting out of bed in the middle of the night.

Of course, when I reached the bridge and found no great evidence of any change, I began to wonder if I had been hyping it up a bit too much. Maybe I'd fallen victim to a case of selective, rose-tinted memory. But as the morning progressed, we disappeared into a series of snow squalls, the temperature plunged—in the space of five hours, the sea temperature fell from 40 degrees to freezing—and we were in the Antarctic.

Between the Convergence and the continent of Antarctica lie 14 million square miles of some of the stormiest waters on Earth. Uninterrupted by landfall, circling endlessly, and driven by powerful winds from the west, the Antarctic Circumpolar Current propels a procession of low-pressure systems through the Southern Ocean, the principal reason why the region suffers so many seemingly continuous storms. At a relatively narrow 450 miles, the Drake Passage—the stretch of water between Tierra del Fuego and the Antarctic Peninsula that we would be traversing on our journey south from Ushuaia—acts as a funnel, frequently concentrating the Southern Ocean's mightiest storms to their maximum rage. We had anticipated the crossing with a certain trepidation, but the two-day voyage passed without a hitch, and as we reached the peninsula's northernmost reaches, the clouds parted and the sun shone down on us as if to welcome us back to Antarctica.

We steamed among the dramatic, rocky, snow-covered South Shetland Islands, some of the earliest land to be sighted in the Antarctic region: Smith Island, named after William Smith, the discoverer of the South Shetlands in 1819 and, the following year, one of the very first people ever to set eyes on the continent of Antarctica itself; Snow Island, entirely draped in ice; and King George Island, the largest island in the group and the place where we would be doing most of our shore work, visiting Brazilian, Chilean, Chinese, Polish, and Russian research stations.

We passed by the western edge of the South Shetlands and rounded the corner on our final approach to King George

Island. Icebergs dotted the calm sea; penguins and the occasional whale broke the surface to cheers of delight from the excited crew. As we steamed south of Livingston Island, it seemed that almost everyone on board—newcomers and Antarctic veterans alike—was out on deck, drinking in the spectacular scenery.

I looked across the wheelhouse, caught Arne's eye, and grinned.

"Sure is nice to be back, eh, captain?"

"Not bad at all," he smiled.

We had set out from Ushuaia on the morning of December 28. Within twelve hours of departure, the first inflatable had been launched for Liz Carr to begin her plankton sampling program. The use of chemicals called chlorofluorocarbons in products such as aerosols had, over the years, depleted the layer of atmospheric ozone in Earth's atmosphere, allowing greater amounts of ultraviolet radiation to reach the planet's surface. Many scientists were gravely concerned that this increased UV radiation could be seriously affecting the phytoplankton and krill in the Antarctic that form the basis of the Southern Ocean food chain, and Liz's experiments were designed to provide data to help answer that question.

Recently turned thirty, Liz was a fit, attractive, hyperenergetic scientist with a mane of red hair. Five years earlier, she had overwintered at World Park Base; subsequently, she had returned on the *Gondwana* and been part of the team that removed the base in the 1991–92 season. Like me, Liz had strong and conflicting emotions surrounding her time in the Antarctic; having just entered her fourth decade, she was keen to move on to new challenges and hadn't been at all sure she wanted to return to a place that held so many powerful memories. It had taken a lot of early-morning and late-evening phone conversations before I was able to persuade her to come along.

But, having taken the plunge, Liz threw herself into her work with enthusiasm. While the *Greenpeace* drifted, Liz spent a couple of hours taking a series of readings—of sea temperature, salinity, light measurements at different depths—and towing a net at slow speed to gather samples of phytoplankton. When she came back on board, she began several hours of filtration and pumping, separating the plankton from the water, logging the results and storing the samples for later analysis at the University of Exeter in England. All together, she was scheduled to conduct about thirty sample stations during the course of the expedition, including every day from Ushuaia to the peninsula and then on the journey back north to Hobart; one roughly every other day between the peninsula and the Ross Sea; and two or three stations, each sampled on three separate occasions, at the mouth of the Ross Sea.

Other members of the science team also launched into their projects. Dr. Roger Grace, an avuncular, cheerful, white-bearded photographer from New Zealand, was in charge of the debris survey. Whenever possible, he would tow a net along the side of the *Greenpeace* or stand at the bow, clipboard in hand, for an hour at a time, scanning the water for any sign of natural or man-made debris.

Keenest of all was Chris Pierpoint. In charge of the visual and acoustic surveys of cetaceans, Chris had set about his task almost from the moment we had left port. He was touchingly thrilled by every experience, from the color of the Southern Ocean, to seeing seabird species he had never before encountered, to recording cetacean species that may never have been recorded before. If he wasn't sitting in his cabin or in the radio room trying to patch together some type of listening device, he could usually be found in cold-weather gear on Monkey Island, binoculars in hand, scanning the waves endlessly for even a glimpse of a whale's back breaking the surface.

While the scientists were busy with their observations, small teams went ashore to visit research stations in the area, inter-viewing base staff and recording the bases' performance in such areas as wildlife disturbance and waste disposal. These results would be included in a report to be presented to the next meeting of the Antarctic Treaty—a task Greenpeace had been fulfilling since the early days of its presence in the Antarctic. Because King George Island is one of the very few places in Antarctica that is ice-free for much of the year, it is host to a disproportionate concentration of bases, many of which were built in the 1980s—during the mad rush of countries to establish a presence on the continent in hopes of gaining special rights if the Antarctic were ever opened up to mineral exploitation. With the 1991 Environmental Protocol putting that dream out of reach, the condition of the various bases reflected the sponsoring nation's genuine level of interest in maintaining a scientific presence on Antarctica, and its financial ability to do so. The Chilean base of Teniente Rodolfo Marsh, for example, illustrated Santiago's nationalistic obsession with the Antarctic and was characterized by clean, new buildings and uniformed military personnel. Russia's Bellingshausen station—literally just a few steps away—was like an impoverished seaside town, with peeling paint, doors hanging off their hinges, and little sign of any human presence.

In addition to the shore work, we had set aside a few days of our presence in the South Shetlands to kick-start one specific area of the scientific program. Humpback whales that feed in the Antarctic Peninsula region breed in the waters off Colombia and Costa Rica, and their passage between those two points is the longest known migration of any mammal (a distinction previously believed to belong to the gray whales that summer off Alaska and winter in the waters of Baja California); because each humpback has a distinct pattern on its tail flukes, as unique to each whale as a fingerprint is to humans, every humpback fluke we could photograph would add to the growing scientific database and provide invaluable information on the behaviors, distribution, and migration of individual whales.

The day had not begun all that auspiciously. It was impressive enough, but the mountains of the Antarctic Peninsula were hidden by low, gray clouds; the glimpses we caught of them only hinted at their true majesty. We all agreed that it looked beautiful, but underneath we seemed—some of us at least—to be trying to convince ourselves as much as share the experience with each other.

I had been looking forward to this day for two months, ever since Walt Simpson had invited me into his living room in Amsterdam and shown me video of the *Gondwana*'s trip to this area—to the Gerlache Strait, Andvord Bay, and Paradise Harbor. I had gazed in amazement at the scenes, as Walt, drifting off into the netherworld that all Antarctic veterans visit when talking about the place, had said, "Yep, this is where you'll be going for your whale research work." And ever since I had briefed the crew on the plans for the expedition and the itinerary for the ship, they had been anticipating the two or three days we had set aside to spend here as a high point of the trip. Yet here we were, within spitting distance of a place called Paradise, and not only did we see no humpbacks, but there was no clear view of the mountains and glaciers that had brought the region's scenery its renown.

But this time around, I had assured myself, luck would be on our side. With a little patience, everything would turn out right. Sure enough, as the afternoon rolled around, the surroundings underwent a gradual transformation.

The deeper we headed into the Gerlache Strait, the narrower it became, and as the mountains crowded in on us, they took on a more impressive, more intimidating appearance. The more the mountains loomed over the ship, the smaller and more vulnerable the *Greenpeace* seemed. This must have been how Alice felt. Adding to the illusion, the clouds gradually peeled away, revealing the mountains' towering peaks, and endless blue far above. This was more like the scene I had anticipated, the dramatically in-your-face mountainous vista that makes the Antarctic Peninsula so beautiful. As word of the spectacular scenery spread around the ship, more and more people began appearing on deck, standing on the bridge wings or leaning over the bow, sucking in the clean air and reveling in the moment.

The sight of blows up ahead hinted that we might have found what we were looking for; but as we drew closer, we could see

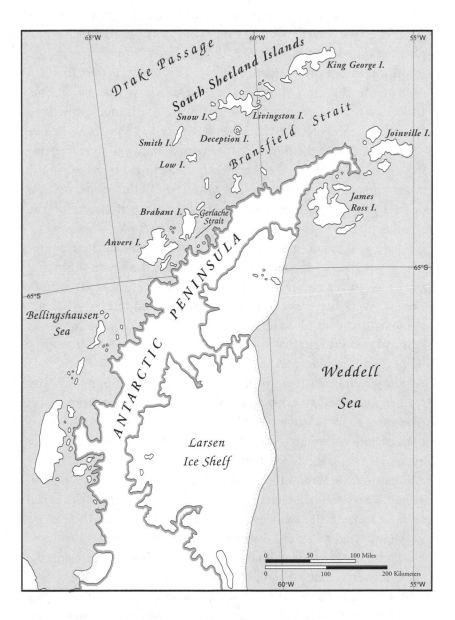

65°W   60°W   55°W

Drake Passage

South Shetland Islands

King George I.

Snow I.   Livingston I.

Smith I.   Deception I.

Low I.

Bransfield Strait

Joinville I.

James
Ross I.

Brabant I.   *Gerlache
Strait*

Anvers I.

65°S

65°S

*Bellingshausen
Sea*

A N T A R C T I C   P E N I N S U L A

*Weddell

Sea*

*Larsen
Ice Shelf*

0   50   100 Miles

0   100   200 Kilometers

60°W   55°W

that they belonged to minkes. It was humpbacks we were after, and with none immediately apparent, Arne suggested that we try Andvord Bay, where the *Gondwana* had found and photographed several in 1991.

So we turned into Andvord Bay and entered another world.

Not for the first time in the Antarctic, words failed me. Indeed, any thought of using something as limiting as words to describe the experience fell away as I gazed at the scene before me. It wasn't just the light, clear and crisp in a way that it seemingly can be only in the Antarctic, reflecting brightly off the mountains and glaciers. It was more than the icebergs that drifted past us, so close we could almost touch them; or the smaller pieces of ice they had calved, shaped like fragile white lily pads and cupping oases of crystal blue water in their palms. There was the air, of course: there was always the air in Antarctica, cold and pure, chilling and cleansing the sinuses with every breath. And there was the calm and quiet, only the gentle rhythm of the ship's generators breaking the silence. It was so still and peaceful that it felt as if we were the first people ever to be here, to discover this enchanted place.

The engine started up and the *Greenpeace* chugged slowly farther into the bay. Antarctica was playing its usual tricks with perspective, the clear air refracting light and making the most distant objects seem as if they could almost be touched. It appeared as if the bay were only a few ship lengths deep, as if at any minute, we would hit the shore. But the bay kept going and going; we passed by glaciers and icebergs even as the cliffs ahead seemed to keep the exact same distance from us. And the more we kept going, the more beautiful it seemed—the water still and clear, the sky a perfect blue, the light shining brightly on the small icebergs that drifted past, glistening white with pockets of deep cobalt. I started willing the bay to be bigger and bigger, for us to be able to turn a corner and keep going deeper and deeper. I was completely alone on the bridge wings, and for a timeless second, I became totally lost in the surroundings. I thought I could hear whales. I felt as if I was actually a part of the bay, and it was a part of me.

I returned to my body to find Hans Monker, the radio operator, now standing next to me, shaking his head in wonderment. Eight days ago he had never been south of the Antarctic Convergence; now here he was in the most beautiful place on Earth.

"How am I ever going to describe this?" he exclaimed out loud, as much to himself as to anyone. "This is incredible. All I can do now is fly to the moon; that is the only way I will ever see anything as beautiful as this."

As afternoon gave way to evening, scientists and crew gathered on the heli-deck. Chris pulled out his hydrophone equipment and we sat in a circle and listened to the sounds of whales in the distance. Liz noticed that the peak of a nearby mountain looked exactly like a humpback's dorsal fin.

The next morning, still looking for humpbacks and still tripping on the scene, we left Andvord Bay and headed out into the Gerlache Strait, to enter Paradise Harbor. As we pulled in, furious winds hurtled off the mountains and down the glaciers; standing on Monkey Island atop the bridge, I threw my arms out wide, exhilarated by the surroundings even as the screaming winds buffeted and tore through me. Then we passed huge icebergs, silently guarding the entrance, and entered Paradise Harbor.

"This is just like sailing in the mountains," said Sarah. "This is exactly the way it looks up in the mountains, except there is water here and we're sailing among the mountaintops."

It was as if the gods had taken a mountain range and deposited it into a clear blue lake, just deep enough for the peaks to thrust a few hundred feet above the surface. As we sailed through Paradise, it was easy to imagine the mountains stretching for thousands of feet beneath us.

It was breathtaking. But I was actually a little worn out from the previous day's experience; no matter how beautiful the landscape, I didn't have the emotional energy to reach again so soon the dizzying heights of euphoria such surroundings seemed to demand.

Besides, something was missing. We still saw no humpbacks.

Uncertain of quite what to do next, Arne and I figured our best chance was to pass through the Errera Channel, east of Danco Island, cross the Gerlache Strait, and stop overnight in Fournier Bay. If we had no success there, we could try a couple of other bays nearby before moving on.

Sunday morning in Fournier Bay dawned gray and misty, with ice spreading off into the murk ahead of us. A minke whale blew lazily off our port side, gentoo penguins porpoised across the bow, and crabeater seals lifted their heads to check us out as we steamed slowly past. But it was a miserable, cold morning: the mist was freezing, the wind was biting, and standing on deck looking in vain for humpbacks for several hours at a stretch was unpleasant and uncomfortable.

When we started into Lapeyrère Bay, Ricardo Roura, one of our science team and the person in charge of our shore work, announced that he thought he saw a couple of humpbacks, so we launched the Rock Boat to investigate. As it disappeared into the gloom, the *Greenpeace* idled quietly in the gray mist.

"I don't know," I said to Arne. "Maybe drifting in the fog brings out too many painful, half-buried memories, but I'm keen to write this off and get out of here." I stood on the bridge wing, trying to figure it out: I had had a good feeling about this trip from Day One, and everything had been going well, and everybody seemed happy—how could they not be, after several days of the most beautiful scenery on Earth? So why were there no humpbacks? As I stood on deck contemplating the situation, there came the unmistakable sound of a whale blowing.

Arne and I heard it at the same time. Nobody had seen it coming, but now here it was, about ten yards off our port quarter. It was a humpback. I rushed around the ship, raising as many people with cameras as possible, and we all rushed back out on deck. For fifteen minutes, the whale played around us. We leaned over the railings, and in the water we could see the whale's long, white pectoral fins. We rushed from side to side as we saw the flippers and the whale disappear beneath the hull.

Two of the crew were working on the poop deck when the whale lifted its head vertically out of the water—spyhopped, in whale-watching vernacular—a couple of yards off the stern and looked in at them. Andy Troia, the first mate, swore he felt a light shudder as it rubbed itself against our keel. For ten minutes more, we rushed around from side to side as the whale swam underneath us again and again, before eventually it tired of us and left.

While all this was happening, the crew of the Rock Boat was having a close encounter of its own. Several humpbacks appeared and started playing around the boat, waving their tails in the air as Ricardo serenaded them with a didgeridu and Roger photographed their fluke patterns. It was the perfect conclusion to our work at the peninsula, and after we had brought Rocky back on board, Arne and I conferred. The base visits were complete; the scientific work had gone well; the past week had been as enjoyable—at times, truly exhilarating—as it had been productive. Now it was time to move on.

That evening, as we passed through the Neumayer Channel, a knot of us gathered on deck, gazing up at the cliffs that hemmed us in on either side. We leaned way over the bow, looking down into the clear water and at the two crabeater seals ahead of us, taking too long to move out of our way and then twisting, turning, diving deep as our ship bore down on them.

We exited the channel and headed west, away from the Antarctic Peninsula. Ahead of us lay a journey of three thousand miles, fully one-third of the way around Antarctica, to the Ross Sea.

I sat in the lounge of the *Greenpeace*, tapping the table with my fingers, to the rhythm of the engines.

Tickety-tum. Tickety-tum. Tickety-tum.

Waiting, waiting, waiting.

It was February 7, almost four weeks since we had left the peninsula. For more than half of that time we had been in transit, heading to the whaling grounds. Now, for ten days, we had been combing the area around the Ross Sea, looking for any sign of the fleet's presence. For all the certainties of the plan on paper, the whalers had once again proven maddeningly elusive, and although it was still early in our voyage, and I continued to be confident that we would find them, the fact that they remained tantalizingly out of reach was beginning to grow frustrating. We needed a stroke of good fortune to help us along the way. And just then, events took the strangest turn.

One of the researchers on board the *Nisshin Maru* cut off part of his thumb in an accident, and although the factory ship's doctor patched it up as best he could, he recommended that the man be sent back to Japan for further treatment. The researcher was transferred to the *Toshi Maru No. 18*, and the catcher steamed north toward New Zealand.

The news, which was leaked to us on board the *Greenpeace*, that a member of the whaling fleet was about to enter Wellington galvanized the staff at Greenpeace New Zealand. Campaigner Nikki Searancke contacted longtime Greenpeace activist Henk Haazen, and they hastily put together an action plan with a bunch of volunteers and a couple of old inflatables that Henk had retrieved from his warehouse in Auckland.

They would do nothing to impede the injured man's departure from the *Toshi Maru No. 18*, nor his transport to the airport. But once he was off the catcher, a team would board the *TM18* and chain themselves to the railings. If all went well, the catcher would have no option but to berth in Wellington so the boarders could be removed. That would cost them some time. More importantly, it might provide an opportunity to detain them for longer still.

Unfortunately, Nikki replied to John Frizell's query, there was no law on the books prohibiting whaling ships from entering New Zealand ports, although a pending bill to that effect was stuck somewhere in the procedural backlog. But it was rumored that the catchers didn't meet even the most rudimentary oil-pollution prevention standards. Under international agreement, a port state has the right to inspect any foreign-flagged vessel and ask to see its documents. If New Zealand authorities investigated the *Toshi Maru No. 18* and found that it didn't meet the basic requirements for all ships entering their waters, they theoretically had the right to detain it until it did.

We didn't know if the rumors were true, but if they were, if the plan came off, and if the New Zealand authorities were moved to investigate the catcher, it would be a terrible blow to the whalers. They would be exposed as operating a fleet of ships in the Antarctic, of all places, that were floating potential pollution hazards which, strictly speaking, wouldn't even be allowed to enter ports like Rotterdam or London. More importantly, the operation, if successful, would tie up one-third of their catching capacity in a foreign port a long way from home. Not only would that mean one ship fewer to kill whales, but if they were down to two catchers, the likelihood of them detailing one to shadow us, as had happened on the first voyage, would be that much more remote.

So a lot was at stake as we waited in the Antarctic for news of the action. The receiver of the radio room was tuned into Radio New Zealand; we took turns straining through the static to hear the first reports.

Paula was the one who came down to the lounge with the news that one protester was reported as being on board the *Toshi Maru No. 18*; the others had been "taken off." The ship was now headed south at full speed; the next report stated that the final boarder had now also been removed and transferred to a police launch.

So that was it. It was over almost as soon as it had begun. They hadn't stopped the ship. But as more details came out, it became clear that the people in Wellington had done the best they could under extremely difficult conditions. Before the *Toshi Maru No. 18* came into port, an article in the local press had announced that Greenpeace was planning some kind of protest. Thus tipped off, the catcher elected not to enter the harbor, but to stay outside and have a pilot boat meet it and take the injured crew member. Not only that, the catcher had reinforcements.

When the activists finally caught up with the *TM18*, they found a phalanx of New Zealand police on board waiting for them.

The photos and footage that appeared in the media told the story. Some of the police hung onto the railings and kicked out to stop the protesters from boarding. Those who did get on board were dragged across the deck, from one side of the ship to the other. One person had her shoulder dislocated; another was severely concussed.

As more information came in, I wrote the unfolding news on the board. We were stunned not only that the protest had been ended with such force, but also that it had been force administered by the New Zealand police. The police of a country that prides itself on its conservationist stance—and specifically its staunch opposition to commercial whaling—had used extreme violence against its own nationals, in defense of a ship that would now go and kill whales in a whale sanctuary for whose adoption that country had lobbied at least as hard as any other.

Meanwhile, the *Toshi Maru No. 18* was on its way back to the Antarctic. The folks in New Zealand had done their best. Now it was up to us.

The next day, still at the mouth of the Ross Sea and still entombed in terrible fog, Arne and I again tried to calculate the whalers' movements and whereabouts, took an educated guess as to where they might be headed, and decided to meet them there. Late the following morning, I stood anxiously in the wheelhouse as we closed in on our putative rendezvous point.

"Kieran," offered Harriet Bakhuizen, the second mate, quietly, "I don't think we are going to find them here."

"What makes you say that?"

Harriet shrugged. "I don't know. Intuition."

It wasn't what I wanted to hear. I didn't say anything. Instead, I bustled around the chart room, hunching over the table and burning a hole in a chart of the Ross Sea.

Paula appeared behind me.

"Don't worry, Kieran," she said. "We're going to find them today. They're here. I can smell them."

Harriet pulled the telegraph to Stop, and the ship drifted slowly to a halt. A short while later, Arne walked onto the bridge.

"Well," I said to him, "we're here."

"Oh yes," he joked, "we certainly are. Harriet, if you have any problems with the navigation, our assistant navigator says we are here."

I smiled, but Harriet seemed preoccupied. Maybe she was worried that she had upset me by voicing her doubts. As Arne and I stood talking in the chart room, she moved around the wheelhouse, shifting back and forth from one radar to the other, wearing a frown of concentration. Finally, she came to the chart room door, looked at the two of us, took a deep breath, and calmly announced that she had a target. She wasn't sure, but she and Majoge van Vliet, her lookout, had been watching it for a little while, and it seemed to be doing around eleven knots.

She took another look at the radar, and began to backtrack.

"No," she said, "it's ice. It's just an iceberg, and we're drifting into it."

That might have been plausible, except another echo then appeared, heading on the same course and at the same speed. Remarkably, the course of the second one was almost exactly the course Arne had plotted.

"Wouldn't it be fucking amazing," he laughed, "if they were on exactly the right course and appeared at exactly the right time?"

We watched them for five or ten minutes. They were definitely getting closer.

"So, Arne," said Paula, "are you convinced they're ships?"

Arne looked at Paula, and back at the radar, and allowed himself a slight smile.

"Of course they're ships," he said quietly. "If you have two echoes doing the same speed and following the same course, then they certainly are ships."

For once, the conditions would work to our advantage. We were now in the middle of a snowstorm; visibility was a mile at best. There was no way they would see us. We would just sit, pretend to be an iceberg, and charge at them when the moment was right.

As news spread around the ship, people began appearing in the wheelhouse. I clutched the radar and stared at the targets as they inched toward us. The smaller echo passed five miles ahead of us, without showing any clue we were there. The larger echo approached within three miles of our stern. We threw on both engines and steamed at it.

There was no reaction. When we were half a mile away we could see it, the familiar outline of the *Nisshin Maru*. Almost immediately, the factory ship finally recognized us, turned, and started to flee. Spray flew over the bow as the *Greenpeace* plowed into the waves and raced through the snow, sticking grimly to the fleeing target.

I took the VHF radio and hailed the factory vessel.

"*Nisshin Maru, Nisshin Maru*. This is the MV *Greenpeace*, on Channel 16."

No response.

I tried again.

"*Nisshin Maru, Nisshin Maru, Nisshin Maru*. This is the MV *Greenpeace*. MV *Greenpeace* calling the *Nisshin Maru* on Channel 16. How copy, *Nisshin Maru*?"

Still no response.

"Why, Arne," I smiled, clinging to the radio as the ship pounded into the waves, "I do believe they don't want to talk to us."

So I recited the statement I'd prepared.

Nisshin Maru, this is the MV *Greenpeace*, campaign vessel of the environmental organization Greenpeace. We are here to protest your whaling program. The area in which you are killing whales has been designated an Antarctic Whale Sanctuary. The whales in this sanctuary are protected from commercial whaling. Your so-called scientific whaling has been repeatedly criticized by the International Whaling Commission, and is nothing more than commercial whaling under another name.

Please stop whaling and leave this area immediately. If you do leave now, we will leave with you. If you do not leave, we will have no option but to interfere with your whaling program.

Greenpeace is a nonviolent organization. We will do nothing to harm or endanger your vessels, your equipment, or your crews. We will, however, use all peaceful means at our disposal to prevent you from killing whales.

I thanked them for their attention and handed the VHF to Kaori Matsunaga, one of our deckhands, who repeated the statement in Japanese.

The *Nisshin Maru* twisted and turned to get away from us. Outmatched and outgunned as always, the little Black Pig was giving it everything it had. Desperately we hung in there, until finally the *Nisshin Maru* abandoned its attempts at outmaneuvering us, pointed its bow north, and charged ahead at full speed. We began to fall back, and by 0230 the next morning, ten hours after we had first made contact and after almost two hundred miles of hot pursuit, it disappeared off our radar. But by that time, my mind had moved on. I knew they were going to run the first time, and it was equally obvious that when they did, they would get away from us. Now we needed to keep the momentum going by finding them again. Two days later, we did.

Barreling across the whaling grounds, we found an echo up ahead, heading on much the same course as we were. We picked it up from quite some distance, so it was too large to be any of the catchers. But it was by itself, and it was traveling at only ten to eleven knots, so it wasn't the *Nisshin Maru*.

In the middle of the Southern Ocean, we had found the fleet's refueling vessel, the *Oriental Falcon*, on its way to a rendezvous with its clients. Ever since the first voyage, we had kept an eye half open to the possibility of catching the fleet in the act of refueling, and as a result, we had already researched the *Falcon* before I had even left to join the *Greenpeace*. One thing that leaped out at us was its top speed. The *Oriental Falcon* could do only twelve knots. This was one ship that couldn't outrun us. All we had to do was stick with it, and it would lead us straight to the whaling fleet.

About 0130 on the morning of February 12, almost exactly two days after the *Nisshin Maru* left our radar screens and just a matter of hours after we began following what we believed to be the *Falcon*, another echo appeared, sitting about eighteen miles away from us. As the *Falcon* passed parallel with it, this second echo also began to move. Farther ahead materialized a third echo, larger this time and probably the *Nisshin Maru*, and then another catcher. One catcher seemed to be missing; the *Toshi Maru No. 18*, presumably, had not yet returned from New Zealand.

We had been steaming up on the *Falcon* pretty much from dead astern, in the blind spot of their radar, so it would have been a long time before they noticed us. We listened in over VHF as all the ships gathered together and contacted each other. There was a pause. We could almost hear the mate on the *Nisshin Maru* counting and recounting the number of echoes on his radar screen. It was dark, and we were in the middle of thick fog, so he had no other way to identify which ship was which. Finally, the *NM* called to one of the catchers, to ask if that was them at such-and-such a position. No, said the catcher, we're over here. There was another pause, while the penny dropped. Uh-oh, said somebody on one of the ships. I think it's the bad guys.

It must have been the last thing the fleet expected: for the tanker that was supposedly their lifeline to lead us straight to them. But however they felt about this unanticipated turn of events, they could do nothing about it. Greenpeace or no Greenpeace, they needed to refuel, and as we drifted in the fog, that's what they started to do.

First, the *Kyo Maru No. 1* drew alongside. The visibility was incredibly poor, so Arne moved the *Greenpeace* to circle slowly around them. The catcher's crew stood by the railings, ready to repel boarders in the fashion taught them by the New Zealand police. On the catwalk to the harpoon they had hung a little welcoming sign, doubtless intended to spoil our photographs: a small banner, printed on a mock ten-dollar bill, reading ALL GREENPEACE WANTS IS YOUR MONEY. We had a chuckle at that one: although it wasn't a particularly good banner—it was too small, and the writing wasn't very clear—we couldn't help but appreciate the effort.

The scene was surreal: the three whalers, the *Oriental Falcon*, and the *Greenpeace*, invisible to each other until within spitting distance; the refueling ships looming out of the thick, cold mist as we pulled slowly up to them and steamed quietly past and back out into the fog. It felt strange indeed to be here, in the middle of nowhere, to have chased the fleet halfway across the whaling grounds, and now to suddenly be so close to them again.

As the *KM1* disengaged and the *Toshi Maru No. 25* pulled up next to the *Falcon*, a minke whale appeared alongside the *Greenpeace*. It blew lazily off our port side, rolled over, swam beneath our hull, and reappeared off the starboard bow. It stayed with us for about five minutes, seemingly attracted to the *Greenpeace* and showing no apparent inclination to move off or swim around the other ships. Stay with us, we smiled, we'll protect you. But this whale, at least, was quite safe. The fleet wasn't going to start whaling while it was refueling, at least not in these conditions, and not while we were so close.

I allowed myself to enjoy the scene and indulge in some smugness over the fact that we had used the supply vessel to find the fleet in the one part of the Southern Ocean where they probably figured they'd be safe. I knew they'd be thinking seriously about us now, wondering what they would have to do to be sure of shaking us. By finding them again so quickly, we'd not only maintained a sense of momentum onboard, we'd also made it perfectly clear to the whalers that this time they weren't going to get rid of us easily.

But once the thrill of the chase had worn off, I looked around and realized all of a sudden that we were in a tricky situation. We'd managed to stumble onto the Great Whalers' Fueling Grounds; now what were we going to do? We'd had discussions at crew meetings about how we should react if we came across the fleet refueling, and we hadn't come to any agreement. Some wanted us to try to interfere with the refueling process, prevent the fleet from taking on the supplies they needed, but Arne, Andy, and I objected to that. For one thing, whatever we thought about the job they did, the crew of the whaling ships were fellow seamen, and we shouldn't do anything to interfere with their functioning safely at sea. For another, any kind of action in the middle of refueling could result in a spill. I would be mortified to be the cause of an accident of that nature in the Antarctic, and there could be no doubt that the news would completely negate any positive coverage we might be able to generate about our encounters with the whaling fleet.

We had little choice but to sit in the fog while the fleet refueled, watching the echoes on the radar and occasionally moving in close to take a good look at whichever ship happened to be tied up to the *Oriental Falcon*. If they were annoyed or worried by our presence, they didn't show it, but just carried on with the task at hand. It was deeply frustrating, and the thick fog seemed only to accentuate the frustration: we had come all this way, and had managed to find the whalers twice already, but conditions were so poor that we were hampered in our ability even to see our quarry. We launched an inflatable to observe the refueling from up close, but the fog was so thick that when the boat wanted to return, it had no idea where we were, even though we were only a hundred yards away. Arne was forced to tell the boat's crew to stay next to the *Falcon* until we could move close enough to pick them up.

When both the *Kyo Maru No. 1* and *Toshi Maru No. 25* finished refueling, they steamed over to the *Nisshin Maru*, presumably to receive their instructions by bullhorn, and sped off in different directions. Shortly afterward, the fog finally and suddenly burned off, revealing the *Nisshin Maru* and *Oriental Falcon* alongside each other off our starboard side, and presenting us with the opportunity to send up the helicopter to document the operation from the air. That at least enabled us to tell ourselves that we were actually doing something, but the fact remained that, within a couple of hours, the *Nisshin Maru* would have finished refueling and would be ready for another round of whaling. We had to decide what our next step should be.

Some of the crew advocated staying until the last moment, when the refueling process was completely over, so we could document even the tiniest spill. But Arne and I both felt that that seemed more than a little sanctimonious; we would be better served, we reasoned, by making the first move and leaving them to guess where we had gone. As I propped myself up in the pantry, force-feeding myself sandwiches in an effort to stay energized after thirty-some hours without sleep, we agreed that we would break off and start heading west, hoping to be off the *Nisshin Maru*'s radar before the factory ship pulled away from the *Oriental Falcon*. But before we could make any moves, the *NM* finished refueling and was soon heading west itself.

I expected the factory ship to take off at top speed, to lose us as soon as possible. Instead, it just meandered along at about ten or eleven knots. Plainly, they wanted us to follow them for a distance, until they were satisfied that they had pulled us sufficiently far from where they wanted to be, at which point they would turn on the juice and leave us behind. We didn't take the bait. We trundled obediently behind them for a while, but dropped our speed steadily and allowed them to ease away from us.

Arne and I sat in his cabin. Either the whalers were going back to the Ross Sea, or they were going to do the SMZ. If they *were* going to do the SMZ—and if I were them, I said, that's what I would do—then I figured the chances were that they'd begin near the northern limit of the Ross Sea and work up from there toward 60S. I reckoned they'd also start from the eastern edge of the whaling area, at 170W. Accordingly, it made sense to resume our search a little way in from that line, in the hope that we could catch them again as they worked their way westward. I suggested to Arne, and he agreed, that once we had completely lost the *Nisshin Maru*, we should turn around and head south along 171W, one degree of longitude inside the eastern edge of the whaling area.

We had certainly disrupted the whalers' plans for the past few days; combined with the action against the *Toshi Maru No. 18* in Wellington, our efforts had made for a rough week for the fleet. Already, we had surpassed by far what we had managed to achieve two years previously. I should have been satisfied, and initially, I was. But as the *Nisshin Maru* steamed slowly out of radar range and we once more found ourselves without any firm idea of where the fleet was likely to show up next, I felt tremendously flat. I had so wanted not only to find them, but also to seriously hamper their activities, to disseminate the news of their presence in the sanctuary to the world's media. As it stood, we had nothing to report. I couldn't help feeling that if we didn't find them a third time, the whalers would have got one over on me again, that they would once more be chuckling to themselves about how they had outsmarted Greenpeace.

That evening, Liz told me that the science team wanted to have a talk about where and when they could return to doing their work. Ever since we had begun searching in earnest for the whalers, I had been neglectful of the science program. I had passed over several opportunities to take samples or photograph whales because I was in a hurry for us to get where I thought the whalers might be. The scientists had accepted their lot with amazing patience, but they were beginning to get a little edgy, wondering when next they would get a chance to do what they had been brought along to do. Roger had already registered his disappointment—in his uniquely stern but gentle way—that Arne and I had refused his request, shortly before we first found the *Nisshin Maru*, to put a boat in the water to photograph a pair of humpbacks at the ice edge near the Ross Sea. A couple of days later, Liz had burst into my cabin and woken me up to tell me she needed to know if she would be allowed to launch a boat for sampling that afternoon.

It was only reasonable that the science team should want to get an idea of how they fit into the scheme of things. In truth, though, finding the whalers again was everything to me. The science program was extremely important, I knew, but I couldn't help feeling a bit let down by their apparent eagerness to write off the whaling campaign and get back to filtering algae and counting whales and debris.

As I left my cabin I bumped into Sarah Macnab, one of the cooks. She was a veteran of the Voyage from Hell, a shared experience during which we had become close friends. I mentioned to her that I was on my way to a meeting with the science team.

"I know," she said.

"It's all fair enough," I told her. "I mean, they don't know everything that's going on, after all, and they're entitled to ask for some information, but I kind of feel like there are vultures circling overhead, waiting for me to say, 'OK folks, the whaling campaign is over—the thing I've been shooting for, to which I've devoted so much of my personal energy, is gone. Now you can go do your science, count your whales, do your plankton samples.'"

I shuffled my feet a little, and she gave me a hug. I told her that if we hadn't found the fleet again within a few days and we had no indications as to where they might be, I would probably call the whaling campaign to a halt. The memories of the last expedition, of searching vainly and endlessly, were still too fresh and painful. There would be no wild goose chases on this campaign. It would be better to end on a relative high note than on the back of several weeks of aimless wandering through the Southern Ocean. Much as that would break me up, I said, sometimes it is harder to know when to stop than it is to keep going.

It was then that Arne appeared at the top of the stairs, looking for me.

"Kieran," he announced calmly, "we have a target."

CHAPTER ELEVEN

Red-Handed

"ARNE, YOU HAVE GOT TO BE KIDDING ME."

He wasn't. He had that positive-thinking, surely-you-never-doubted-us glint in his eye, but he wasn't kidding. We had sailed down exactly the right line of longitude; at 1800, Andy the first mate had noticed interference on the radar and then, one after another, three echoes appeared dead ahead, heading southwest at about eleven knots. Within a couple of hours they had stopped in formation, ready to start the next day's whaling. This time they weren't going to run.

"Well, Kieran, take your pick."

I had decided to put the *Greenpeace* close to one of the catchers and launch the Rock Boat toward it before the fleet started whaling. I looked at the radar and settled on the target that was nearest.

That target turned out to be the *Toshi Maru No. 18*—the "Wellington Explorer," as we had dubbed it—now safely back in the bosom of the fleet. But as we closed in on it, the weather deteriorated and the catcher disappeared into the snow. Launching a boat now would serve no purpose—from its low vantage point, an inflatable wouldn't even be able to see a catcher, let alone chase after it—but, despite the bad weather, Paula agreed to take the helicopter on a recce. As she flew alongside and hovered over the deck of the catcher, its crew put on quite a show for her, theatrically scampering up into the crow's nest and peering through binoculars into the distance. They were hamming it up, attempting to make it look as though our efforts were little more than a joke. But they didn't hide the fact that the harpoon was uncovered. They were ready to hunt whales.

We followed the *Toshi Maru No. 18* for several hours, but it seemed to be drawing us steadily away from the rest of the fleet. When it suddenly turned north—almost the exact opposite of the direction in which it had been heading—we decided not to follow. We turned west and almost immediately came across the *Kyo Maru No. 1*. We were within a mile when visibility suddenly improved; the catcher slowed down and then changed course. It was hunting.

The *KM1* was off our port bow. Through my binoculars, I scanned the water ahead of the catcher. I couldn't see anything, and I began to relax.

"They're having us on," I said. "They're testing us."

The catcher turned to starboard and I brought the binoculars back to my eyes. For the first time in my life, I fully understood what it meant to feel the blood drain from my face.

"Oh shit! There's a blow."

The *KM1* chased the whale across the bow of the *Greenpeace*. Arne sounded the whistle in protest. Everyone scrambled on deck to see what was going on. Paula stood by me in the wheel-house.

"Can't we put a boat in the water?" she asked.

"It's too late. We'd never be able to launch it in time to stop them. We'll just have to stick with the ship."

I stopped and looked at her. She was still wearing her flight suit. Tim Gorter the radio operator gave voice to my thoughts before I could.

"What about you? Are you ready for a flight?"

She looked at me and I nodded keenly.

"Don't waste any time taking anyone else!" I shouted after her as she disappeared off the bridge. "Just go for it."

The catcher had people in the crow's nest and at the harpoon. It turned and chased the whale back across our bow. Again, Arne pulled the handle on the whistle repeatedly.

I ran out onto the bridge wing. I thought I heard somebody say that the catcher had got the whale, and at that moment the *KM1* stopped and turned, its stern facing us, and I thought they had shot it. I was pacing the deck in disbelief: our first day with the fleet, and they had just gone ahead and killed a whale right in front of us. But it was a mistake. Nobody had said what I thought they had said, and the whale was still alive. The *KM1* swung about and the blow reappeared in front of it, and then suddenly Paula was airborne and heading straight for them.

The assembled crew on the *Greenpeace* let out a cheer as Paula circled the catcher and swooped into position on the harpoon. Finally, after the bitter disappointments she had suffered two years previously, Paula was doing what she had come to the Antarctic to do: using the helicopter to block the line of fire and save a whale.

It's pretty intimidating at the best of times, having a helicopter in your face. The young guy at the harpoon seemed terrified as Paula hovered in front of him and looked him straight in the eye.

You, she motioned with her hand. Get away from that harpoon. Get out of here.

While Paula distracted and harassed the harpooner, we launched one of the Avons to cover the small distance between the *Greenpeace* and the *Kyo Maru No. 1* and sit in front of the catcher. By the time it arrived, the whale had escaped, and the catcher returned to its trackline.

The *Nisshin Maru* and the other catchers had dropped out of sight, so Paula headed back to the ship to pick me up, and she and I set out on a flight to find them. Almost as soon as we took off, however, a snowstorm descended and we were forced to return. In the meantime, the *Kyo Maru No. 1* had gained some distance from the *Greenpeace* and was now maneuvering sharply in the snow. We had been forced to stop and retrieve the inflatable because of the worsening conditions, allowing the catcher to pull farther away from us, and now we were paying the price. Watching on the radar, we saw the echo of the *KM1* change course and head straight for another target. The catcher had clearly killed a whale and was delivering it to the *Nisshin Maru*, and in this weather we could do nothing about it.

The two echoes were alongside each other for a while, and then the *Nisshin Maru* sped off at close to sixteen knots. We elected to stick with the *Kyo Maru No. 1* and wait for the conditions to improve so we could use the boats and helicopter. In the late afternoon, the sky began to clear and Paula flew off after the catcher. It had been busy: a whale was lashed to the side.

The *Nisshin Maru* turned toward the *KM1* to pick up the dead whale, and the *Greenpeace* moved to intercept them. But they were having none of it. They well knew that, no matter how much they argued that they were conducting a legitimate scientific research program, the moment we had our first pictures of dead whales to send to the media, the PR battle would be lost before it had begun. They were determined to delay us in getting those first pictures for as long as they could.

It took them three hours to transfer the whale. The catcher sped off in one direction and the factory ship in another, and they didn't come together until almost 2200, with twilight kicking in and the light no longer suitable for flying or photography.

I stood by the windlass and looked at the two ships in the evening light. They had killed at least two whales without our being able to prevent them. But the fact that the fleet had gone to so much effort to avoid our documenting the transfer and butchering of the second whale showed how concerned they were about our presence. And not only did Paula's harassment of the *Kyo Maru No. 1* mean that at least one whale was still swimming free as a result of our action, but it had also fired up everyone on board the *Greenpeace*. As long as we could stay close, we would have many days ahead to get in the whalers' way.

That evening we sent out stills and video of the previous day's activities, and the people at Greenpeace Communications in London, working around the clock, distributed them to the wires with a press release. As a result, I expected some media interest to develop. I pictured a slow but steady growth in interviews of the sort we had experienced during the first trip. I was completely unprepared for the barrage of media calls that came our way.

Elisabeth Mealey started it. In charge of media for Greenpeace in the Asia-Pacific region, she had convinced Simon Benson, a young reporter on the Sydney *Daily Telegraph-Mirror*, Australia's biggest-selling newspaper, to push the story. The next morning it was splashed over the front page: a full-color photograph of the helicopter hovering over the harpoon of the *Kyo Maru No. 1*, and the banner headline RED-HANDED!

Once the *Telegraph-Mirror* ran the story, other media outlets in the country followed suit. The morning drive-by radio shows mentioned it, and then the national TV networks picked it up. By the time of my final interview of the day, at about ten o'clock with ABC Radio in Brisbane, the presenter was opening with "As you will have heard on the news. . . ."

Part of it was the typical media feeding frenzy—everyone determined to get the story that everyone else was going for—but that wouldn't have happened if there hadn't been meat on the bones. The big hook hauling in all the reporters was that the fleet was killing whales in a whale sanctuary. Of course, this was the angle we had pushed and was, indeed, one of the rationales for making the trip. Still, I was taken aback by the extent of the reaction to this element of the story. Almost every interview, it seemed, began with questions along the lines of: Isn't a sanctuary, by definition, supposed to be some kind of safe area? How come these guys are allowed to hunt whales down there?

At the same time as I was juggling media calls, we remained in action against the whaling fleet. At one stage, Greenpeace Communications was on the phone trying to impress on me the urgency of filming an interview that could be fed to one of the main Australian TV networks and I, in turn, was trying to impress on them the need for me to hang up and head to the wheelhouse to direct operations against a catcher that was trying to shoot a whale right in front of us.

Fortunately, the mist rolled in again, giving the whales a respite from the whalers and me the opportunity to concentrate on the media element of my work for a short while. And so I stood on the bridge wing with Dave Flett, the cameraman, answering questions that one of the crew read to me from a fax that a TV station had sent to the ship. When we finished we would forward the piece, via London, to the TV station, which would edit the interview and broadcast it with the talent in the studio reading the questions and then cutting to my answers on the ship, as if the interview were being conducted live.

A nasty, biting wind zeroed in on my face and fingertips, eating at my flesh even as I tried to keep myself composed and respond to the questions. At the same time the *Toshi Maru No. 18* was close by, and I kept stealing glances over my shoulder to check what it was doing. We had maneuvered the *Greenpeace* into position so that the *TM18* was prominent in Dave's shot, and although the media work was undeniably important, I was starting to feel very uncomfortable about the fact that, now that we were finally in among the fleet, I was concentrating more on answering media questions and arranging pretty camera angles than on putting boats in the water. Any minute now, I worried, the wind that was trying to strip the meat from my hands and face would blow off the mist, and the fleet would start hunting. I didn't want to even think about how the crew would react if the catcher killed a whale in front of us because I had been too preoccupied with appearing on television.

Sure enough, as I finished the interview and turned around, the mist cleared and the *Toshi Maru No. 18* spotted a whale. The catcher turned to follow its prey and I ran to the boat deck where Andy was standing with Tim, the radio operator.

"We've got to put one of the boats in the water!" I panted. "The *Toshi Maru No. 18* is right next to us, and it's going to kill a whale if we don't do something."

"The Rock Boat's fueled up," said Andy, "but its HF radio doesn't work. I'm not letting it go out of visual range."

"Fine, it doesn't need to. We just need to put it in the water *now*."

The launch was astonishingly quick. A crew was suited up, in the boat, and away while the *TM18* was still chasing the whale. Lena gunned Rocky across the calm, gray sea, the boat's white wake churning behind as it raced toward the catcher. As soon as the *TM18* saw the inflatable heading toward it, it broke off the hunt. The whaler returned to its trackline, and the whale swam free.

The Rock Boat dogged the *TM18* for most of the day, sticking with it and essentially taking it out of the picture. But because it was the only ship near to us, it was the only one we were able to shadow: the Rock Boat's radio prevented it from heading farther afield, conditions were still too unpredictable to allow one of the smaller inflatables to go chasing off into the distance, and constant snow flurries kept the helicopter anchored firmly to the deck.

The day before, Paula had had the chance, at long last, to prove what the helicopter could do, and it had paid huge dividends; now she wanted the opportunity to do it again, but the weather wasn't cooperating. It wasn't the snow that was the problem so much as the air temperature, which was far enough below freezing to cause the moisture in the air to form ice on the body of the helicopter and its blades. She had no choice but to watch, in her flight suit, from the wheelhouse as the Rock Boat chased the *TM18*, and to explain to the people who kept asking that, no, she couldn't fly in these conditions and that was why she was in the wheelhouse and not in the helicopter.

As soon as the snow disappeared, Paula cleared herself for

takeoff and shot off after the catchers. And as she did so, I found myself in the most heated and animated interview I had done so far.

It was for the Australian television program *A Current Affair* and, thanks to Paula, it started out perfectly. Asked to describe what was happening at that very moment, I was able to lean back in my chair in the campaign office, look out the window, and announce, "Right now, we have one of our inflatables in the water and our helicopter is heading for one of the whaling boats. . . . Yes, the helicopter is swooping over the deck right now, and our pilot is in front of the harpoon as I speak. . . ."

Then the producers brought on Masayuki Komatsu, Japan's deputy IWC commissioner. It was a typical tabloid TV stunt: they hadn't told me that Komatsu would also be on, and he, I'm sure, was kept equally ignorant about my presence on the show. Having fallen victim to this kind of program in the past, I was prepared for the worst, but it was Komatsu who was being set up for the sacrifice. The interviewer had decided from the beginning that he would go for Komatsu's throat; and Komatsu, presumably totally unused to this kind of questioning, tied the noose for his own neck. He allowed himself to be goaded into venturing that there were "too many" minkes in the Southern Ocean and that Japan's whalers were therefore merely "giving Mother Nature a helping hand." Then, every time Komatsu mentioned Japan's "sampling activity," the interviewer interrupted him:

"*Sampling activity.* Is that the same as *killing*, Mr. Komatsu?"

Finally, the interviewer couldn't maintain his already virtually shredded semblance of objectivity any longer:

"I don't want to seem rude, Mr. Komatsu, but might I suggest that this talk of 'scientific research' is a joke?"

Then Komatsu and I were set loose on each other. After a few predictable exchanges between the two of us, the interviewer asked Komatsu whether he was worried that if Greenpeace continued its actions against the whalers, somebody would be hurt or even killed. Yes, replied Komatsu, he was; after all, he went on, the fleet's crew would have to take whatever measures were necessary to defend the research.

That did it. Although Komatsu seemed to recognize his blunder as soon as he had made it—when I protested that his statement was particularly outrageous given our continued policy of nonviolence, he sputtered that, yes, that had always been greatly appreciated by their side—it was too late. Even my outraged bluster was outdone by the retort from the stunned, incredulous interviewer.

"So what are you going to do, then, Mr. Komatsu? Shoot them? Have you got a gun?"

Over the next few days, we continued to pursue the fleet through the waters north of the Ross Sea. All too often, they were able to shoot whales and bring them back to the factory ship without our having a chance to do anything about it. When that happened, the best we could do, when conditions permitted, was send Paula up so that Dave and Roger could document the flensing process on the deck of the *Nisshin Maru*. But, as much as possible, we frustrated the catchers with inflatables and helicopter; after several days of actions, any catcher that was approached by an inflatable simply shut down operations straight away rather than risk shooting a whale in front of us.

All the while, our efforts continued to have a snowballing effect in the outside world. Our footage was appearing on television around the globe, and even the Japanese media was reporting that we had found the fleet hunting whales in an area the rest of the world had declared a sanctuary. The Australian environment minister held a press conference to express his concern. Best of all, the New Zealand government issued a formal protest to Japan.

"New Zealand considers that with modern techniques, the information essential for management and conservation of whales can be obtained from nonlethal methods," announced Foreign Minister Don McKinnon. "While communicating these points to the Japanese government, we have expressed particular concern that this year's programme is being conducted not only in the agreed Southern Ocean Sanctuary but more specifically in the Ross Sea."*

We had crossed the Rubicon. We weren't just getting in the whalers' faces. We were doing more than spreading the message worldwide. We were causing protests at the governmental level. We were creating a diplomatic incident.

The following morning, February 17, once again dawned with dreadful conditions. Slowly, however, the weather cleared, first improving enough for the fleet to begin whaling and then finally enough to allow us to launch our boats. Even then, Rocky's ride to the *Nisshin Maru* was treacherous, with unpredictable swells pounding at the inflatable's hull as it fought its way across the troughs, jarring the crew even as they tried to shelter from the snow. They considered turning back, but eventually settled into the lee of the factory ship, where they soon began to cause quite a stir. In the boat was our Japanese deckhand Kaori Matsunaga, and the *Nisshin Maru* practically started listing to port as its crew leaned over the railings to stare at her. When she took the wheel to drive, their eyes nearly fell out of their heads. The Greenpeacers must be making her do it, we imagined them saying to each other.

Hanging above the stern slipway of the *Nisshin Maru* was a banner proclaiming GREENPEACE IS A SHAM. Like the mock dollar bill on the catcher's catwalk, its intention was doubtless to diminish the propaganda benefits of our photographs and videos. It was small and hard to read, though, and in photos we had taken at the slipway, it was completely obscured by the fire hoses that the factory ship's crew had been training on our boats to keep them away. A classic rookie mistake, we joked: either

---

* Seven countries—Argentina, Australia, Chile, France, New Zealand, Norway, and the United Kingdom—claim territory in the Antarctic; New Zealand's claim is centered on the Ross Sea. All claims are effectively frozen by the Antarctic Treaty, however.

spray the Greenpeacers with fire hoses or mock them with banners, but don't try to do both.

As the Rock Boat's crew members dodged the fire hoses and tried to read the banners, they strained to hear a continuous-loop tape that the factory ship was playing over loudspeakers. "Dear Greenpeace," it blared, "this is the captain of the *Nisshin Maru*. Please stay away from our ships. We are turning right now." At least, that's what the folks in Rocky thought it said; unfortunately, they couldn't quite agree among themselves, because they had difficulty hearing the message above the noise of the inflatable's engine. But it was obviously more than loud enough for the crew on the deck of the *NM*, who had to walk around with their fingers in their ears.

The diplomatic ripples caused by our actions spread ever wider. Following New Zealand's lead, Chile issued a strongly worded statement through its IWC commissioner, Pablo Carera: "The Government of Chile is concerned by Japanese scientific whaling in the Southern Ocean Sanctuary. The killing of any whale is a reason for concern. We are making the necessary contacts with the other countries that concurred in favor of the creation of the sanctuary, in order to define a joint position. . . . Japan's reservation to the creation of the sanctuary notwithstanding, there is in place a moratorium on whaling and Japan is bound by it. There are other methods to conduct scientific research on whales that do not require capturing and killing these animals, as Japan is doing. . . ."

I sent out a message to Greenpeace offices suggesting that everybody should press their government to join the protest. Sarah and Roger, as the ship's resident Kiwis, sent a message of thanks to the New Zealand government, and the Swedes, Danes, and Dutch on board sent their own letters back home, urging their countries to add their voices. The Americans drafted an e-mail for Vice President Al Gore, which the Washington, D.C., office prepared to post, together with photos of our actions so far, on the Greenpeace website.

Meanwhile, footage and stills of a whale being flensed on the deck of the *Nisshin Maru* had provided an extra boost to media coverage, which was now spreading to Europe. The British tabloids had picked up the story and were running it in their own inimitable style. The notice board in the mess room was crammed with news releases, government protests, wire stories, newspaper articles, and messages of congratulations from Greenpeace offices. At the same time, I was constantly writing and rewriting updates on the blackboard, determined that this time around, everybody on board was going to know everything that was going on, and then some.

The next morning we launched Rocky at 0530, so that it would already be in the water before the fleet started to move at its usual time of 0600. At 0545, seemingly unnerved by the boat's launch, the *Nisshin Maru* started up and set off along the track-line. We took off in pursuit, and a catcher followed a ways behind us. Perhaps we should have been a bit more suspicious about the fact that that catcher spent the whole day just on the edge of our radar range, but at the time we didn't think anything of it.

The morning developed into perfect whaling weather: calm and clear, with very little wind. That meant it was perfect flying weather too, so we sent Paula to check out and identify the nearby catcher and then go look for the others. She took off with a happy Chris next to her and flew toward the nearest member of the fleet.

She arrived just in time. The catcher was the *Toshi Maru No. 18*, and a minke was in front of it. Paula swooped down low and called up the *TM18* over the VHF: "*Toshi Maru No. 18*. This is the Greenpeace helicopter on your starboard side. Do not attempt to kill this whale. Please keep your man away from the harpoon. That harpoon is a danger to my helicopter."

Chris saw someone begin the walk toward the harpoon and then stop and turn around, as if he had been called back. The minke veered sharply to its left. The catcher ignored it and returned to its trackline. We'd saved another whale.

Paula flew on and found the *Kyo Maru No. 1* about twenty miles ahead of the *Nisshin Maru*, came back, refueled, and set out again. For the first time, the conditions were perfect for Paula to roam across the fleet at will, flying from one ship to the other, keeping track of what each catcher was up to, and swooping down to the harpoon if necessary.

As a result, we were in good spirits. We felt more than ever that we were doing what we came to do. The *Toshi Maru No. 18* was blocked off from the *Nisshin Maru* by the *Greenpeace*; if it shot a whale, then it would have to get past us to deliver it. The *Nisshin Maru* was covered by the Rock Boat, and the *Kyo Maru No. 1* could be easily reached by the helicopter. The *Toshi Maru No. 25* was nowhere to be seen, and hadn't been for some days; we surmised that it was mapping the ice in the Ross Sea, to be ready for when the rest of the fleet finished in the SMZ. As a result, as long as the weather stayed clear enough to fly, we effectively had the whole fleet covered.

But of course, this was the Antarctic, the only place in the world, it seemed, where it was possible to experience four distinct weather patterns in the course of an afternoon. Sure enough, as the day wore on, the sky darkened, the sea became gray and menacing, and a fierce wind appeared as if from nowhere, tossing inflatables about on the waves and driving lookouts from the crow's nests on the whalers. Paula was once more grounded, inflatables were brought back on board, and whaling was ended for the day. The fleet now saw its opportunity to take leave of us.

I didn't fully appreciate what was happening until it was too late. Andy had, however, been grumbling all afternoon that our constant slowing down to launch and retrieve helicopter and inflatables was allowing the *Nisshin Maru* to increase its distance from us, giving them an opening to make a run for it. Sure enough, by the time all our boats and flying machines were back on board, the factory ship had stretched the distance between us to about twelve miles. Later in the evening, as I stood in the chart room with Arne, the *NM* had already increased that lead to eighteen miles. More ominously, the *Toshi Maru No. 18* was sticking with us, about six miles off our starboard quarter.

Suddenly it became all too clear. The fleet had been fairly racing through the SMZ, doubtless hoping to make us work extra hard and use up fuel, and possibly tire us out before they entered the Ross Sea. The *Toshi Maru No. 25* had been dispatched to map the ice in the Ross Sea in advance. Meanwhile, the others had been heading toward the northern boundary of the whaling area, which would give them more time to put some space between us if they then decided to turn around and charge south. Today's events, which had shown them that in good weather we could tie them up easily, had doubtless convinced them that running away was indeed their best option. And when we fell back because of our launch and retrieval operations, they saw their chance and took it, leaving the *Toshi Maru No. 18* to stick with us and report our every move.

I sat in Arne's cabin and reviewed the situation. It was certainly a compliment: they wouldn't be going to all this trouble if we weren't bugging them. So far, they had caught about five whales in ten days; they probably would have expected to catch forty. And the fleet's escape might even prove beneficial in the long run, if we could eventually lose the catcher. It would give us a break from the intensity of the past couple of weeks, it would allow us to resume the science program, and we would be able to head deep into the Ross Sea, doing some science and looking for the opportunity to sprint away and pick up the rest of the fleet again.

Just because instead of three whaling ships nearby there was now only one, and just because that one whaling ship was now following us and not the other way around, it didn't mean our wider campaign was slowing down. On our first full day without the fleet, the *Oriental Falcon* put in to Timaru, a backwater in the South Island of New Zealand. Three campaigners from

Greenpeace New Zealand—Catherine Delahunty, Nicola East-hope, and Michael Szabo—walked calmly up the gangway and chained themselves to the railings. They had found the ship after Catherine had spent hours on the telephone calling virtually every port authority in the country, claiming that her errant boyfriend was on board and she needed to find him, until eventually she struck gold.

The Japanese captain of the *Falcon* at first wouldn't confirm or deny that his ship had been in the Southern Ocean, and refused to meet with the protesters on board. The Korean crew, on the other hand, were fascinated by this latest diversion in what would normally have been a fairly routine resupply opera-tion, and several took photographs of themselves and each other next to the Greenpeace team. The crew asked the protesters if they were cold, standing out on deck on a chilly New Zealand morning. Not as cold as you must have been while refueling the whaling fleet in the Antarctic, they countered. Oh yes, confirmed the crew, it was very cold down there.

Across the Tasman Sea, the diplomatic war of words continued to spread. On February 20, Australia confirmed that it too was now lodging a formal protest with Japan. In a statement delivered through the Ministry of Foreign Affairs and Environ-ment to a visiting Japanese Foreign Ministry delegation, the government supported the New Zealand position and went on to say: "There is strong opinion in many countries, including Australia, against all forms of commercial whaling, and we very much hope that Japan will cease its practice of lethal and large-scale whaling, particularly in the Sanctuary."

Nonetheless, however successful the campaign was proving in the wider world, after a few days of being followed by the *Toshi Maru No. 18* I fell briefly into a black pit. I was extraordinarily uncivil to anyone who poked a head into my cabin to see how I was doing, and practically chewed the head off even my closest friends. Finally, Liz bit the bullet, sat me down, and said she didn't know what was the matter with me, but if I was worried about the campaign, I needed to snap out of it—things were going great, the notice board was stuffed with news stories, the crew was happy. I think I mumbled something about just wanting a bit of privacy for a while. Inside, however, I knew it had more to do with the catcher that was following us.

On the one hand, the catcher's presence gave me a sense of relief that I no longer needed to worry about finding the fleet. In a way, the *TM18* provided a cover behind which I could hide, an excuse I could use for any further shortcomings for as long as the catcher was with us. Thus freed from the need to keep everything under control or to obsess over the tiniest detail of life on board, I felt able to relax and let down my guard without having to worry about the consequences.

More powerful than the relief, however, was the frustration of knowing we were at the catcher's mercy. The expedition would obviously have had to end at some stage anyway; but, desperate to avoid the horrors of the last voyage, I had from the beginning wanted us to be able to break it off at a time when we wanted, to be able to declare a clear-cut victory before leaving the fleet behind. Now, unless we could shake the *TM18* and find the rest of the fleet again, it was going to end on their terms instead.

We headed into the Ross Sea, driving hard into a furious gale that threw sheets of snow and ice at us, but just as the smaller catcher struggled and fell behind, the storm abated, giving the *TM18* an opportunity to haul us back in. We steamed into McMurdo Sound, where Arne felt that, given his knowledge of the area, he'd be able to lose the whaler in the various bays and inlets; but after hiding in the radar shadow of one of the islands in the area, we found our route blocked by fast ice, and we were forced to turn around and steam back into the *TM18*'s path.

When our plan to head to the end of McMurdo Sound, and perhaps spark further diplomatic protests by dragging the whaler past Scott Base and Mactown, was foiled because of extremely heavy ice, we decided to catch our breath for a while. Arne nosed the *Greenpeace* gently into the fast ice, and we parked the ship at the bottom of the world. Skuas circled slowly overhead. A minke whale blew and rolled lazily astern. In the distance, a group of black dots slowly revealed themselves as about twenty emperor penguins marching determinedly in our direction. When they reached the ship and found us blocking their way, they looked us up and down, uttered a collective "Qwaark," and settled down on the ice.

It was a beautiful spot. The sky was clear, the sun was shining, the sea was calm and blue. Wildlife was everywhere. If we couldn't get rid of the whaler, we might as well resume the science program. We launched the Rock Boat so that Ricardo, Liz, and Chris could take some plankton samples and record any whales that were in the vicinity.

The rest of us stood out on the heli-deck, watching the penguins keep an eye on us. Suddenly the emperors became deeply agitated and moved away from the edge of the ice, squawking loudly. We soon saw why: a little farther along the ice, three orcas—a large bull and two females—were spyhopping, obviously looking for their next meal.

The orcas disappeared beneath the water for a while, and the penguins began to relax. All of a sudden, the large male surfaced next to the Rock Boat, spyhopping a matter of feet away. Excited, the folks in the boat stopped what they were doing and started taking photographs. Then the whale began making passes beneath the inflatable, creating waves that rocked the boat from side to side. Rocky's crew began to grow nervous. The orca disappeared, then charged toward the Rock Boat, creating a huge wave that lifted the boat up, moved it sideways, and tipped it over toward one side, where the two females were waiting. Lena, the boat's driver, didn't wait to see what might happen next; she started up the engine and took off. One of the orcas briefly gave chase; as everybody looked anxiously astern, another whale spyhopped, unseen at the time but captured on video, just off the boat's port bow.

It's always difficult to interpret other species' behavior. The orcas may simply have been curious about the boat, or agitated because we were in their territory. But it certainly looked as if they were treating the people in the boat as large penguins on a funny-looking ice floe, and the behavior was consistent with reports of killer whales knocking floes to tip penguins and seals into the water. Chris had his hydrophones in the water the whole time, and the recordings he made were in many ways more chilling than watching the scene unfold from the deck of the *Greenpeace*. There were clicks from the whales' sonar as the male found and explored the Rock Boat; vocalizations as the male called to the females; more clicks and vocalizations as the three whales evidently determined their strategy; and then silence as they moved into position, followed by a roaring *whoosh* as the big male rocked the inflatable.

The scientists and crew came back on board, and contented themselves with watching whales from the safety of the Black Pig. And there was an abundance of whales to be seen. In the early evening, we saw a group of rare beaked whales taking frequent shallow breaths through holes in the ice before making deeper dives. Chris was in heaven, bouncing around the deck far into the night, braving the bitter cold to watch yet more whales in the midnight sun.

The scientists were happier than they had been all trip, and their good mood helped to make up for the times over the past few weeks when I had had to turn down their requests to stop because we needed to concentrate on the whalers. And if we couldn't get back to the whaling fleet because of our shadow, then we might as well make the most of the scientific opportunities created by being at the ice edge. That way, only the *Toshi Maru No. 18* was being inconvenienced.

Arne and I sat in his cabin. I was now ready to call the whaling campaign to a halt. We had had a good run, but we just weren't getting the breaks anymore. It had been such a great expedition so far that I didn't want to spoil it all by dragging it on unnecessarily.

Arne agreed. It really *had* been a good campaign, hadn't it? We had achieved at least as much as we initially thought we might, and it certainly did feel good to have found the fleet so many times. Nonetheless, as hard as we tried to convince ourselves that we were content, we felt a sense of emptiness. Something was missing. The end of the campaign was being dictated by the whalers, and that wasn't right. If only we could break free and find them a fourth time. Just one more time, and we'd be truly happy.

Any hopes we had of a repetition of the previous day's conditions at the ice edge evaporated while the day was still young. Where that day had been clear, crisp, and still, this one was foggy and windy, with a swell that made it all but impossible to launch a boat safely, and not a whale in sight. We decided to sail to the western side of McMurdo Sound and work our way north. Lots of little bays and inlets were sprinkled along the coast, where Arne was hopeful that we might still lose the catcher and earn ourselves one more throw of the dice after all.

What began as an unpleasant, stormy day soon stepped up to an altogether different league of viciousness. Sheets of snow hurtled across our path at more than sixty miles an hour. At times it was a struggle to see even a hundred feet. The wind screamed down from the mountains, filled with hate, desperate to break through the wheelhouse and slice through us. Our path was littered with growlers, pushed erratically into our way by the howling gale. Each bay we approached seemed packed with fast ice. Nothing even on the previous expedition had been quite like this; only our being in the relative shelter of McMurdo Sound prevented us from being tossed around as we had been two years ago.

Amid it all, Arne remained calm. He knew the dangers of operating in this kind of environment better than anyone, but his mind was still focused on trying to find the fleet one final time. He looked at me as I entered the wheelhouse that afternoon, and pointed at a long, thin echo.

"Interesting, don't you think?"

About twelve miles away was a grounded iceberg, a massive

piece of ice all of ten miles long. On its leeward side were a slew of smaller bergs, and probably also some fast ice. It made for a confusing mass of radar echoes, and a treacherous place to go poking around with a ship.

"Could be a nice place to hide from our friends," Arne smiled.

Visibility was so poor that even when we were within half a mile of the massive iceberg, we couldn't see the faintest hint of it. Using only the radar as a guide, we inched around the end of the giant berg and tucked ourselves behind it, stopping just short of the fast ice, which blocked our way.

To no great surprise, the echo of the *Toshi Maru No. 18* appeared once more, and then stopped at the mouth of the small bay that the iceberg had formed. After a few minutes, it started heading slowly south again. Arne's plan had worked. They had lost us, and now, just like that, they were gone.

As soon as the catcher was on the edge of our radar range, Arne began moving slowly northeast and back out into the sound. Before long, the *Toshi Maru No. 18* had all but faded from memory. What was important now was maneuvering the *Greenpeace* safely through the storm and ice.

Danger was never far: as we crawled forward that evening, the mate on watch gave a shout and there, looming out of the murk, was a previously invisible edge of fast ice only a couple of hundred yards ahead. Arne steered hard to starboard, and the ice passed narrowly by on the port side. In the mass of snow and mist swirling about ahead of us, the ice had been all but impossible to spot. Though we weren't traveling at great speed, it could have done real damage to the ship, and in these conditions, and this late in the season, with the last flights gone from McMurdo and no ships in the area apart from ourselves and the whalers, that would have been trouble.

"Hmmm," said Arne. "Now that, you see, was a classic example of a whiteout situation."

For seventeen hours without a break Arne stayed in the wheelhouse, pressing the buttons to steer us around growlers and through fields of old sea ice broken up by the storm. At 0500 the next morning, a target appeared on the radar, heading northeast and out of McMurdo Sound. It was the *Toshi Maru No. 18*, presumably on its way to rejoin the fleet once again. Arne stopped the ship to avoid being detected, and the *TM18* carried on its way. At that, Arne declared himself satisfied with where we were, and took himself off to bed.

Time now was running extremely short. We had not been given a definite date of return by Amsterdam, but if we were going to find the fleet again, it would have to be within a couple of days. Arne and I had calculated the fleet's trackline in the Ross Sea as heading south down the eastern edge, then west along the Ross Ice Shelf and north up the west side. We decided to position ourselves northeast of Ross Island and wait for the ships to arrive on their journey to the sea's western edge.

A couple of days after losing the *TM18*, and with the whalers' estimated time of arrival drawing near, several of us sat drinking from a variety of bottles that had been placed on the round table in the lounge. For some reason best known to herself, Majoge had attempted to instill a more romantic atmosphere on board by turning out the lights and placing candles in the lounge and mess. It actually seemed to have a positive effect, the warm glow of the candles providing a contrast with the increasingly bitter cold outside. The ship was surrounded by pancake ice, the deck was coated with white, and a small snow petrel rested by the helicopter.

Just then, Tim came rushing in, wearing a big grin and excitedly flapping a piece of paper, which he thrust into my hand. It was a wire story, headlined

France condemns Japanese whaling in Antarctic Sanctuary

The story quoted French Environment Minister Michel Barnier as calling the hunt "extremely regrettable" and its scientific motivation "questionable." Japan's whaling was, said Barnier, "all the more shocking less than a year after the creation of the sanctuary, set up on a French initiative." The actual French communiqué was even stronger. "Within the framework of IWC," the statement read, "France will take care that the provisions of the convention with regards to takes for scientific purposes be clarified in order to prevent their use as alibis for practices mainly motivated by commercial objectives."

Not all the messages to come in that night were so welcome. John Frizell and Walt Simpson both informed us that the *Greenpeace* was required back in Hobart no later than March 18; the Australian office needed the ship for an action in Tasmania, and then the Pig was on a tight schedule to transit through the Indian Ocean and make it to the Mediterranean by May. Walt said he was sorry, and if it were up to him we would always have a ship dedicated to whale work, but we had done more than anybody had expected, and now it was time to let other campaigns make use of the ship.

Arne and I looked at the messages the next morning, and then looked at each other.

"Basically, it means we have to find them today, or not at all," I said.

"Basically, yes," he agreed.

Paula was far from happy about us trying to find them at all. She had passed that psychological point beyond which it's very difficult to summon up renewed enthusiasm. She wanted to go home, and she certainly didn't want to go flying on this day. The deck was covered with ice, making takeoff and landing treacherous. It was damn cold as well: zero degrees Fahrenheit and a searing fifty-knot wind, producing a windchill closer to minus sixty. It was no fun standing out on the open deck and putting the blades back on. When she found that the helicopter's air intake was packed full of snow, Paula's mood darkened even more. The whalers weren't around, she reckoned, and she didn't see the point of going to all this effort to put the helicopter together for a flight when the flight wouldn't show anything and she'd only have to put the helicopter to bed again.

After she returned, she felt that her opinions had been borne out. There had been no sign of the whalers, nor, judging from the extent of the ice edge she had seen, did they seem likely to be anywhere in the immediate vicinity. It looked as if we had miscalculated; the whalers must still have been somewhere to the east.

A few crew members were agitating for us to head east ourselves, cover more ground, and then put the helicopter up again. This was our last chance; we had to make something of it. But Paula didn't want to fly again anytime soon, and after going over the chart with her, I agreed that it didn't make much sense. If the whalers weren't here, they were a long way away, and by the time we reached a point where it would make sense to send the helicopter up again, it would be the next morning and we'd have to start making our way north. And even if we did find them, and we did have an extra day, they would be in transit anyway, so what good would it do? I ticked off these points out loud on the bridge.

"From a campaign perspective," I said finally, "there's no point in making another flight." Arne was there, and Andy, and Tim and Hans the radio operators, and maybe Harriet and Majoge—I don't remember. A short silence ensued.

"Then," announced Arne quietly, "I think we've reached the end of the road."

"Yes, I think we have."

Arne followed me into the chart room.

"All right then, should we go straight north or follow along their trackline?" he asked.

"I reckon we might as well go northeast up their trackline to their bounce point, then northwest to the coast, and then straight north. Not that I think they're that far north."

"No, nor do I."

Following our estimate of their trackline would give us one more chance of maybe bumping into the whalers before we left the Ross Sea. But it seemed highly unlikely that we would succeed; our calculations, it appeared, had been wrong and the fleet was somewhere else—in which case, the campaign was over.

I called a crew meeting for the evening to explain that we had basically run out of time and options; the campaign had been terrific, but it was time to head home. I thanked everyone, but most of all I thanked Arne. I had really grown to admire him during this voyage, and also to rely on him very much as a friend. Although I felt it had been, to a large extent, "my" campaign, it certainly would not have been at all possible without him. Arne, uncomfortable with being singled out for attention, rightly pointed out that everybody shared in the expedition's success: engineers, mates, cooks, deckhands—all had kept the ship running and everything working, pretty much without complaint. Anyway, it wasn't over yet, Arne observed: we still had a couple of weeks until we reached Hobart, and during that time we'd be busy with our scientific program, which in many ways was as important as the whaling campaign.

Beers were on me, I announced, and then, drained, I staggered out of the lounge, lay down on my bed, and promptly fell asleep. I woke up briefly later, found plenty of beers against my name, and went back to my bunk at 0230.

Sometimes a sleep can be so deep that, aroused from it early, you feel as if you have been out for hours. When Majoge came into the cabin and told me they had found a catcher, my first thought was that it was around lunchtime and that maybe it was some kind of joke: Kieran's asleep, let's wake him and tell him there's a catcher on the horizon. But it was 0345. I'd been asleep for an hour, and Majoge was excited and perfectly serious.

"You have *got* to be kidding me," I said, and not for the first time on this trip.

"No, I'm not," she said breathlessly. "We were traveling along the trackline and were exactly at the bounce point and then Harriet thought she saw some radar interference and then the visibility improved and all of a sudden, there was a catcher."

I scrambled up to the wheelhouse.

"We had to change course," said Harriet, "because if we had stayed on the course we were on, we would have bumped right into them."

"Well," I said calmly, "I think we'd better turn around and bump right back into them again, don't you?"

Arne appeared in the wheelhouse.

"It was right on the bounce point," said Harriet, "exactly where you said."

Arne and I smiled at each other.

The catcher saw us, turned slowly, and began heading away, to the south. Then we saw a larger echo, about ten miles away, which suddenly took off north at something like seventeen knots. It was obviously the *Nisshin Maru*. There was equally obviously no way we could get near it, and no point in even trying.

Andy was on watch by now and asked what we wanted to do.

"Let's go have a look at this guy," I said, nodding toward the catcher, and Andy swung the wheel about.

The catcher was heading south at around eleven knots. It was obviously pulling us away from the *Nisshin Maru*, but the alternative was to steam blindly after the *NM* and end up without any target to follow. I suggested that we follow the catcher for a while and then turn around and head north toward the point where we last saw the factory ship. That way, it was always possible that the catcher might turn around and follow us out of the Ross Sea.

Our deadline for returning to Hobart meant that we had no time to go chasing after the *NM*. We had run out of time, but at least we had found them again, as Arne and I had wanted. We would be heading north anyway; it would be no skin off our nose if the catcher followed us the rest of the way. We'd be doing science, and there'd be one less catcher killing whales.

"I seem to remember," said Arne softly in the chart room, referring to a statement I had made in the crew meeting the night before, "that the probability of our finding them again was zero."

"*Close* to zero," I corrected. "Anyway, *I* seem to remember *you* using the term 'zilch' to describe our chances, when we were talking earlier yesterday."

"Yes, but that was not on public record."

We looked at the chart. Our guesstimated trackline had indeed been exactly right. The whalers had simply cut off the corner where we had been waiting, either because of the ice that Paula had seen from the helicopter, or because that was where we had last been seen.

"Actually, the *Nisshin Maru* was a few miles off the trackline," observed Arne.

"They probably just drifted in the night," I reassured him. "It was to be expected."

"Oh, so you *expected* that we would find them here, then?"

"Me?" I looked at him and smiled. "I was never worried."

I left a message on John Frizell's answering machine at home: we had had our final crew meeting of the whaling campaign, we were heading north and continuing with our science program, all was well, and, oh yes, we had found the fleet again.

I went to bed around 0830 and fell into a deep sleep. When I woke up, it was 1630. I opened the door. A note lay on the floor. It was a message from John. He "didn't have the heart" to wake me, but he thought I would like to know that Britain had formally objected to Japan's whaling in the sanctuary.

CHAPTER TWELVE

Vote-Buying, Canny Proposals, and Fish-Eating Whales

THE MOMENT THE *GREENPEACE* DOCKED IN HOBART AT THE END of the voyage, my Greenpeace career was over. The convolution and downsizing that had made others reluctant to commit to use of the ship prior to my departure had continued apace, to the point where several campaign departments were now undergoing serious restructuring. In the process, many jobs were being eliminated or redefined, mine included; an essentially identical position was mine if I wanted it, but such were Dutch labor laws that I would have to go through an application and interview process alongside any other applicants. I elected to pass; I didn't like the idea of having to prove I was the most competent person to do my own job. Besides, I was burned out on the whaling issue. Anyway, I wanted to be free from the strictures of being part of an activist organization, to return to my first love of writing, and had been contemplating leaving Greenpeace for some time; the relative success of this most recent expedition provided what I thought was the perfect opportunity to bow out.

A couple of weeks after the *Greenpeace* arrived in Hobart, I stood on the dock and waved as the Black Pig—once more under the command of Bob Graham, who had led our first Antarctic voyage—left on its latest journey. I wouldn't see it again. For four more years, it continued to prove its worth on campaigns around the world, until finally its age caught up with it. During our last voyage I had noticed that my cabin, which was directly over one of the fuel tanks, smelled of oil; when my carpet began to feel damp, the chief engineer and I took a closer look and found that the floor was rusting away. Over the ensuing years, many other such problems started appearing until finally, in 1999, after the ship took a fearful battering in a monstrous storm, the *Greenpeace* was sent into retirement and now sits in a maritime museum in Rotterdam.

After the ship left port, I spent some time unwinding with friends in Tasmania, then met up with Liz Carr and Sarah Macnab, with whom I spent my birthday in Melbourne. Finally, in April 1995, I flew home to Washington, D.C., to an uncertain future.

Two months later the International Whaling Commission met in Dublin: the first IWC meeting I had missed in almost ten years. Despite having withdrawn from the scene, I was nonetheless keen to follow the action, particularly as it pertained to Antarctic whaling and the protests generated by our last expedition, so every morning I scanned the e-mail updates sent to me by John Frizell. Anti-whaling governments sponsored two nonbinding resolutions: one recommending that scientific research intended to assist with the implementation of the Revised Management Procedure be undertaken with nonlethal means, the other that IWC members refrain from issuing scientific whaling permits in the Southern Ocean Sanctuary and other such sanctuaries. Each passed handily: by 23 votes to 5 with two abstentions, and 23 votes to 7 with one abstention, respectively.

It would be nice to report that at that point, faced with the combined pressures of the sanctuary decision, the continued attentions of the MV *Greenpeace*, the ongoing political pressure from environmental organizations and other governments, and the clear expression of irritation on the part of the vast majority of the IWC's members, the Fisheries Agency of Japan and the Institute of Cetacean Research saw the writing on the wall, conceded that enough was enough, and agreed to mothball their harpoons indefinitely. It would be nice; but, not altogether surprisingly, that isn't what happened.

Not only did the ICR ignore the latest resolutions and continue its "scientific research" regardless, as it had done countless times before in response to numerous previous admonitions to rescind its scientific whaling program, but this time it responded with the diplomatic equivalent of an extended middle finger and actually increased its self-assigned quota. When the fleet left port for the Antarctic later that year, it was with the goal of killing up to 440 minke whales—a 33 percent increase over previous seasons.

Indeed, the whalers responded to their defeat in Puerto Vallarta with a renewed resolve to fully exploit the avenues and loopholes that remained open to them. In 1996 the ICR expanded its operations to the North Pacific, establishing a "scientific whaling" program that involved the hunting of up to 100 minke whales during the northern summer months between Antarctic voyages. Four years after that, this North Pacific program was expanded, adding an annual total of 50 Bryde's whales and 10 sperm whales, and in 2002 it grew yet again to include 50 sei whales and a further 50 minkes, for a total of 260 whales of four different species each year. Combined with the ongoing haul from the Antarctic, this meant that, twenty years after the IWC had voted for the moratorium, Japan's whaling industry assigned itself a total of 700 whales a year, more than twice as many as when we had first set sail in 1991 to confront the fleet in the Southern Ocean.

The FAJ was also busy working to secure greater support for its position within the IWC through aggressive use of diplomacy and development aid. The Fisheries Agency and its allies sought at the same time to undermine the IWC by taking their case to other international bodies and arguing that the IWC's maintenance of the moratorium was irrational and contrary to scientific evidence. Their goal was to establish that whaling was not only possible but essential—that the whaling industry was a force for good that could show the world a way out of a looming food crisis.

The ICR laid out this case in a paper released during the 1999 IWC meeting in Grenada. Entitled *Estimation of Total Food Consumption by Cetaceans in the World's Oceans*, the paper asserted that globally, cetaceans consume between 280 and 500 million tons of aquatic life, "equivalent to roughly three to six times the total estimated recent worldwide marine commercial fisheries catch." Two years later, the institute published a book by Masayuki Komatsu of the FAJ, which made the case in more strident tones. "Whales' amazing appetite sends shock waves through the world," Komatsu ululated. "Whales are eating fish to depletion. . . . We need to cull whales in order to achieve sustainable use of the fish."

In a sense, nothing about this was particularly new. Blaming marine mammals for declines in commercial fisheries has been a favorite diversionary tactic for whalers, sealers, fishermen, and politicians for decades. The notion of "multispecies management"—whereby sealing and whaling, in addition to being profitable industries, served to keep marine mammal numbers "in check," thereby permitting the growth of fish populations and thus commercial fisheries—was a cornerstone of the North Atlantic Marine Mammal Commission, founded in 1992 by Norway, Iceland, and the home rule governments of Greenland and the Faeroe Islands as an intended regional counterpoint to the IWC. The ICR's own research whaling program has long included, as one of its goals, the assessment of "the role of whales in the ecosystem"—which seems to come down to researchers looking inside the stomachs of freshly killed whales to see what they have eaten, and how much. Since the mid-nineties the ICR, the FAJ, and their allies have given the argument particular and ever increasing emphasis, ultimately offering it as the principal justification for extending the North Pacific whaling program to sei whales in 2002: the increased hunt, said the ICR, was "based on urgent scientific need to collect data on the competition between whales and fisheries." The species taken under the program, the ICR continued, "are abundant" and are "very large animals—this means they consume huge amounts of marine resources."

It is undeniably true that the world's whales eat a lot of aquatic life, not least because many of them are, as the ICR noted, extremely large. The stomach of one female humpback whale was found to contain 600 herring. In one blue whale, researchers found food totaling in excess of one ton—the equivalent, notes whale researcher Roger Payne, of "the meat in eight thousand quarter-pound hamburgers." On average, however, Antarctic minke whales probably eat 80 to 260 pounds of krill a day during a roughly 120-day feeding season. For the larger sei whales, the known range is between 220 and 440 pounds a day, while in the Arctic, the average bowhead whale might swallow anywhere between 1,100 and 3,300 pounds of food in a twenty-four-hour period. Any way you look at it, that's a lot of food—although whether it adds up to as much as the ICR claims is less certain. The figures cited above suggest a daily food intake for baleen whales of around 1.5 to 2 percent of body weight, which most researchers consider to be the likely average. The lower ranges of the ICR estimates used similar figures; the upper limit, however, was calculated on the basis of baleen whales consuming 3.5 percent of their body weight per day, as much as twice the more commonly accepted figure.

Even without the quibbles over the ICR's precise figures, the fundamental premises of the argument—that whales are eating fish that would otherwise be available to commercial fisheries, that commercial fisheries are therefore suffering, and that the solution is to cull whales in order to allow fish stocks to grow—are shaky at best. Cast aside for a moment the fact that, by any measure, whale populations today are just a tiny fraction of their size at the beginning of the twentieth century, when the amount of marine life they consumed would have been massively greater—and when, also, despite a greater number of whales eating a greater number of fish, fish populations were much larger. Ignore also the fact that, despite Komatsu's hysterical charge that the number of whales worldwide "has nearly doubled since the moratorium," only a few whale populations have shown any notable sign of recovery; and apart from the Eastern Pacific gray whale (which is reckoned to have at least rebounded to and possibly even exceeded its initial numbers), none are anywhere near their pre-whaling levels.

Instead, indulge the ICR with its most extreme estimate of global food consumption by cetaceans. Of the 500 million tons of marine life that the institute claims disappears into cetacean stomachs every year, 109.5 million tons are supposedly consumed by the baleen whales of the Southern Ocean, and 254 million tons are eaten by sperm whales around the world. But Antarctic baleen whales eat almost exclusively krill, for which there is virtually no commercial demand; and the prey of sperm whales is dominated by deep-sea squid, for which there is also no commercial fishery.

The whalers' own evidence, past and present, underscores the above point. Year after year, researchers on board the *Nisshin Maru* have dutifully sliced open the stomachs of the Antarctic minke whales they have brought aboard, but each and every one of those stomachs has contained krill and virtually nothing else. In the North Pacific, a 1977 Japanese study of the stomachs of nearly 22,000 seis killed by whaling found that 44.5 percent were empty; of those whales that did have food in their stomachs, just 3 percent had been eating fish, 12.5 percent had eaten krill, and 82.7 percent had been feeding on copepods, tiny planktonic animals that are even smaller than krill. Indeed, the nature of sei whales' baleen plates—which have very fine hair on their inner surfaces, making them better adapted to sifting smaller organisms from the water—is testimony to the species' preference for very small plankton, a fact that has been known to whale scientists (except, apparently, those associated with the ICR) for years.

But even if whales did eat 500 million tons of commercially valuable fish and other aquatic life each year, "culling" those whales would not necessarily result in an increase in those fish. To insist that it would requires a facile vision of marine ecosystems in which a limited number of predator and prey species keep each other's numbers in some kind of "balance." But food webs, including marine ones, are far more complex than that. They are chaotic systems, in a constant state of flux, with an incredible number of interacting components. The nature of those interactions is still poorly understood, and human intervention's impact upon them is even less known.

Reducing the number of whales *might* result in an increase in the fish species on which they prey, but it doesn't follow that those fish would then be available to commercial fisheries. A large proportion would succumb to natural mortality, while some would be eaten by other predators such as marine mammals or predatory fish. Indeed, predatory fish consume by far the largest amount of fish in the ocean; in fact, killing whales is just as likely to result in a *decrease* in commercially valuable fish, because some whales also eat their predators.

But if the argument was less than compelling, that didn't prevent the pro-whalers from making it widely and frequently, as part of a determined and concerted effort to push the "multi-species management" agenda in as many different international forums as possible. In 1995 Komatsu and colleagues successfully lobbied to include, as a key element of the so-called Kyoto Agreement that emerged from the International Conference for the Contribution of Fisheries to Food Security, the "use of all components of the marine ecosystem evenly to keep the balance of the ecosystem." Komatsu took advantage of his position as chair of the Committee on Fisheries (COFI) of the U.N. Food and Agriculture Organization (FAO) to have COFI pass a resolution in 2001 calling on the FAO to conduct studies into "interactions between marine mammals and fisheries." The following year, Japan, Norway, and Iceland also lobbied— unsuccessfully this time—for similar language to be adopted as part of the World Summit on Sustainable Development (popularly known as the Earth Summit), which was held in Johannesburg, South Africa.

The FAJ and its minions made the case with particular frequency and urgency at regional fisheries bodies, especially those involving eastern Caribbean, Pacific island, and East African states. In 1998 the FAJ used the "whales-eat-fish" argument at a meeting of the South Pacific Forum, to foment opposition to a joint Australia–New Zealand proposal to the IWC for a South Pacific Whale Sanctuary. A Japanese government communiqué sent to forum members argued that "excessive and unnecessary protection" of whales would "heavily damage [the] balance of the marine ecosystem and be destructive to fisheries in the region." At the 2001 meeting of the Indian Ocean Tuna Commission, held in the Seychelles under Komatsu's chairmanship, Japan "expressed concern that consumption of fish by top predators such as marine mammals could diminish catches of commercial species."

There was a method to all this. Among some of the less developed countries that were the FAJ's target audience, its argument that whales were eating fish stocks into depletion—and, even more, that those whales were being allowed to increase in number because of unnecessary protection forced on the world by rich Western environmentalists who cared more for wildlife than for people—was calculated to touch nerves rubbed raw by legitimate grievances over past colonial misdeeds and ongoing economic imperialism. It was also intended to provide intellectual cover, of a sort, that would allow some of those countries to support the FAJ's pro-whaling stance in international conventions such as the IWC's meetings. Increasingly, a number of these nations chose to do just that, although evidence pointed to such decisions being motivated more by financial than intellectual concerns.

Japanese officials repeatedly denied that their government was offering countries financial inducement to attend and to support Japan's position at the IWC and related forums. In his book Komatsu insisted, "Such a rumor is inexcusable, as it has no foundation . . . the anti-whaling organizations' mean tactics using such a false allegation for propaganda never ceases to amaze me. In this case, they deceive the public so effectively that some remote nations ring on the phone to the Japanese authorities asking if they could receive financial assistance by offering to cast their votes in support of Japan."

But Komatsu himself admitted in a 2001 Australian radio interview that Japan used the promise of overseas development assistance, or ODA, as a way to shore up support for its whaling policy around the world. That same year Lester Bird, prime minister of Antigua & Barbuda, which had been supporting Japan at the IWC since 1998, admitted: "Quite frankly, I make no bones about it . . . if we are able to support the Japanese, and the quid pro quo is that they are going to give us some assistance—I am not going to be a hypocrite about it, that is part of why we do so." The year before, Atherton Martin, then minister of environment for Dominica, resigned in disgust, protesting that his country's IWC policy was "undignified and unacceptable and must be resisted. . . . There is absolutely no reason for us to be held ransom by Japan . . . in return for promises of aid."

In 1999 a series of articles provided rare insight into the aid-for-votes process, beginning with a wire story quoting Hiroaki Kameya, then vice minister for agriculture, forestry, and fisheries, as saying: "We would like to use overseas development aid as a practical means to promote nations to join [the IWC], expanding grant aid toward nonmember countries which support Japan's claim." The story went on to state, "Because anti-whaling countries' attitudes are stubborn, it is judged that it is more advantageous for future negotiations to dig up supporting votes by increasing member countries than by trying to split opposing votes." About a week later, a fisheries newspaper reported that Mr. Kameya had set a target of an additional thirteen countries joining the IWC and siding with Japan; that story specifically mentioned Morocco. Two months afterward, another fisheries paper informed its readers that Mr. Kameya had departed for Namibia, Zimbabwe, and Guinea to "explain Japan's position of whaling and the IWC and CITES [the Convention on International Trade in Endangered Species] and appeal to take united steps."

The FAJ protested that Japan provided far greater amounts of ODA to countries such as Argentina, Brazil, Chile, India, and Mexico than to those nations accused of having their IWC votes bought by Tokyo. "Have these countries ever supported Japan in the IWC?" asked Komatsu rhetorically in his book. "No, on the contrary, India, Argentina, and Brazil are constantly opposing Japan at the IWC. Other countries in the list also take different positions than that of Japan."

But, as was pointed out in a report published prior to the 2002 IWC meeting by the Italy-based Third Millennium Foundation, the "vote-buying campaign is linked to one specific category of Japanese aid—Grant Aid for Fisheries—not to Japan's entire ODA program. It is true that in any one year more than 150 countries receive some form of Japanese ODA, but only 10 to 15 of those receive fisheries grant aid. Moreover, there is not one developing country that supports Japan regularly in the IWC that is *not* a recent recipient of Japanese financial or technical assistance in the fisheries sector." The Grant Aid for Fisheries program, said the Third Millennium Foundation report, operates in "virtual autonomy." The distributor of such largesse? None other than the Fisheries Agency of Japan.

The first countries to see the light were the eastern Caribbean nations of St. Lucia and St. Vincent & The Grenadines. Both had joined the IWC prior to the 1982 meeting, and for several years were strong members of the conservationist camp. In 1986 their prime ministers were invited to Tokyo; shortly afterward, a matter of days before that year's IWC meeting, the countries' anti-whaling commissioners were replaced, and the islands have been solidly in Japan's camp ever since. Another Caribbean nation, St. Kitts & Nevis, showed up at the Glasgow meeting in 1992 but did not speak or vote, then disappeared from sight for seven years. Dominica and Grenada joined in 1993; Antigua & Barbuda, which had been strongly anti-whaling for many years, withdrew its commissioner and joined the pro-whaling bloc in 1998; St. Kitts & Nevis returned in 1999, assumed a more active role, and this time remained; Guinea joined in 2000, as did Panama— which had also been a conservationist member of the commission until withdrawing, reportedly under Japanese pressure, in 1981; and Morocco made its first appearance in 2001. All of them voted consistently with Japan. Other former environmentally minded countries, notably Oman and the Solomon Islands, found it progressively harder to resist Japanese "diplomacy," to the point where they ultimately voted almost exclusively with Japan, at least on most matters of greatest import to the FAJ. Even the Seychelles, which joined the commission in 1979 and rapidly became the FAJ's nemesis—proposing the Indian Ocean Sanctuary and the commercial whaling moratorium, and for many years remaining one of the leading anti-whaling nations—was ultimately forced, apparently after strong diplomatic and economic pressure from Tokyo, to leave the IWC in 1994.

It was always possible that, no matter how many fisheries development projects the FAJ sprinkled around the world, there still wouldn't be enough votes at the IWC. And so, even as they gathered a growing number of allies into their warm embrace within the commission, the whaling forces sought simultaneously to undercut the IWC, question its credibility, and advance other conventions as more legitimate forums for addressing the issue—in particular the Convention on International Trade in Endangered Species.

As its name suggests, CITES is the body responsible for managing, monitoring, restricting and, when necessary, banning trade in wild flora and fauna; since the adoption of the commercial whaling moratorium, it had placed all species and populations of cetaceans on Appendix I, its highest level of protection, meaning all international trade was strictly prohibited. This was especially vexing for the Norwegian whalers, who had next to no viable market for whale meat in their own country and desperately needed to export it to Japan; but it was also troublesome for the FAJ, which recognized that the credibility of its claims that whales were the "cockroaches of the sea"—as Komatsu had called minke whales during the aforementioned Australian radio interview—was damaged by CITES having deemed those very creatures worthy of the same degree of protection as such undeniably endangered species as the giant panda and the mountain gorilla. And so in 1997 (and again in 2000 and 2002, CITES meetings being roughly biennial), Japan proposed resolutions calling for various whale populations to be moved— "downlisted," to use the CITES vernacular—from Appendix I to the less-restrictive Appendix II. (Norway had first proposed such a vote, for the so-called Northeast Atlantic and North and Central stocks of minke whales, in 1994.). Although all the efforts ultimately failed, some came close to being approved: the Norwegian proposals actually attained simple majorities in 1997 and 2000, although well short of the required two-thirds majority, while the Japanese proposals typically secured about 40 to 45 percent of those voting. The CITES Secretariat resisted any change in cetaceans' status, pointing out that the convention deferred on whaling matters to the IWC, and stating that as long as the IWC maintained its moratorium on commercial whaling, CITES should retain its ban on the trade in whales and whale products.

But the whalers continued to work at least as hard on improving their vote count within CITES as they did in the IWC, and it was not hard to see where their preferences lay. Even as Komatsu denigrated the latter as "an organization where anti-whaling members shout for the protection of whales" and a place where, "when anti-whaling powers propose a resolution that insists on 'black is white,' it passes, while when Japan or Norway say 'white is white,' it is rejected," he noted that "approximately one half of all CITES members . . . support our proposals. And that one half is greater in number than the entire membership of the IWC."

By the time the IWC assembled in Monaco for its 1997 meeting, much of the whalers' multifold strategy had yet to fully reveal itself, but for those who cared to see, the writing was on the wall. The ICR had expanded its research whaling program in the Southern Ocean and introduced one in the North Pacific; in the Northeast Atlantic, Norway was steadily increasing the number of whales it assigned itself under objection to the commercial whaling moratorium. The IWC remained nominally in control of whaling, but the liberal use and abuse of objections and other clauses in the IWC's convention was, in the eyes of at least some observers, increasingly putting that control at risk. The whalers thus found themselves in a status quo whereby whaling was ostensibly illegal but proving eminently possible on at least a limited level, and increasingly so.

As a result, some observers, concerned about the present situation but, even more, about possible developments in the near future, were beginning to talk openly of the IWC being in "crisis." Among those who harbored such grave concerns about the IWC's direction was the commissioner for Ireland (and later IWC chair) Michael Canny, who came to Monaco with the most radical and polarizing plan that the commission had seen in many years.

Canny proposed a package of measures: the Revised Management Procedure (RMP) would be formally adopted into the Schedule as part of a broader Revised Management Scheme (which had long been discussed, and which included such proposed measures as observer and verification programs); the RMP could be used to calculate catch quotas, but only in the coastal waters of those countries currently conducting commercial whaling (i.e., Japan and Norway); the meat from any whales so caught could be used only for local consumption—in other words, there could be no international trade in whale meat and products; scientific whaling would be phased out, and commercial whaling on the high seas would be ended in perpetuity.

In other words, Japan and Norway would lose the ability to conduct whaling on the high seas, and the opportunity for limitless "scientific whaling" quotas, but they would get limited, officially sanctioned quotas for their coastal whaling communities. As a result, the argument went, the number of whales being killed worldwide would almost certainly decrease, and the whaling that remained would theoretically come under tighter control.

But the very fact that the proposal appeared to have something for everyone meant that it also contained more than enough concessions for both sides to hate it. For all that the FAJ regularly bemoaned the fate of Japan's coastal whaling communities and the moratorium's impact on them, its interest was never in securing the cultural and nutritional well-being of those communities, but in finding a way to catch as many whales as possible on the high seas, particularly the Antarctic. Norway needed to be able to export its whale meat to Japan, which Canny's proposal would prohibit, and it remained likely that a strict RMP would provide its whalers with far fewer whales than it was presently catching.

Most environmentalists, meanwhile, treated the Irish proposal as if it were carrying the plague. Some insisted that no such undertaking was needed. Far fewer whales were being hunted than prior to the moratorium, they noted; all that was required was for the anti-whaling bloc to remain firm in its resolve. Others reacted to the proposal to ban whaling on the high seas by predicting an explosion of whaling in coastal waters; furthermore, they argued, because whales migrate between coastal waters and the high seas, Canny's plan would effectively open up almost all whale populations to exploitation.

But supporters (of which there were relatively few) countered that the proposal specifically called for the restriction of any future whaling to Norway and Japan, and that even if that did somehow fall by the wayside, the RMP required any country that wanted to start whaling to first pay for and conduct several years' worth of expensive surveys, which would have to be analyzed and approved by the IWC's Scientific Committee before the committee could even consider whether any quotas could be set. And any such quota would be based on the numbers of whales counted in the small areas where whaling would be allowed, not on the numbers in the population as a whole. Taken together with the local consumption proposal—removing the possibility of selling any whale meat to Japan, and hence the rationale for Japan to support the establishment of any would-be whaling fleets—those conditions, Canny's supporters argued, ensured that both the incentive and the opportunity for coastal whaling outside Japan and Norway would diminish significantly.

Other criticisms were voiced. Some questioned the political wisdom of laying all the cards on the table before the game had truly begun: even if the proposal's contents provided a package that would be worth having, the fact that Canny had made that package his opening gambit meant, they reasoned, that any final result would be significantly less. Critics questioned the legality of allowing two countries to hunt whales and forever denying the option to everyone else, and wondered how the trade ban would withstand the inevitable challenge from the World Trade Organization. They argued that even limited, legal commercial whaling would establish a market for illegal hunting, and pointed out that at every single turn, the whaling industry had cheated and there was no reason to imagine it wouldn't continue to do so. A fair number still didn't trust the RMP and were far from convinced it was as watertight as its advocates insisted. But the underlying, majority view was simply that it was a compromise that the whalers didn't deserve: the commercial whaling business was an industry with a reprehensible past that was still doing everything it could to escape every regulation and restriction, and the proper course of action was to shut it down, not grant it any concessions.

That latter point pretty much summed up my own feelings toward the whaling industry. Yet I was a strong and public supporter of the Canny proposal—not because, as some critics characterized the motivation of the plan and its proponents, it provided an opportunity to cut a deal and walk away, but because I (and the others in Canny's small band of backers) honestly believed that, if enacted, it provided the best way for us to limit and ultimately eliminate commercial whaling.

Simply put, the anti-whaling forces had failed to build on the momentum of victory in Puerto Vallarta. The whalers were the ones showing initiative; the environmentalist side was concentrating its efforts on blocking the whalers' moves, and such proactive ideas as were floated—for example, replacing the moratorium with a permanent or fifty-year ban—had next to no political support (and would anyway have been subject to an objection from Japan and Norway, leaving us in the position we were in already). The anti-whaling strategy had basically become one of "just saying no" to commercial whaling and "maintaining the pressure" on nonwhaling governments to lobby Tokyo and Oslo to bring whaling to an end. The problem with that was that the Americans, Australians, British, New Zealanders, and others might talk tough on whaling, but when it came down to it, they were not going to commit anything like the same resources to stopping commercial whaling as the FAJ was expending on propping it up and expanding it. Frankly, the whalers were beginning to run strategic circles around us, and the way some of us saw it, we basically had two options: we could stand, Canute-like, proudly refusing to give any quarter as we were slowly submerged by the whalers' advancing tide; or we could try to outmaneuver them and, while conceding the possibility of some commercial whaling, put together a package that would make whaling next to impossible—and certainly less prevalent than it was becoming.

Such a strategy was risky—but, we argued, a lot less risky than the course of inaction at the time. Almost everyone else on the environmental side viewed it in exactly the opposite way. Of the "big three" organizations, only the World Wildlife Fund fully endorsed the Irish proposal; Greenpeace and the International Fund for Animal Welfare supported elements of it, but ultimately, because it would allow commercial whaling and the two organizations were opposed to commercial whaling, they wouldn't back the package as a whole. Pretty much all the other organizations actively loathed the idea.

Although the proposal went nowhere in Monaco, it was a major agenda item at the next meeting, in Oman, with a good number of the delegates speaking up in defense of the principle of forging an agreement, if not the specifics of the Canny plan. But the proposal's advancement required some spirit of compromise, and by 1999 it was clear that that was not in evidence. The stronger anti-whaling governments, emboldened by the outright hostility to the plan from the vast majority of environmental organizations, refused to budge; and Japan announced that it had no intention of caving in on the elimination of scientific whaling, pelagic whaling, or international trade—the three cornerstones of the proposal. Quietly, Canny's initiative withered on the vine, and people on both sides of the aisle breathed an enormous sigh of relief.

The Monaco IWC meeting was the first I had attended in three years. I had walked away from the whaling issue after I left Greenpeace in 1995, pausing now and then only to read updates from IWC meetings or to touch base with old friends. The Irish proposal, however, piqued my interest enough for me to show my face at the IWC again. When it became clear that no progress was going to be made on what I for one considered a bold and innovative undertaking, my briefly renewed enthusiasm once more waned.

Unfortunately, much as I wanted to put whaling and Greenpeace behind me, their absence left a hole in my life that proved hard to fill. I found work as a freelance writer on environmental issues, particularly issues facing the ocean, but although much of it was interesting and rewarding, the stimulation factor couldn't hold a candle to the life I had been living for the past several years; just as importantly, I was growing weary of Washington, D.C., which was hot, humid, and saturated with self-importance.

So it was that in the summer of 1998 I found myself on a Greenpeace vessel in the polar regions once more. This time, however, it was as a journalist on board the *Arctic Sunrise*, the organization's small icebreaker, examining climate change impacts in Alaska and the Russian Arctic. We recorded testimony from Alaska Natives living in villages along the Bering Strait and along the coasts of the Bering and Beaufort Seas; and steamed along the ice edge to remote Wrangel Island, far to the north of Russia, studying seabirds, polar bears, and walruses with a team of researchers from the University of Alaska. The subject matter fascinated me and I found enough material to write two dozen articles for magazines and websites during the three-month voyage. And I became so taken with Alaska that, almost as soon as the expedition was over, I moved to Anchorage. If I couldn't live in Antarctica, I reasoned, then this was the next best place: I found a small wooden cabin near Cook Inlet, and as I looked across the water at the Alaska Range, I could almost imagine that the snow-capped volcanoes were the Transantarctic Mountains.

I felt as if I had come home, and as a result once more found enthusiasm and inspiration in my work; I had plenty to write about, and in the summer of 1999 I began drafting a book on the natural and human history of both the Arctic and the Antarctic. If it wasn't quite the same as being on a ship in search of whalers, it was nonetheless fun and fulfilling; so much so that, when Greenpeace asked me if I would lead another Antarctic expedition for the 1999–2000 season, I turned down the offer. Walt Simpson did his best to convince me to change my mind; in Anchorage to oversee that summer's *Arctic Sunrise* voyage to the Arctic, he made regular visits to my cabin with bottles of wine and a brace of arguments as to why I should make the trip. But I resisted his entreaties, and the closest I came to this expedition was checking the daily updates on the Greenpeace website as the *Arctic Sunrise* encountered the whaling fleet. I had always imagined that I would feel deeply frustrated and jealous, not being part of an Antarctic whaling voyage; in fact, content in the life I had constructed for myself in Alaska, I was merely curious to see how the expedition developed.

Even from the other end of the world, it was clear that events in the Southern Ocean were unfolding differently than before. This time, for whatever reason, instead of running away, the whalers, at least initially, stood their ground and fought back: the crews on the catchers drenched the inflatables with powerful fire hoses, and the *Nisshin Maru* even caused a collision with the *Arctic Sunrise* by overtaking far too closely on the Greenpeace ship's port side—a direct and dangerous violation of international maritime regulations. Although the fleet did not shoot a whale directly in front of Greenpeace cameras, the *Sunrise* did come across a whale that had just been harpooned, and filmed it thrashing in the water for six and a half minutes before it was finally killed.

When the fleet did eventually decide to flee, the *Sunrise* soon found it again, and its crew did everything it could think of to interfere with its operations. At one point, first mate Frank Kamp even leaped onto a dead whale that the *Nisshin Maru* was trying to haul aboard; but, unable to keep his grip, he slipped into the water and the whale was transferred to the factory vessel as planned. Australian deckhand Deb McIntyre and Dutch engineer David de Jong managed to tie their inflatable to one of the cables being used to haul another whale on board—almost managing to decapitate themselves in the process—and the *Nisshin Maru* crew had no alternative but to drag the boat halfway up the stern ramp before cutting them loose. New Zealand Prime Minister Helen Clarke was moved to formally state her government's support for Greenpeace's actions against, as she put it, "commercial whaling under the guise of scientific research," prompting a furious exchange of letters between Tokyo and Wellington, and ultimately leading Komatsu to charge that the "New Zealand Government officially supports violent actions in protest against our legal activity." Clearly upset by the whole endeavor, the Japanese delegation moved unsuccessfully at the next IWC meeting to have Greenpeace expelled.

Even as the *Arctic Sunrise* prosecuted its actions against the *Nisshin Maru* and the catchers, the situation in the IWC was deteriorating, and it continued to do so over the next two years. The ICR expanded its North Pacific research whaling program, first in 2000 to include Bryde's and sperm whales and then in 2002 to also encompass sei whales and a larger number of minkes. The number of pro-whaling countries joining the commission continued to grow and, based on analyses of recent diplomatic activity and distribution of the FAJ's Grant Aid for Fisheries program, some feared that as many as ten more might appear, ready to vote with Japan, at the 2002 IWC meeting in the whalers' home port of Shimonoseki: enough to push the pro-whaling bloc into the majority. Iceland, which had left the IWC in 1992, had applied for re-entry, but wanted to be admitted with a reservation to the moratorium, even though it had not filed an objection within the prescribed ninety-day period when the moratorium had been adopted back in 1982. Some of the nonwhaling countries were sounding surprisingly malleable on the subject, and if the whalers secured a majority there seemed little doubt that Iceland and its postdated objection would be allowed readmission as requested.

A whalers' majority would assuredly result in the IWC passing resolutions commending the ICR's outstanding research in the Antarctic and North Pacific, or urging that the RMP (which had still not been formally adopted into the Schedule) be adjusted to a lower tuning level, thus giving the Norwegians cover to continue increasing their self-assigned commercial quotas. Although there was no indication that the whalers would have anything like enough votes to secure a three-quarters majority and thus overturn the moratorium, the Southern Ocean Sanctuary, the Indian Ocean Sanctuary, the pelagic factory ship ban, and the numerous other precautionary measures the commission had adopted over the last twenty-some years, there was a real danger that the anti-whalers would seek to cut a deal before the situation became any worse: a deal that, given that they would now be negotiating from a position of weakness, would undoubtedly include far fewer safeguards than would be needed. For that matter, if the whalers felt confident enough, maybe now they wouldn't even be interested in any deal, but would instead just wait until their majority was secure and large enough that they could do whatever they wanted.

It was clear that the FAJ wanted the Shimonoseki meeting in particular to be an overwhelming success, allowing it to trumpet news of a great victory across the land. What better scenario than for the fleet to return to port from the Antarctic shortly prior to the meeting; for the conference itself, with the whalers (including Iceland) freshly in a majority, to pass a resolution applauding the fleet's work; and for the ships to then leave again, this time for the North Pacific, to continue research that had, as in the Antarctic, also been endorsed by the newly enthusiastic IWC?

If the FAJ was devoting enormous diplomatic resources to making the Shimonoseki meeting a great success, environmental organizations were mobilizing with greater urgency than in many years to deny the whalers the advances they craved. They worked with friendly governments to try to dissuade potential new members of the pro-whaling bloc from joining the IWC, and to persuade nonwhaling nations that this was the time to become members themselves. And Greenpeace, making the whaling campaign an organizational priority once more, determined that it had no option but to do once again what only it could do: find and harass the *Nisshin Maru* in the Southern Ocean.

Ten years and four expeditions' worth of experience had made it abundantly clear that it was extremely hard to seriously hamper the activities of the whaling fleet. But something had to be done, if only to try to deny them at least some whales, and to embarrass them and fire up the anti-whaling forces heading into Shimonoseki—anything to tarnish the whalers' enthusiasm and momentum and damage their growing air of confidence.

John Bowler, the able and practiced veteran who had stepped in when I turned down the 1999–2000 voyage, was less inclined to spend another three months away from his family, but expressed interest in being the coordinator and contact person on land. There were some relatively young campaigners who were available to make the trip—Sarah Duthie, from Greenpeace New Zealand, and Yuko Hirono, a fresh recruit to Greenpeace Japan—but nobody with any experience of leading an expedition of this nature, or of being at sea for long stretches. Most of the crew, too, would be new—at least to the whaling campaign in the Antarctic. And so, inevitably, the call came once more. Would I be available to be the expedition leader?

The book I had been working on two years earlier had been published, and I had no other major project to prevent me from taking six months out of my life to go chase whaling ships. The success of the previous expedition—the one I had missed—had reminded me that it was possible to have at least some impact, even with a ship like the *Arctic Sunrise*, which was arguably even slower than the *Greenpeace*. And the growing successes of the pro-whaling forces had not only made me feel bad for having turned my back on the campaign six years previously, but also reignited my enthusiasm for becoming involved again.

I put my life in storage, sublet my cabin, and exchanged an Alaska winter for an Antarctic summer. And just a few days after we crossed the Convergence, as we sat in the middle of icebergs and fog; as the first catcher appeared, and then the second, and then the *Nisshin Maru*; as we chased them through the ice and finally stopped for the night, I stood on deck and watched the factory ship, waiting for the whalers to make the next move and preparing to take them on one more time.

CHAPTER THIRTEEN

One Last Roll of the Dice

AS I STOOD ON THE BRIDGE THAT FIRST MORNING WITH THE fleet, squinting through the mist at the factory ship and watching the movements of the rest of the fleet on the radar, a loud hail came across VHF Channel 16.

"*Arctic Sunrise*. This is *Nisshin Maru*."

I stared at the radio in disbelief—in ten years of chasing the fleet around the Antarctic, I had never known them to initiate any radio communication—and then rushed down below to find Yuko. She called the factory ship back to acknowledge that we were listening, and the radio room recorded the message for her to translate:

> This is Hajime Ishikawa, head of the Southern Ocean Survey Fleet. We are conducting scientific research as allowed under Article VIII of the International Convention on the Regulation of Whaling and strongly demand that you, Greenpeace, should cease your obstruction of a permitted survey and leave the survey area immediately.

You, Greenpeace, obstructed our survey the other year, caused a collision at sea, and endangered the safety and lives of crew members.

You have damaged and removed our things, attempted the boarding of our ships and other completely unacceptable behavior. In a civilized society this is considered to be on the same level as acts of pirates and robbers. If you, the *Arctic Sunrise*, and members of Greenpeace intend to repeat the same obstruction this year, we of the survey, in order to protect ourselves and continue our survey in safety free from pirates and any group which commits piratical acts, will have to use water hoses to repel anyone trying to obstruct us.

I repeat, we demand that you, Greenpeace, stop obstructing a legitimate survey and leave the survey area.

The tone was condescending; in particular, the term that Ishikawa used repeatedly to refer to "you, Greenpeace," and "you, *Arctic Sunrise*," was one that in Japanese was reserved for speaking down to someone you consider your inferior. We elected not to respond in kind, Yuko delivering an altogether more restrained response on my behalf:

This is Kieran Mulvaney, expedition leader on board the MV *Arctic Sunrise*. I thank you for your earlier transmission. It is a pleasure to have contact from you.

We will be very happy to leave the whaling grounds as you recommend. We are all a long way from home, and we miss our relatives and friends. We would all like to be home for the New Year holiday. I'm sure you feel the same way. However, we are planning to be here until you cease your whaling activities in the Southern Ocean Sanctuary. Until then, we will continue to protest your whaling program.

Your so-called "research" whaling program was never requested by the IWC Scientific Committee and is continued despite repeated requests from the IWC to stop the program. Most recently, in 2001 the IWC passed a resolution stating that the commission "strongly urges the government of Japan to halt the lethal takes of minke whales conducted under the JARPA program, at least until the Scientific Committee has reported to the commission on the impacts of the JARPA program on the stocks of minke whales in Areas IV and V." Furthermore, the IWC has designated this area as the Southern Ocean Sanctuary.

Despite your characterization of us as "pirates" and "robbers," Greenpeace is, and always has been, a nonviolent organization committed to the principles of peaceful protest, as you well know. We will do nothing to endanger or harm your vessels or your crews, and we request that you publicly make the same commitment to us.

We must point out that it was the *Nisshin Maru*, not the *Arctic Sunrise*, that was at fault for the collision two years ago. The Lloyd's database records the incident as a ramming of the *Arctic Sunrise* by the *Nisshin Maru*. The *Nisshin Maru* was the overtaking vessel. You will be aware that Rule 13 of the International Maritime Organization Convention on the International Regulations for Preventing Collisions at Sea states that "any vessel overtaking any other shall keep out of the way of the vessel being overtaken." We urge that you not take any action to similarly endanger the *Arctic Sunrise*, a vessel which is far smaller than your own, this year.

Once again, we respectfully request that you cease your whaling. Until and unless you do, we shall continue to exercise our right to peaceful protest.

We wish you safe sailing.

For all the ICR's phobias about what horrendous deeds we might do unto the whalers, during our first full day among the fleet the weather conditions prevented any attempt at whaling, so all five ships—*Nisshin Maru*, catchers, and *Arctic Sunrise*—simply steamed in formation along the trackline. On the following morning, December 15, conditions began to improve, but they were still not good enough for us to launch—nor, I thought, for the fleet to begin hunting—and so we found ourselves once more steaming along with the whalers, this time a few miles astern of the *Yushin Maru*, the newest, biggest, and best of the catchers. Then, suddenly, the *Yushin Maru* began maneuvering; obviously they were ready to whale after all. We scrambled the Hurricane and it raced to the catcher, but barely had it arrived than it was forced to return after its propeller hit a piece of ice.

The arrival of a snowstorm delayed further launches, but after lunch we tried again. The ice, however, was growing thicker and thicker—far more than at any other time I had been with the fleet. I had never seen them operate in such difficult ice conditions before and was surprised to find them doing so now. But they continued to push relentlessly southeast, deeper into the ice edge, making it difficult for us to launch our boats. When eventually we did manage to launch a patched-up Hurricane, this time toward the *Kyo Maru No. 1*, the encroaching pack forced it to return prematurely once more.

After retrieving the boat the second time, we decided to stick with the *KM1*. Throughout the afternoon and early evening, the catcher and the *Sunrise* threaded their way slowly through whatever leads, or channels, we could find in the ice, speeding up whenever ice gave way to open water and then slowing down once more when the pack returned. Suddenly the *KM1* put on a tremendous burst of speed, rapidly accelerating to sixteen knots. People were in the crow's nest, and it looked as though someone was at the harpoon. They had found a whale and were giving chase.

Within minutes, the Mermaid—our other large inflatable, which, being a jet boat, was thus without a propeller that could be damaged by ice—was in the water and in hot pursuit. As those of us in the wheelhouse strained to see exactly what was happening, the excited voice of Mehdi Moujbani, the Mermaid's driver, came over the VHF:

"I see it. I see the whale. I'm going to get in front of the ship."

The whale was about fifteen meters in front of the catcher; the harpooner stood at the bow and lined up his shot, but as he prepared to fire, the Mermaid raced into position and the whale dove beneath the ice. We'd saved our first whale.

The Hurricane set out to join Mehdi and crew member Clive Strauss in the Mermaid. Soon both boats were struggling with the thick ice, and we all found ourselves engaged in a slow-motion chase in the middle of the Antarctic. Neither the *Kyo Maru No. 1* nor the *Arctic Sunrise* was able to put on any appreciable speed except for occasional short-lived bursts in open water, and the crews of the two inflatables were surrounded by ice and struggling even harder than the larger ships to find a way through. The Mermaid was forced to act as an icebreaker for the Hurricane, carving narrow channels for the propeller-driven boat to follow, as the Hurricane crew hacked at the pack with oars and paddles in a frantic attempt to shove the ice floes out of the way and reach the whaler. Soon, however, the arrival of another snowstorm brought a temporary halt to both whaling and to the Lewis-and-Clark escapades of the boat crews.

The superiority of the whaling ships was on display at every turn. Overnight we would situate ourselves roughly in the middle of the fleet, making sure we were ready as soon as they started moving the next morning. But such was the fleet's speed and planning that they could shoot away the next morning before we could react, and almost before we knew what was happening, they could get a jump on us and start whaling before we could free ourselves of a huge expanse of pack ice and reach them.

Watching the targets on the radar on the morning of December 16—the catchers maneuvering sharply as they chased after whales, and then returning to the *Nisshin Maru* to offload the whales they had killed—I understood why the fleet had been grinding through such thick ice ever since we had found them. After all, they must have known that the *Arctic Sunrise* was a true icebreaker and thus theoretically better equipped to force its way through the pack than they were. It could scarcely have been an attempt to lose us: they could much more easily accomplish that by simply heading out into open sea and going full throttle. On our previous expeditions, they had assigned one catcher each day to serve as a sightings vessel, probing the ice edge and counting whales to relay information back to the other ships; since increasing their catch total to 440 whales a year, however, they had brought along an additional ship to focus solely on those chores. That vessel, the *Kyoshin Maru No. 2*, steamed a hundred miles ahead of the rest of the fleet, providing detailed reports on weather and ice conditions and the abundance or lack of whales along the trackline; plainly, it had advised that if the factory ship and catchers could battle their way through the thick pack ice, they would find a polynya—the term given to a large expanse of open water in the middle of fast ice or pack, and a haven for whales. The fleet was obviously now in that polynya and, judging from the activity of the radar echoes, had come across the mother lode.

Desperately, agonizingly, we sought to close the gap. Andy Troia, who had been first mate on my last voyage and was this time serving as captain, had retreated to the crow's nest to afford himself a better view and was steering the ship from up above, trying to tease the *Arctic Sunrise* through any available leads and, when none were immediately apparent, forcing the little ice-breaker to bludgeon its way through the pack that lay between us and the whalers. It seemed to take an age to make any progress, and all the while I could do nothing except watch the radar, peer through binoculars, and pace the wheelhouse, frustrated that as we battled our way slowly through the ice, the fleet was shooting whales with abandon.

Finally, after several long hours, we broke through and into the polynya, emerging close to the *Nisshin Maru*, with two of the catchers—the *Yushin Maru* and the *Toshi Maru No. 25*—nearby. The *TM25* appeared to be heading to the factory ship to offload a whale. We prepared both the Hurricane and the Mermaid to intercept it; but the launch was once again delayed by drift ice, and by the time the boats reached the target, the transfer had taken place. Now the *Kyo Maru No. 1* was also approaching, and so the boat crews stood ready for action once more. As the catcher moved into position off the starboard quarter of the factory vessel, its crew broke out the fire hoses and began spraying the people in the inflatables. The crew of the *Nisshin Maru* lowered ropes and flags into the water to snag the boats' propellers, as they had done two years previously. And cascading down the bottom of the stern ramp was a waterfall of spray, evidently designed to either block the view, inhibit any Greenpeacer who contemplated being dragged up with a whale, or both.

Earlier that day we had received word from a source in Tokyo that the factory ship was freshly equipped with two giant water cannons, powerful enough "to knock activists out of their inflatables." If those were what we were looking at now, they scarcely lived up to the hype. But then, high above the ramp, two nozzles turned slowly like tank turrets and suddenly unleashed a torrent of water. Now *those* were cannons. We laughed as the jets landed a direct hit on the bridge of the *Kyo Maru No. 1*, but then the cannons' operators adjusted their aim, inundating the inflatables and their crews with water and spray.

The jets of both fire hoses and water cannons were aimed directly at the boats' drivers, Olivier Devaux and Jesse Reid. The crews of the Mermaid and the Hurricane did their best to protect them, standing over the cockpits with their backs to the oncoming jets, but the volume of water was too great. Even so, both boats stayed at their positions, managing to delay the transfer by a quarter of an hour before the whale was finally dragged through the water and up the stern ramp of the factory ship.

As the inflatables headed back to change crews, our helicopter, which had been filming the action, headed off in search of a catcher. They came across the *Yushin Maru* hunting a whale. The gunner took aim as the minke fled for its life, and then he fired; the retort from the cannon was so loud that both Jari Stahl, the cameraman, and Jeremy Sutton-Hibbert, the photographer, recoiled with shock. The harpoon flew through the air and landed harmlessly in the water; still the *Yushin Maru* continued its chase, and the whale swam as fast as it could, trying to avoid the fate the whalers had in mind for it. Again the harpooner missed, and again; each time he hauled in the harpoon and reloaded as the *Yushin Maru* maintained its high-speed pursuit. For forty minutes the chase continued; five, six times the gunner fired; five, six times the whale was spared. Finally, on the seventh attempt, the harpoon found its mark. The sea was still, the ship came to a halt, and the catcher's crew pulled the stricken whale to the bow. It had died instantly, and a bright crimson cloud colored the water as its body was hauled to the surface and tied alongside the catcher.

The next day, December 17, we launched all four boats—the Hurricane, the Mermaid, and the two smaller Novuranias— toward the *Nisshin Maru* as the *Kyo Maru No. 1* approached to unload a whale. My plan was that all the boats would attempt to interfere with the transfer, and the longer-range inflatables would then stick with the catcher as it returned to the hunt. As the Mermaid, which carried Jeremy and Jari, kept its distance, Jesse Reid and Vincent Custers piloted the Hurricane close to the *KM1*. As they did so, both catcher and factory ship opened up with everything they had.

Vincent and Jesse took a terrible beating from the combined attentions of the fire hoses and the water cannons. Vincent fought to shield Jesse, who was driving, from the onslaught; but so much water was coming from so many directions that the task was hopeless. One jet of water knocked out Vincent's contact lens; another hit him in the mouth and busted open his lip. Jesse hunkered down behind the wheel, trying to simultaneously shield his face and watch where he was going.

"It wasn't too bad," he insisted later. "I could kind of see out of the corner of one eye, but there was so much water it was really hard to breathe. I'd turn away from the fire hoses and then the water cannons hit me in the face."

Driving on instinct, barely able to tell where he was, Jesse was surprised at one point to find the boat virtually on top of the dead whale that was tied alongside the catcher.

Eventually, the transfer was made, and at this point the Hurricane was supposed to take off after the *Kyo Maru No. 1* as it returned to the hunt. But the ice-cold water from the fire hoses and water cannons had taken its toll.

"My hands are freezing," Jesse radioed. "I can hardly feel them. I'm coming back right now."

The Hurricane came back, a new crew took over, and Jesse and Vincent clambered back on board. They stood in the hold, literally screaming in agony as the blood came back to their hands and faces.

During the brief delay and indecision as we scrambled to prepare another crew, the *KM1* had darted back into the ice. We used the *Arctic Sunrise* to blaze a path through the pack for the inflatables, but it was slow going. We didn't appear to be gaining at all on the catcher, and the ice closed behind us as soon as we chugged through, forcing the boats to work almost as hard as if we hadn't been there.

If I was surprised that the fleet was operating in such thick ice, I was completely stunned that they seemed to be much better in the ice than we were. The *Arctic Sunrise* was an ice-breaker, after all, but it was a slow and cumbersome one; we had little option but to bludgeon our way through as best we could. The catchers, by contrast, while only ice-strengthened and not truly ice-class, were fast, powerful, and maneuverable: they could steam through a lead, stop, turn on a dime, and disappear through another lead, taking the path of least resistance and leaving the *Sunrise* lumbering behind them. With an icebreaker, the pack ice was supposed to be our turf. The crews on the catchers were clearly excellent mariners; that they were beating us so soundly in the ice was, to Andy and myself, humiliating.

By the time we pulled the boats back on board, the catcher, which had been just a few hundred yards away when soaking Jesse and Vincent, was ten miles distant and steaming in formation with the rest of the fleet. We broke free of the ice and gave chase. As the evening drew on, the wind began to pick up, reaching about twenty knots and making conditions marginal for whaling. But then, up ahead, we could see one of the catchers make a sharp turn. It was hunting. All we could do was charge toward it as fast as we could; the catcher's pursuit of the whale was taking it on an intercept course with us, allowing us to make up ground much more quickly. We put boat crews on standby and prepared to launch the Hurricane if we could just get closer. But we were too late; just as we were about to put the boat in the water, the catcher stopped dead. It had killed the whale. We could do nothing except watch ineffectually as it took its quarry to the factory ship.

The following morning, the fleet moved northeast away from the ice edge and out into the Southern Ocean. For the next couple of days, high winds and heavy snowstorms stopped the fleet from whaling, and we became reacquainted with the undulating swells of the ice-less sea. The *Arctic Sunrise* may have been far more capable in the ice than the *Greenpeace*, but it lacked the Black Pig's robustness in the open ocean; like all icebreakers, it had a rounded, keel-less hull, which enabled it to rise up onto ice floes but also contributed to a strange rolling motion when confronted with anything stronger than a stiff cross-breeze. Fortunately, we never once experienced any weather as severe as that on the Voyage from Hell in 1992–93—nor, for that matter, any wind as ferocious as the Force 12 that had struck during the 1999–2000 expedition—but even a relatively mild Force 8 or 9 was enough to send the *Sunrise* into paroxysms of protest. Sailing on the *Arctic Sunrise* was at times like attempting to ride bareback on a gigantic floating cork; on my first trip on the ship, its movements while hove to off an Alaska village were enough to induce a visiting customs officer to rapidly lose his lunch. Earlier on our present voyage, one particularly impressive roll removed an unsuspecting Jesse from his feet and sent him across the floor from one side of the hold to the other, back again, and then back one more time before he finally crashed to a halt.

By the morning of December 21 the wind had begun to abate, but when I staggered up to the wheelhouse at 0600, it was still snowing fairly hard; even a few hours later, as we prepared a boat to launch toward the *Kyo Maru No. 1*, there didn't appear to be much likelihood of any immediate action. Then, suddenly, at around 0900, the snow stopped and visibility improved. Watching from the wheelhouse, Jesse and Waldemar Wichmann, the first mate, saw some whales; and at that moment, just as we were in a position to launch one of the boats, the *KM1* took off. By the time the Hurricane touched the water, the catcher was three and a half miles away and vanishing toward the horizon at seventeen knots. It took the Hurricane, battling through heavy swells, a good half-hour to reach its target, even though the catcher's progress was interrupted as it twisted and turned in pursuit of the fleeing whale.

The whale was about a hundred meters in front of the whaling ship as the Hurricane swept into position. We wrestled briefly with a moral dilemma as Jari argued that the broader campaign would be better served if he filmed the minke being shot, but the discussion didn't last long: Jesse and Vincent made it clear that they were going to save that whale, and they steered the inflatable directly in the harpoon's line of fire. For the better part of an hour they stayed there, Vincent shouting the whereabouts of the unfortunate whale to Jesse, who was striving to keep the Hurricane in front of the rapidly maneuvering catcher. Eventually, the whaling ship broke off its chase and returned to its trackline, and the exhausted whale swam free. But long before then, Andy and I had become occupied with other concerns.

The radios on the Hurricane had become waterlogged during the rough ride to the catcher and were all but useless: despite the fact that Vincent and Jesse were reporting back regularly to the *Arctic Sunrise*, we could hear them only occasionally, and barely, while they couldn't hear us at all. Acutely aware of the uniquely savage nature of the Antarctic environment, Andy had, from the outset of the voyage, repeatedly emphasized the extreme importance of boat crews maintaining contact with the ship at all times, and had established a specific routine that needed to be followed in the event of any communication breakdown. Fortunately, it was a lesson well learned: as soon as Jesse and Vincent recognized the problem and realized they were in a small boat in the Southern Ocean that was out of visual range of, and audio contact with, the *Arctic Sunrise*, they activated their SART, or Search and Rescue Transponder. Their position then showed up clearly on our radar, and we were able to pick them up. It had been a tense sixty minutes, but the Hurricane crew did everything by the book, and managed to save a whale while they were at it.

An hour later, however, the *Kyo Maru No. 1* did kill a whale, and when the *Nisshin Maru* turned toward it to take delivery, we moved to intercept. As we closed in on the catcher, we could see that the whale seemed to be hanging strangely by the catcher's side. And then we realized why: its tail flukes had somehow been ripped off, presumably while the catcher's crew had been trying to tie it alongside. We launched the two large inflatables, and as the factory ship bore down, we were all concentrated together: *Nisshin Maru*, *Kyo Maru No. 1*, *Arctic Sunrise*, Hurricane, and Mermaid. As Jeremy and Jari filmed from on board the Mermaid, Waldemar drove the Hurricane in close to the catcher, and the whaling ship's crew responded with a fusillade from the fire hoses.

As the factory ship let rip with its mammoth water cannons, the Hurricane disappeared completely from view in a torrent of water and spray. The boat's crew tried to shield their driver as best they could, but the whalers had so many cannons and hoses that wherever Waldemar turned, a jet of water hit him directly in the face. One blast caught him unawares, jerking his head back and buckling his knees, and for an instant he worried he was about to be knocked out. Somehow he kept his composure and his consciousness, and in the middle of all the chaos held the Hurricane in position. The boat crew remained resolutely polite, even to the extent of smiling at the catcher crew each time they took a hit from the fire hoses. At one point, the swell simultaneously dropped the bow of the *KM1* and lifted the

Hurricane, so that crew member Mikey Rosato found himself level with the harpooner. Mikey smiled and offered a handshake; the harpooner stared at him in shock until the Hurricane dropped back on the receding swell.

Eventually, the body of the whale was transferred and then, to my surprise, the catcher remained on station to transfer the whale flukes before returning to its trackline, with the Hurricane and Mermaid in pursuit. When the Mermaid radioed to the ship at about 1830 that it needed to refuel, I figured that by the time it had returned to the *Sunrise*, fueled up, headed back out, and caught up with the catcher, it would be close to 1915 and there would be only 45 minutes remaining in the whaling day. So I suggested to Andy, and he readily agreed, that instead of sending the Mermaid back out, we'd just bring it on board for the evening.

Waldemar, however, had other ideas. He wasn't satiated by his efforts to stop jets of water with his face earlier in the day, and about ten minutes after we had brought the Mermaid on board, I saw him in the hold, suiting up to take it back out again. I wasn't keen on people overextending themselves, but I wasn't about to stop someone from trying to save whales either, so the Mermaid went back in the water to join the Hurricane and the catcher.

The boat was barely under way when two minke whales surfaced close to the *Kyo Maru No. 1*, and the catcher immediately turned and gave chase. Just as quickly, the Hurricane crew sped their boat in front of the whaling ship's bow, maneuvering frantically to keep between the harpoon and the whales. Time and again the harpooner swung his gun about and took aim, but each time Olivier and his crew—Duygu Gungor from Turkey, and Frenchwoman Nathalie Renard—interceded. It was working. They were going to save those two whales.

And then, suddenly, they heard a loud clunk. The Hurricane's propeller had hit a chunk of ice and the boat began shaking violently. Olivier had no choice but to stop. The catcher sped past, and Olivier knew it was over. The Mermaid was gaining rapidly now, but it was too late. There was a bang, and the harpoon struck home.

The *Arctic Sunrise* retrieved the stricken Hurricane, and the Mermaid arrived in time to see the whalers tying up their catch alongside. Some of the catcher's crew stood ready with fire hoses, but for some reason another crewman, apparently their senior, told them to hold off. If the whalers were mellowing toward us, it didn't last: two of the catchers later managed to sandwich the Mermaid between them, drenching the inflatable's crew with fire hoses as the factory ship also opened up with its water cannons.

With that, the whalers' day ended. The crew of the *Kyo Maru No. 1* covered its harpoon, and the crew of the Mermaid returned to the *Arctic Sunrise* to dry off and warm up. As the Mermaid was hoisted back on board, I joined Olivier, Nathalie, and Duygu, sitting sadly out on deck. Poor Olivier—there was no disguising his torment. He blamed himself, accused himself of incompetence: he had been driving, it was his fault they hit the ice. I blamed myself: had it not been for my initial decision to bring the Mermaid back on board, the boat would have swiftly refueled and changed crews and would have been able to enter the whaler's line of fire when the Hurricane broke down.

It had been a long, hard day: a solid twelve hours of actions, very intense and mostly successful. But there was a lot of emotion on board our little icebreaker that evening; we were trying to save whales, and to see them killed in front of us was desperately upsetting. Eva Amira, a young volunteer from Greece, summed it up best.

"I think today we had our best day," she said as we gave each other a hug. "But it was also the saddest."

The whalers had evidently had enough. The next day, despite our being once more in ice, and despite a furious snowstorm that dropped visibility to almost zero, the fleet ran away from us. They stayed on their trackline but roared along at sixteen knots, an insane speed in such thick ice and snow.

The fleet was heading southeast and would soon be bouncing back to the northeast; and so, once they were safely off our radar screen, we turned and steamed east to wait for them along the line I had reckoned they would follow. Whereas during previous expeditions the whalers' disappearance frequently provoked consternation and frenzied computation of their likely trajectory, this time no such panic ensued. I was supremely confident that I had picked the right place to intercept the fleet, and that we would be with them again, in a matter of days at most. The only way the plan could go wrong, I thought, would be if we bumped into the *Kyoshin Maru No. 2*—the survey vessel that steamed ahead of the fleet—which would assuredly inform the rest of the ships of our presence and give them ample opportunity to avoid us.

That evening, we bumped into the *Kyoshin Maru No. 2*.

By the time the mate on watch saw the echo on the radar, it was about ten miles distant. Andy immediately brought the *Sunrise* to a halt to try to avoid detection, but it was too late: the target stopped dead at almost exactly the same time we did. It was by itself, and on the trackline I'd predicted for the whalers. It had to be the survey vessel, and there could be no doubt that at that very moment, the *Nisshin Maru* was being informed of our location.

We decided to sit tight. There was a slim chance that they hadn't seen us move and were themselves wondering if we were an iceberg. I retreated to my bunk but couldn't go to sleep. Every time I closed my eyes, I pictured that ship in the darkness across ten miles of icy water. This was the one thing that could foul everything up. I was not a happy man. I got out of bed; sat in the lounge and drank a beer; prowled around the largely deserted ship; sat in the mess and made a snack; read a book; prowled around some more; and finally willed myself to sleep at about 0300. I fell asleep again immediately after my 0600 wake-up call, only to be reawakened forty-five minutes later by Andy, who told me that the target had started moving toward us.

Whether we stayed or steamed away, our cover was going to

be blown, if it hadn't already been. So we sat and watched as the echo grew ever closer and then, finally, through the mist, we could see the ship itself: it was indeed, as expected, the *Kyoshin Maru No. 2*. Once it had spied us and confirmed our identity, it began to steam away; then, presumably instructed by the *Nisshin Maru* to stick with us, it returned, steamed to within a few hundred yards, and stopped.

What to do next? Some on board suggested sending over a boat to say hello; others offered that it was neat to have seen the *Kyoshin Maru No. 2*, because now we could say we'd encountered the entire fleet. But I wasn't remotely interested in saying hello, and I didn't think this meeting was neat at all. In fact, it was disastrous; I had hoped to go through the whole expedition without ever seeing the survey vessel, because I knew that if we did see each other, it would mean we were about a hundred miles away from our real targets and, once the *Kyoshin* had revealed our position, we'd be unlikely to ever get any closer. That was exactly the scenario that was unfolding, and I was irritated that few seemed to grasp the gravity of the situation.

After we'd had enough of watching them watching us watching them, Andy and I decided to force the issue and start moving. Because we knew the fleet had all but finished whaling to the west of us, we started steaming slowly east. I had assumed that the *Kyoshin* had been detailed to follow us, at least for a while; but to my surprise, although it started moving at the same time as we did, it steamed equally slowly in the opposite direction. Was it trying to lead us astray? Was it returning to the fleet? Was it just as eager to be rid of us as I was of it? Whatever its motivations, it crawled toward the northwest and off our radar screen, and we again found ourselves alone.

We continued east, regularly searching the area with the helicopter as we did so, taking advantage of our lack of company to recover from what had been an intense couple of weeks and to enjoy Christmas and New Year's. We made contact with the Australian bases in the region and sent messages to our old friend, the Australian government resupply and research ship *Aurora Australis*, advising them that the whalers were in the area and suggesting they keep an eye open. On the evening of December 30, a target appeared southeast of us and heading west; it was the *Aurora*, and we called to say hello. We would have steamed over to meet them, but conditions were dreadful, with screaming winds flinging sheets of snow at us and whipping the sea into towering waves. Although the much larger *Aurora*, with the weather at its back, was trucking along at a healthy twelve knots, our little *Sunrise* was barely making three or four.

The next night, the New Year had just been ceremoniously rung in, as per tradition, by the youngest person on board (Eva, our Greek volunteer). We had all joined hands to sing "Auld Lang Syne," despite our almost universal ignorance of the words, when Andy, who had been summoned to answer a telephone call, reappeared. He leaned forward to say something to me, which I couldn't quite make out over the general hubbub but which I assumed to be some generic New Year's greeting.

"Yes, Happy New Year to you, too!" I shouted back.

Andy looked a little perplexed, then leaned in and tried again. "The *Aurora* has found the whalers," he said.

"What?" I said.

"The *Aurora* has found the whalers," he repeated.

I froze, stared at him, and uttered the phrase that had become something of a trademark over the last few voyages: "You have got to be kidding me."

The *Aurora* had discovered the fleet far to the west of us. The whalers had presumably waited until the *Kyoshin* saw us wander off to the east, decided to continue with their trackline as planned, and ended up behind us.

The crew of the *Aurora Australis*, like that on board the *Arctic Sunrise*, had been celebrating the New Year. When they encountered the *Kyo Maru No. 1*, the catcher fled to the safety of the *Nisshin Maru*. The *Aurora* called the fleet, advised them that they were in waters the Australian government considered its Antarctic territory, and asked them to leave. Apart from a cursory acknowledgment of the *Aurora*'s communication, the whalers, as was their wont, stayed silent. A few of the resupply ship's crew stood out on deck and decided to show the *Nisshin Maru* and company precisely what they thought of Japan's whaling program; reportedly, Tokyo sent Canberra an aggrieved cable complaining that Australian nationals had displayed their bare buttocks to Japanese nationals in the waters off Antarctica.

Much as some on the *Aurora* would have liked to continue monitoring the fleet's activities, they had work to do. It was proving a heavy ice year in the area, and the *Aurora* needed to break through into Prydz Bay to release another resupply vessel, the *Icebird*, which was stuck in the pack. But thanks to the encounter, we knew where the fleet was. At around midnight on January 3, we found them again.

Waldemar, Jeremy, and Neil Brewster, the radio officer, stood glued to the bridge windows, binoculars in hand. Almost simultaneously, each let out a roar as he saw the catchers up ahead. Then the *Nisshin Maru* materialized off our port beam. We were with the whalers once more, but evidently our previous actions had been about as much as they wanted to take, so rather than be subjected to them again, they took off.

The *Nisshin Maru* fled to the southeast while the catchers gathered together and disappeared to the west. As we chased after the factory ship, Andy called it up over VHF.

"Why do you run?" he asked. "Do you have something to hide? We are here to observe your scientific research."

Yuko also tried to make contact, injecting some humor into her effort.

"Please don't run," she pleaded. "We are a slow ship, and we can't keep up."

Coincidentally or not, the *Nisshin Maru* soon afterward began dropping speed: from fourteen knots it eased off to about twelve and a half, still a good half-knot and change more than the *Arctic Sunrise* could manage, but leisurely enough for us to at least keep it in sight a while longer. Then, suddenly, it slowed down, stopped next to an iceberg, and slipped behind it. We eased our way around the other side and found the factory ship close in behind the berg, apparently trying to hide from us. As soon as it saw us, the *Nisshin Maru* circled the berg, then began heading west.

A furious snow squall descended, transforming the surroundings into vintage, hostile Antarctica: snow in abundance; high winds and whitecapped waves; dreadful visibility; ice scattered about the ocean surface; and us once again playing cat-and-mouse among the icebergs with the whaling fleet. Shortly before 0500, the *Nisshin Maru* disappeared behind a berg, and soon afterward a radar echo appeared on the other side, continuing along at the same course and speed. But David Iggulden, returning as a mate for the first time since the Voyage from Hell in 1992–93—and, apart from me, the only veteran of that dreadful experience on board—was suspicious: the second echo looked a little too small. And so, instead of taking the bait, he slowly nudged up to the iceberg and, sure enough, found the *Nisshin Maru* hiding on the other side. It had met up with a waiting catcher, which had promptly taken off in an attempt to lure us into following the wrong target. The catcher now sped off to the south, and the factory ship, having been rediscovered, continued west. At one stage it changed course dramatically to cross our path, as if wishing to create a collision; because it was approaching from our starboard side, it technically had the right of way, so David altered course to keep the two ships apart. The *NM* passed harmlessly astern of us before resuming its course, with us following.

The pursuit continued through the night and the next morning, until noon on the 4th, when the *Nisshin Maru* turned north into the powerful winds that were roiling the seas, put on the power, and began to pull away, darting into an enormous mass of what must have been a couple of hundred icebergs. Our radar screen became a bewildering morass of echoes until eventually, by around 1800, we lost the *Nisshin Maru* altogether.

David, who was again the mate on watch, wondered if the

factory ship had just found an iceberg to hide behind and had bedded down for the night. Andy was dismissive.

"They've been steaming away from us for eighteen hours. We can't catch them. Why would they suddenly stop?"

"Well," observed David in his crisp English tones; "it *is* six o'clock."

He had a point. For all their frequently smart tactics and adroit manipulation of the technical advantages they had over us, the whalers were mostly remarkably predictable about one thing: the hours they kept. Although there were exceptions, they generally started at somewhere around 0600 and finished twelve hours later. We didn't have any better ideas, and so, conceding that David's argument had some merit, we elected to dive deeper and deeper into the maze of icebergs to see if the factory ship was hiding somewhere inside.

As the sky grew darker, the weather grew worse, and the visibility further diminished, we searched among the icebergs. The snowstorm became so bad at one point that it was all we could do to see to the bow of our ship. Undeterred, we carried on, looking behind each iceberg that had been on the known path of the factory ship. It was quiet on the bridge, the combined challenges of looking for the whaler and steering through the most hostile environment on Earth creating a tense and exciting atmosphere. From one berg to the next we went; I sat stock still, staring intently out into the darkness, wondering if we had a chance. Finally, a little after midnight, almost exactly twenty-four hours after the chase had begun, the *Nisshin Maru* appeared ahead of us. We could just make out a dim shape in the near distance; and then, either concerned that we would run right into it or conceding that the game was up, the factory ship turned on its navigation light. We were back in business—but not, as it turned out, for long.

True to form, the *NM* started moving at 0600 that morning, steaming hard this time to the northeast. It took off at around fourteen and a half knots, far too fast for us to compete, and built a healthy distance between us as we gave chase. Late that morning the factory vessel dodged behind one iceberg and then another, and by the time we caught up to the second berg, a catcher was headed directly for the *Nisshin Maru*. I expected it to meet up with the *NM* and receive instructions on what to do and where to run next, but to my surprise, it assumed the position at the factory ship's stern. They appeared to be transferring a whale. What was going on? For one thing, the weather seemed inclement for whaling, but for another, where the hell had that catcher been? Had it been more than twenty miles away and then come running back to deliver a whale? Or had it steamed far from the factory ship, killed a whale, and then ducked behind the nearest iceberg to wait for the *NM*?

The catcher sped off at about sixteen knots and rapidly receded into the distance. The *Nisshin Maru* forged ahead at about thirteen knots, disappeared behind another iceberg and, when it emerged after a brief delay, appeared on the radar to have become two echoes. It had met up with a second catcher, and now the strategy was clear: the catchers would get fifteen to twenty miles ahead of the *Nisshin Maru*, which would blast along at close to full speed until it was a comfortable distance away from us, and when a catcher killed a whale, it would wait behind an iceberg for the factory ship to meet up with it. If that was their plan, we could do absolutely nothing about it, especially in this kind of weather. It would be foolhardy to let the inflatables travel as far from the *Arctic Sunrise* as they would need to, and in any case the boats might not even be able to make up sufficient ground while the catchers continued to roar along at that kind of speed. In other words, as long as this was how the whaling fleet planned to operate, our continued presence was pointless.

I had a decision to make. For some time, confronted with the limitations of our equipment and the additional hurdles presented by the whalers' more aggressive tactics, we had been planning to head into Melbourne to recoup, recover, refuel, re-equip, and then return. We would install windshields on the boats, to protect their crews from the fire hoses and water cannons; equip the boats with state-of-the-art radios and emergency location equipment, so we could feel more comfortable letting them travel long distances; and add a third long-range inflatable and an extra photographer to cover the entire fleet more effectively. At the same time, the *Arctic Sunrise* itself was in need of attention: Dave McEvitt, the chief engineer, was growing increasingly concerned about the state of the ship's generators and was urging us to have them fully inspected in port and repaired, as necessary, by an engineer from the company that had made them.

My initial reaction to the fleet's discovery by the *Aurora Australis* was that, now that we knew exactly where the whalers were, and therefore where they would be going next, we should head north immediately, and then return to spend the rest of the season disrupting them. But a quick read of the crew's faces when I floated that idea made clear that it wasn't a viable option; nobody wanted to break off while we had a chance to hit them a second time. Now, though, another opportunity to exercise the Australia option was rapidly presenting itself.

I went to my bunk and took a nap. When I woke up, I knew what we had to do. I found Andy, told him my decision, and as the whalers continued to speed north, past the northerly limit of the whaling area (on their way, we speculated, to meet their refueling tanker), we dropped back.

Before we headed out into the raging Southern Ocean, we needed to lower the helicopter into the hold, and so we initially turned south in search of a giant iceberg to give us shelter, or an expanse of pack ice that would dampen the motion of the waves and stop the ship from rolling so much while we moved the helicopter down from the deck. On our way, we ran straight into the *Kyoshin Maru No. 2* hiding behind an iceberg of its own. Its crew was presumably as stunned to be found by us as we were to find them; we circled each other briefly, and then the *Sunrise* continued on its way.

We arrived in Melbourne, held a press conference, and welcomed visitors to the ship, all the while remaining coy about our intentions and allowing everyone to infer, even as we quietly made preparations for our second leg, that the expedition was over.

And then, all of a sudden, it was.

The engineer we had requested came on board the morning after our arrival, took one look at the generators, exclaimed that he had no idea such old models were still in operation and that his company had neither the tools nor the manuals for them anymore, and left. When he returned a few days later, appropriately equipped, he made a preliminary investigation and placed the first order for replacement parts. Those parts had to come all the way from Germany; and with each further inspection and test, more problems seemed to come to light, each requiring more and more work. The time needed for parts to arrive, and repairs to be made, kept growing: several days became a week, one week became two. Calculating how long the fleet would likely remain in the whaling area and the earliest date we would be able to return, I reached the conclusion that even assuming the most optimistic date for completion of repairs, returning just wouldn't be worthwhile.

I called a crew meeting and made the announcement: we wouldn't be going back to Antarctica. Even though, as the days had slipped away, most of the crew had seen it coming, the sudden finality of the decision was, to many, a shock and a bitter disappointment. A couple of people cried. But, I pointed out, the only reason we felt dejected was because we had planned on doing what no other expedition had done before: returning to the Antarctic to take on the whalers for a second time in the same season. If we had been able to pull it off, it would have been phenomenal, but what we had been able to achieve in the time we had at our disposal was more than enough for us to be plenty satisfied with our efforts.

Even so, I too found myself stunned by the suddenness of it all. I had returned after six years away to take charge of another expedition, and now suddenly, through no fault of our own, it was over. It seemed scarcely believable, and even though I had obviously been cognizant of a possibly abortive ending longer than

anyone else, it was still a shock. It was deflating and disem-
powering, not least because none of us could do anything
about it.

I also felt I was calling an end to more than this particular
expedition. For me, certainly, it was the final voyage: although it
had been wonderful to come back one more time, I couldn't see
myself returning in the future. It was one thing being on the
road and at sea for six months at a time when I was twenty-four
and essentially rootless. Now I was thirty-four with a cozy
book-lined cabin in Alaska and close friends whom I knew were
waiting for my return to Anchorage and with whom I could
barely wait to be reunited. If Greenpeace called again, I suspected, I would probably say no. If indeed Greenpeace ever did
call again: this last expedition had proven beyond any doubt that
these campaigns had now become technological mismatches. It
was one thing to ask people to do the best they could in difficult
circumstances, but not if that meant being pounded mercilessly
with torrents of ice-cold water and then watching as the whaling
ships sped away. Already, I knew, some voices in the organization
were questioning the wisdom and benefit of continuing such
lengthy endeavors at the expense of other strategies.

But those were decisions for others to make. I stayed around
long enough to tie up a few loose ends, relax a little, and revel in
the sun and civilization of Melbourne. And then, after a few
weeks, I looked around and realized I was no longer needed.
The campaign was over, the crew was focused on fixing the ship,
and I had gone from expedition leader to a piece of deadwood
taking up bunk space. It was time to leave.

The day of my departure, I dragged my bags slowly out on
deck. Most of the crew members were waiting to say goodbye.
We exchanged hugs, and I hauled my luggage down the gangway and into the waiting taxi. I took one last look at my waving
comrades as I pulled away, and then watched in the rearview
mirror as the ship slowly receded into the distance.

EPILOGUE

Even as I retreated once more to the comfort of my life in Alaska, pro-whaling and anti-whaling forces alike were preparing for the May 2002 International Whaling Commission meeting in Shimonoseki. On the environmentalist side, nerves were fraught at the prospect that as many as ten new members might show up and join the whaling bloc, induced to do so by a Fisheries Agency of Japan promise of a new fish processing plant or some similar venture. That worst-case scenario did not unfold: just four new nations joined the IWC and sided with Japan at the Shimonoseki meeting. Three— Benin, Gabon, and Palau—were recent recipients of assistance from the FAJ's Grant Aid for Fisheries program, and their attendance had been anticipated; the appearance of the fourth, Mongolia, was unexpected. The landlocked nation had, of course, received no fisheries aid—the first and only member of the FAJ's cheerleading squad to hold that distinction—but faxes detailing Japanese funding for the Mongolian delegate to the previous CITES meeting had earlier come to light, so there was ample reason to suspect that the country's sudden devotion to the pro-whaling cause was less than ideological.

The FAJ did not, as some had feared, wind up with a majority at the meeting—some of the predicted pro-whaling attendees such as Mauritania and Namibia did not show, perhaps discouraged by intense lobbying from environmentalists and some of the stronger anti-whaling nations; and Portugal and San Marino joined the commission on the conservationist side. As a result, some of the more nightmarish forecasts, such as votes in favor of Japan's scientific whaling, did not come to pass. But, far from boasting an overwhelming anti-whaling majority as it had a few years previously, the commission now comprised an almost even number of commission delegates on each side; and so even as environmentalists managed to thwart the whalers' most ambitious schemes, their own initiatives also foundered.

At the 1998 IWC meeting in Oman, Brazil had floated the idea of a whale sanctuary in the South Atlantic, and Australia and New Zealand had jointly suggested a similar concept for the South Pacific. Neither posed the same kind of threat to the whaling industry that the Southern Ocean Sanctuary had: the Antarctic was far and away the largest target for the FAJ in their idealized postmoratorium world, and nobody was looking seriously at resuming large-scale commercial whaling in either of the regions covered by the new sanctuary proposals. Nonetheless, the proposals put the whalers on the defensive and forced them to expend time, effort, and money on the counterattack. Both proposals also had immense symbolic importance: for one thing, if adopted, the South Atlantic and South Pacific sanctuaries would provide an additional layer of protection if the moratorium were overturned, and would combine with the existing sanctuaries in the Indian and Southern Oceans to make the entire Southern Hemisphere off-limits to commercial whaling. Perhaps yet more important, the energy behind the initiatives was being generated by countries within the sanctuary boundaries; in particular, the South Pacific proposal was being pushed strongly by many of the island nations that the FAJ had targeted for its vote-buying initiative. A number of those nations, not waiting for the IWC to adopt the proposal, began declaring whale sanctuaries in their national waters—among them the Cook Islands, French

Polynesia, Papua New Guinea, Samoa, and Niue: powerful retorts to FAJ claims that the anti-whaling movement consisted only of middle-class, suburban Anglo-Saxons and Western Europeans.

But the growing number of FAJ vassals prevented either proposal from being adopted when put to a vote in 2000 and 2001, and the Shimonoseki meeting saw the cards fall much the same way: although both secured majorities, they fell well short of the three-quarters margins required for adoption.

The 2000 meeting in Adelaide had seen the nonwhaling bloc begin to splinter into two: the core "no whaling at any costs" group, epitomized by Australia, Germany, the Netherlands, New Zealand, the United Kingdom, and the United States, among others; and what environmentalists began to dub the "middle-minded": countries such as Chile, Denmark, Finland, Ireland, Mexico, Oman, South Africa, Spain, Sweden, and Switzerland, which appeared to be leaning increasingly toward supporting—or at least not opposing—commercial whaling if it could be conducted under the strict criteria of a conservative Revised Management Procedure and Revised Management Scheme. Two competing Revised Management Scheme resolutions were tabled in Shimonoseki: one by Japan, which would have eliminated the sanctuaries in the Indian and Southern Oceans, rescinded the ban on the use of factory ships on all species except minkes, and overturned the moratorium. It failed by 16 votes to 25 with three abstentions— among them Norway, which claimed the proposal didn't do enough for coastal states and called the vote "premature." A Swedish counterproposal would have restricted whaling to two-hundred-mile Exclusive Economic Zones and for local consumption only, and in the meantime would have maintained the moratorium and the factory ship ban; it failed by 12 votes to 24 with seven abstentions.

The IWC left Shimonoseki in much the same way as it had entered: locked in a stalemate, with no side boasting a working majority and the true believers on each side seemingly ever more firmly entrenched. But environmentalists came away from the meeting declaring victory, largely because, having feared the worst, they were able to stymie the whalers' efforts, even as the pro-whaling side suffocated their sanctuary proposals. Iceland's attempt to rejoin the commission with a postdated objection to the moratorium was defeated, as were a Japanese motion for all votes to be determined by secret ballot and Japan's request for fifty minke whales as an "emergency relief allocation" for four coastal communities.

Japan had been lobbying for this "emergency" allocation every year since the imposition of the moratorium; on each and every occasion, the commission had turned it down. This time the Japanese delegation, frustrated at having failed to get its way on its home turf, snapped. In a move that stunned even the most cynical and hardened IWC observers, Japan gathered its stooges together and, in a blatant act of revenge, blocked the bowhead whale subsistence quota for the Inupiat and Siberian Yupik of Alaska and Russia's Chokotka Natives.

The bowhead hunt has been an intrinsic element of the culture of those native societies for well over a millennium. It became briefly controversial in the early 1980s following a sharp increase in the number of whales being hunted, and because scientists believed that the bowhead population was in sharp decline and in danger of being pushed into extirpation. But subsequent studies showed that researchers had significantly underestimated the number of bowheads in the region, and the native whalers took major steps to improve management of the hunt. As a result, the bowhead population, although still endangered, was increasing; environmentalists no longer opposed the hunt; and the commission's recurrent granting of a five-year quota had long become a mere formality, routinely done by consensus. Until now. Thirty nations voted in favor of the quota in Shimonoseki, but 14 voted against and China abstained. A second vote produced 32 in favor but 11 against and two abstentions—one vote short of the necessary three-quarters majority.

U.S. commissioner Rollen Schmitten called the action "the most unjust, unfair, and unkind vote that was ever taken" in IWC history. The representative of the Chukotka people referred to it as "a knife in our backs." The FAJ's Caribbean supporters said they had no objection to whaling by aboriginal peoples, but voted against the quota in protest of the rejection of the coastal whaling quota. Masayuki Komatsu proclaimed, "This year the United States delegation has a message to take home: end the hypocrisy. . . . Our coastal whaling bid has been rejected for 15 years. The United States ought to feel the same pain."

It was particularly unjust for the Japanese delegation to take this particular tack at this particular meeting, for not only had the ICR already decided to increase by fifty its "scientific" catch of North Pacific minke whales, but those extra minkes were going to be caught by vessels operating out of those same four coastal communities in whose name Japan sought to deprive Arctic Natives of their nutritional and cultural needs. The communities, in other words, were already guaranteed their fifty whales, albeit through sleight of hand and creative use of "scientific research"; the Japanese delegation and its minions blocked the bowhead quota purely out of spite.

In October the IWC gathered in Cambridge, England, for a special meeting to resolve the bowhead issue. This time, having presumably made its point and felt the considerable behind-the-scenes wrath of Washington, Japan did not stand in the way, and the bowhead quota was agreed upon by consensus once more. But that same meeting had more than its share of controversy.

Four days before the meeting took place, and notwithstanding the Shimonoseki votes, Iceland announced its renewed adherence to the International Convention for the Regulation of Whaling. It restated its intention to rejoin the IWC with a reservation to the moratorium decision, but promised it would not resume commercial whaling before 2006. (It did not, however, promise not to begin "research" whaling.) Norway requested that Iceland's membership be considered by the special meeting, beginning a series of four confusing votes, all on matters of procedure, that appeared to end with the commission agreeing, by 19 votes to 18, to readmit Iceland, complete with its objection to the moratorium. However, none of the votes expressly addressed Iceland's membership; all were so confusing that Sweden, which cast the decisive vote that apparently readmitted Iceland, angrily protested afterward that it had had no intention of doing any such thing. Adding to the confusion, Iceland itself (which was unequivocally not a member prior to the vote) was somehow allowed to cast one of the votes in favor of its apparent readmission.

Despite the fact that they are supposedly rooted in science, Japan's research whaling programs in the Antarctic and North Pacific are, if anything, becoming less resistant to serious scientific scrutiny. In Shimonoseki, a group of researchers presented a paper to the Scientific Committee that excoriated the expansion of the North Pacific program. Japan's scientific whaling was now morphing into a long-term whaling operation without an end point, the paper argued.

Prior to the expansion of the North Pacific program to include sei whales, the ICR declared that the sei whale population in the region numbered 20,000 and was increasing; not a shred of evidence was presented in support of this contention, nor will any likely ever be. No mention was made of the inconvenient fact that just three years previously, ICR director Seiji Ohsumi had submitted to the IWC Scientific Committee a paper estimating the population at just 9,110 whales. The whalers' modus operandi: repeat an unsubstantiated "fact"—there are 20,000 sei whales in the North Pacific; whales are eating fish to depletion; Greenpeace rammed our ship—over and over again in the hope that, by doing so, this will make it come true, or at least convince others that it is. (Sometimes it works: in August 2002, even the *New York Times* carried an op-ed that essentially parroted the worst of the ICR/FAJ propaganda concerning whale numbers and their effect on fish populations.)

Of all these fake "facts," the whalers' favorite is the shibboleth that the IWC Scientific Committee has long agreed that there are 760,000 minke whales in the Antarctic. In fact, this estimate was one that the ICR produced, and that was derived from compiling different figures from different parts of the Antarctic, taking no account of variances in the methods used in each area or the possibility of overlap—that is, that some of the whales estimated to be found in, say, Area IV might also be in Area V, and might therefore have been counted twice. True, the IWC Scientific Committee did concede for a time that, in the absence of anything to the contrary, the ICR's was the best available estimate. However, at the 2000 meeting, and again in 2001, the Committee anounced that extrapolation from more recent data produced a figure that was appreciably lower than 760,000, perhaps as low as 300,000, and that minke whale numbers in the Antarctic might actually be falling. Furthermore, genetic analysis has proven that there are at least two completely distinct species of minkes in the Southern Ocean: the dwarf minke whale, a subspecies of the minkes found in the Northern Hemisphere, and the Antarctic minke whale, endemic to the waters south of the equator. None of this has ever been acknowledged in the propaganda of the ICR or FAJ; even as we set sail on our last expedition, and again on our return, the FAJ's Komatsu and the ICR's Ohsumi continued to state that 760,000 minkes lived in the Antarctic, even though they knew that their figure had been discredited and that the evidence was now suggesting that even this largest of whale populations was also finally falling into decline.

When the *Arctic Sunrise* arrived in Melbourne, Greenpeace issued a press release that calculated, by combining subsidies to the research fleet and fisheries aid to the country's supporters in the IWC, that Japan had spent more than $320 million of its taxpayers' money propping up the whaling industry—a staggering $58,000 for each whale caught in the Antarctic and North Pacific. And yet, in 2001, demand for whale meat at the wholesale level actually fell, and as of January 2002, 30 percent of the meat from the previous season remained unsold. In a March 2002 poll for the *Asahi Shimbun* newspaper, 53 percent of respondents said they had not eaten whale for "quite a long time," 33 percent said they didn't eat it at all, 9 percent said they ate it "only occasionally," and 4 percent said they ate it "from time to time." Those who did continue to eat whale were mostly aged fifty or older; younger people, the *Asahi Shimbun* found, were more likely to think of whales in the context of "conservation of animal life" than as food, and most had little or no interest in eating whale meat again, even if it did become available. Times have changed: most young people in Tokyo prefer hamburgers to minke meat, and the notion that the Japanese people are being denied a food source they crave is a myth.

Which begs the obvious question: if it is no longer profitable, if it can be sustained only through massive subsidies, if it brings massive international opprobrium, and if, at the end of the day, there isn't even much of a market or demand for the meat, why does the whaling industry in Japan—or, for that matter, Norway and Iceland—stubbornly persist?

The short answer is that it can. Like any dying industry anywhere in the world, it has its benefactors who are happy to prop it up because doing so ensures them political support in return. In Norway and Iceland, the primary appeal appears to be base nationalism as much as anything: both cultures are proud peoples who refuse to be bowed by outside pressures. As for Japan, it just so happens that the whaling industry's biggest booster is the FAJ and its superiors at the Ministry of Agriculture, Forestry and Fisheries—which, because commercial fisheries are such an important source of revenue for Japan, wield an enormous amount of power. Part of the motivation is undoubtedly pride, and the refusal to be beaten by activists from abroad whom the whalers perceive as irrational and emotional. There is also concern that whaling is just the thin end of the wedge—that after driving Japan's whaling industry into oblivion, Western environmentalists will then target other fisheries such as bluefin tuna.

Ultimately, at the heart of the conflict there is, I suspect, a fundamental cultural dichotomy—although not the "West vs. East" clash that Komatsu and others would have us believe. Rather, there is a profound contrast in beliefs over how humanity should relate to the natural environment. The FAJ and the Nordic whalers are charter members of what has come to be known as the "wise use" movement—which actually finds some of its most stringent adherents among fishers, foresters, and hunters in the United States. The movement claims to represent the rational concept of "sustainable use," which posits that if a natural resource is to be used, it should be used in a sustainable manner, allowing its continued existence for the benefit of future generations. In fact, however, the wise use crowd takes the principle one step further, essentially advocating that if a "resource" exists, it must be utilized, and if it can be utilized in a sustainable manner, then so much the better. That's in sharp contrast to the views of those of us who believe that just because a "resource" can be used, it doesn't necessarily follow that it should be; and that in the case of whales, it is time we viewed them not as floating slabs of meat and oil but as the fascinating, certainly sentient, and possibly intelligent fellow mammals that they are. After centuries of overexploitation, it is time to leave them in peace.

But whatever the motivation, one thing is certain. When I first became involved in the whaling issue, and even when setting out on my first few Antarctic expeditions, I felt—many of us felt—that it was only a matter of time, that we had only to overcome the last stubborn pockets of resistance and then the whaling industry would finally succumb to its inevitable death throes. Those days of optimism are presently waning.

The dam has not broken: the whaling industry is but a fraction of its size twenty years ago, and so is the number of whales being killed. But it is leaking, and it is springing more holes with each passing year. Whaling's opponents are applying mortar to the cracks as they appear and doing their best to reinforce the levee; it is holding so far, but it may not for much longer.

Commercial whaling has been dying for hundreds of years. It began dying in the Atlantic Arctic in the seventeenth century, and in the Western Arctic two hundred years after that, in each case just decades after the discovery of bowhead whale populations led to those populations becoming almost exterminated by massive hunting. It was all but dead through most of the Northern Hemisphere by the late 1800s, and would have expired completely had it not been for the rise of industrial whaling in the Antarctic. Here, too, the industry's glory days were relatively brief; after thirty years it had reached its peak, and it has been declining—slowly at first, and then rapidly—ever since. The last years of the twentieth century, and the opening stanza of the twenty-first, mark the first period of time since then that commercial whaling worldwide has actually been increasing again, and the industry's supporters are banking that their sheer relentless persistence, coupled with the force of financial persuasion, will combine to give it a new lease on life.

The next few years will prove whether that will be the case: whether the pro-whaling forces will ultimately prevail, or whether expending vast amounts of financial and political capital propping up an industry that nobody wants will simply prove too much to maintain. In that best-case scenario, perhaps what we are witnessing are merely the last defiant death throes before commercial whaling breathes its last and, unmourned and unloved, finally passes away.

Cast of Characters

MV Greenpeace Antarctic Whaling Campaign 1991–92
Departed Singapore November 18, 1991;
Arrived Fremantle, Australia, February 7, 1992

Bob Graham   MASTER
New Zealand

Jörn Haye   FIRST MATE
Germany

François Lamy   SECOND MATE
Canada

Lena Sierakowska   THIRD MATE
Britain

Thom Looney   RADIO OFFICER
United States

Peter Laue   CHIEF ENGINEER
United States

Anders Stensson   SECOND ENGINEER
Sweden

Bob James   THIRD ENGINEER
Britain

Marco de Bruijn   ASSISTANT ENGINEER
The Netherlands

Jens Grabner   ASSISTANT ENGINEER
Germany

Edwin Hotz   ASSISTANT ENGINEER
Germany

Sue Spicer   COOK
United States

Sîan Bennett   ASSISTANT COOK
Britain

Hanno-Lutz Gruener   BOSUN
Germany

Sake Bosma   DECK
The Netherlands

Milo Dahlman   DECK
Sweden

Karen Foley   DECK
Britain

Abby Gage   DECK
United States

Ted Hood   DECK
United States

Hidemichi Kano   DECK
Japan

Jobst Mailander   DECK/DOCTOR
Germany

Grace O'Sullivan   DECK
Ireland

Naoko Funahashi   EXPEDITION COORDINATOR
Japan

Athel von Koettlitz   LOGISTICS COORDINATOR
Britain

Kieran Mulvaney   MEDIA COORDINATOR
Britain

Patricia Becher-Ketterer   CAMPAIGN ASSISTANT
Germany

Robin Culley   PHOTO
Britain

Alex de Waal   VIDEO
The Netherlands

MV Greenpeace Antarctic Expedition 1992–93
Departed Hobart, Australia, December 8, 1992;
Arrived Auckland, New Zealand, March 14, 1993

Arne Sørensen   MASTER
Denmark

David Iggulden   FIRST MATE
Britain

Sophie Piette   SECOND MATE
Canada

Julio Bernal   THIRD MATE
Argentina

Thom Looney   RADIO OFFICER
United States

Mark Loveridge   RADIO OFFICER
Australia

Ernst Radloff   CHIEF ENGINEER
Germany

Anders Stensson   SECOND ENGINEER
Sweden

Joris Wolters   THIRD ENGINEER
The Netherlands

Dave Caister   ASSISTANT ENGINEER
Britain

Marc Defourneaux   ASSISTANT ENGINEER
United States

Anders Gram   ASSISTANT ENGINEER
Denmark

Martin Freimuller *Switzerland*	COOK
Sarah Macnab *New Zealand*	COOK
Chris Robinson *Australia*	BOSUN
Harriet Bakhuizen *The Netherlands*	DECK
Diana Desnoyers *United States*	DECK
Earl Dorney *Australia*	DECK/DOCTOR
Grant Harper *New Zealand*	DECK/SCIENCE
Pat Herron *United States*	DECK
Ted Hood *United States*	DECK
Wilfried Laing *Germany*	DECK
Paula Huckleberry *United States*	HELICOPTER PILOT
Ted Cassidy *New Zealand*	HELICOPTER MECHANIC
Naoko Funahashi *Japan*	EXPEDITION COORDINATOR
Kieran Mulvaney *Britain*	EXPEDITION COORDINATOR
Athel von Koettlitz *Britain*	LOGISTICS COORDINATOR
Dana Harmon *United States*	ANTARCTIC CAMPAIGN
Marty Lueders *United States*	PHOTO
Alex de Waal *The Netherlands*	VIDEO

MV Greenpeace Antarctic Expedition 1994–95
Departed Ushuaia, Argentina, December 28, 1994;
Arrived Hobart, Australia, March 17, 1995

Arne Sørensen — MASTER
Denmark

Andy Troia — FIRST MATE
United States

Harriet Bakhuizen — SECOND MATE
The Netherlands

Hauke Mack — THIRD MATE
Germany

Tim Gorter — RADIO OFFICER
The Netherlands

Hans Monker — RADIO OFFICER
The Netherlands

Rob Willighagen — CHIEF ENGINEER
The Netherlands

Bob James — SECOND ENGINEER
Britain

Anders Stensson — THIRD ENGINEER
Sweden

Anders Gram — ASSISTANT ENGINEER
Denmark

Martin Freimuller — COOK
Switzerland

Sarah Macnab — COOK
New Zealand

Tom Briggs — BOSUN
United States

Milo Dahlman — DECK
Sweden

Marc Defourneaux — DECK
United States

Kaori Matsunaga — DECK
Japan

Lena Sierakowska   DECK
Britain

Werner Stachl   DECK
Austria

Majoge van Vliet   DECK/NURSE
The Netherlands

Paula Huckleberry   HELICOPTER PILOT
United States

Kieran Mulvaney   EXPEDITION LEADER
Britain

John Morris   TRANSLATOR
Britain

Ricardo Roura   ANTARCTIC CAMPAIGN/SCIENCE
Argentina

Liz Carr   SCIENCE
United States

Chris Pierpoint   SCIENCE
Britain

Roger Grace   PHOTO/SCIENCE
New Zealand

Dave Flett   VIDEO
Britain

MV Arctic Sunrise Antarctic Whaling Campaign, 2001– 2
Departed Cape Town, South Africa, November 29, 2001;
Arrived Melbourne, Australia, January 16, 2002

Andy Troia   MASTER
United States

Waldemar Wichmann   FIRST MATE
Argentina

David Iggulden   MATE
Britain

Joanne Hender   MATE
Britain

Vincent Custers *The Netherlands*	MATE
Dave McEvitt *Ireland*	CHIEF ENGINEER
Samuel Nsiah *Ghana*	SECOND ENGINEER
Walter Karfich *Germany*	THIRD ENGINEER
Mehdi Moujbani *Tunisia*	OUTBOARD MECHANIC
Neil Brewster *Australia*	RADIO OFFICER
Hans Monker *The Netherlands*	RADIO OFFICER
Amanda Bjur *Sweden*	COOK
James Vernyi *United States*	COOK
Olivier Devaux *France*	BOSUN
Eva Amira *Greece*	DECK
Mariek Benjamin *The Netherlands*	DECK
Duygu Gungor *Turkey*	DECK
Jesse Reid *Canada*	DECK
Nathalie Renard *France*	DECK
Mikey Rosato *Australia*	DECK
Clive Strauss *Canada*	DECK/DOCTOR
Phil Robinson *New Zealand*	HELICOPTER PILOT

Arjen Blok   HELICOPTER MECHANIC
The Netherlands

Kieran Mulvaney   EXPEDITION LEADER
Britain

Sarah Duthie   CAMPAIGNER
New Zealand

Yuko Hirono   CAMPAIGNER
Japan

John Morris   TRANSLATOR
Britain

Andrew Davies   WEB EDITOR
United States

Jeremy Sutton-Hibbert   PHOTO
Britain

Jari Stahl   VIDEO
Swede

Chronology

c. 1000 C.E.: Basques begin hunting right whales in Bay of Biscay region, the first true commercial whaling operation. Over the ensuing centuries, they expand slowly northward and westward, arriving off Labrador around 1540.

1611: England's Muscovy Company sends two whaling ships to the newly discovered Arctic archipelago of Spitsbergen to hunt bowhead whales. By 1613, the waters around Spitsbergen are choked with whaling ships. By the late seventeenth century, Dutch whalers alone send roughly 250 vessels and 18,000 men to the Arctic in search of bowheads.

1675: Yoriharu Wada begins organizing whaling crews in Taiji, Japan.

1712: The beginning of American commercial whaling, operating out of Nantucket in search of sperm whales.

1842: British explorer James Clark Ross, sailing off the Antarctic Peninsula, observes "a very great number of the largest-sized black whales," prompting interest in the prospects for an Antarctic whaling industry.

1863: Norwegian whaling pioneer Svend Føyn launches the *Spes et Fides*, the first truly steam-powered whaling ship.

1868: Føyn perfects the harpoon cannon.

1874: A German whaling ship, the *Grönland*, heads south in search of the whales spied by Ross. It becomes the first steamship to cross the Antarctic Circle, but fails to catch any whales.

1904: Norwegian Carl Anton Larsen establishes the first Antarctic whaling operation, at Grytviken on South Georgia. In its first twelve months, the company shoots 184 whales. Within ten years, South Georgia whalers kill 1,738 blue whales, 4,776 fin whales, and 21,894 humpback whales.

1909: The first British Antarctic whaling station is established on West Falkland Island.

1923: Larsen leads the *Sir James Clark Ross*, the first Antarctic factory ship, into the Ross Sea.

1925: The *Lancing*, the first modern factory ship equipped with a stern ramp, reaches the Antarctic.

1927: Whale kill for the Antarctic season: 13,775.

1929: Whale kill for the Antarctic season: 40,201.

1930: Thirty-eight factory ships and 184 catchers, mostly British and Norwegian, are operating in the Antarctic.

1931: The Geneva Convention for the Regulation of Whaling, the first international attempt to regulate the industry, is signed. That same year, an all-time record 29,410 blue whales are killed in the Antarctic.

1934: The first Japanese factory ship, the *Tonan Maru*, heads to the Antarctic.

1937: The International Agreement for the Regulation of Whaling is signed in London. The next season, 46,039 whales are killed in the Antarctic, the highest total ever.

1944: The Blue Whale Unit is created.

1946: The International Convention for the Regulation of Whaling is signed in Washington, D.C. Three years later, the International Whaling Commission meets for the first time.

1964: Antarctic whalers are able to find and kill just twenty whales. The following year, the IWC protects the species from whaling.

1971: Greenpeace makes its first voyage, to Amchitka Island to protest nuclear testing.

1972: The U.N. Conference on the Human Environment votes for a ten-year moratorium on commercial whaling.

1974: The IWC replaces the Blue Whale Unit with the New Management Procedure.

1975: The first Greenpeace anti-whaling voyage, confronting Soviet whalers in the North Pacific.

1979: The IWC establishes the Indian Ocean Sanctuary and bans pelagic factory-ship whaling for all species except minkes.

1982: The IWC establishes an indefinite commercial whaling moratorium, to take effect beginning with the 1985–86 Antarctic season. Japan, Norway, Peru, and USSR file objections; Japan and Peru later withdraw their objections.

1985: The Greenpeace flagship *Rainbow Warrior* is blown up by agents of the French government; one Greenpeace crew member is killed.

1986: After failing to break through the ice the year before, the MV *Greenpeace* sets out on an ultimately successful voyage to establish World Park Base.

1987: The Japanese factory ship *Nisshin Maru No. 3* and three catchers set out on the first "scientific whaling" voyage in the Antarctic, to kill up to 330 minke whales.

1989: During the second "scientific whaling" voyage, the *Nisshin Maru No. 3* encounters the Greenpeace icebreaker *Gondwana*, which interferes with its actions for several days.

1991: The MV *Greenpeace* leaves Singapore on an eighty-one-day voyage to intercept Japan's Antarctic whaling fleet.

1992: The French government proposes Southern Ocean Sanctuary; *Greenpeace* departs on its second voyage to find Antarctic whalers.

1994: The IWC adopts Southern Ocean Sanctuary; *Greenpeace* embarks on its third Antarctic anti-whaling expedition.

1995: Japan increases its quota for Antarctic "research" whaling from 330 to 440.

1996: Japan begins "research" whaling in the North Pacific.

1997: "Irish proposal" floated at the IWC meeting in Monaco.

1998: Brazil floats the idea of a South Atlantic whale sanctuary; Australia and New Zealand suggest a similar sanctuary in the South Pacific.

1999: The Greenpeace icebreaker *Arctic Sunrise* engages the *Nisshin Maru* and catchers.

2000: Japan expands North Pacific "research" to include Bryde's and sperm whales.

2001: *Arctic Sunrise* again engages the Antarctic whaling fleet.

2002: Japan expands its North Pacific hunt to include sei whales, and increases the North Pacific quota of minke whales. At the annual IWC meeting, Japan and allies initially deny bowhead quota to natives of Alaska and Russia. At a special meeting in England, the IWC apparently readmits Iceland as a member, with a reservation against the moratorium; somehow, nonmember Iceland is itself allowed to cast the deciding vote.

FURTHER READING

The following is a small selection of books and reports on whales, whaling, Greenpeace, Antarctica, and various combinations thereof. It is by no means comprehensive, but it includes some of the most relevant and accessible publications.

Antarctica: The Extraordinary History of Man's Conquest of the Frozen Continent.
Surry Hills, NSW, Australia: Reader's Digest, 1990.
One of the very best overviews ever published on the subject, this is an excellent starting point and reference book for anyone interested in reviewing the history of Antarctica's exploration.

Barnes, James N. *Let's Save Antarctica.*
Richmond, Victoria, Australia: Greenhouse, 1982.
Now out of date, but still an excellent primer on Antarctic environmental issues from one of the leading advocates of a World Park Antarctica.

Birnie, Patricia. *International Regulation of Whaling: From Conservation of Whaling to Conservation of Whales and Regulation of Whale-Watching*
Dobbs Ferry, New York: Oceana, 1985.

Classic, authoritative two-volume review of the history of international attempts to regulate whaling.

Bohlen, Jim. *Making Waves: The Origins and Future of Greenpeace.*
Montreal: Black Rose Books, 2001.

Firsthand observations from one of the true founders of Greenpeace.

Bonner, W. N., and D.W.H. Walton. *Key Environments: Antarctica.*
Oxford: Pergamon Press, 1985.

Semitechnical overview of Antarctic biology, ecology, geology, climate, exploration, and conservation.

Brown, Michael, and John May. *The Greenpeace Story.*
London: Dorling Kindersley, 1989; 2nd ed., 1991.

A comprehensive account of the early Greenpeace years, including a list of many campaigns and activities.

Brown, Paul. *The Last Wilderness: Eighty Days in Antarctica.*
London: Hutchinson, 1991.

An account of the 1988–89 voyage of the *Gondwana*, including an encounter with the *Nisshin Maru No. 3*.

Carwardine, Mark, Erich Hoyt, R. Ewan Fordyce, and Peter Gill. *The Australian Geographic Guide to Whales, Dolphins & Porpoises.*
Terrey Hills, NSW, Australia: Australian Geographic, 2000.

Includes descriptions of selected species; chapters on behavior, biology, and conservation; and a whale-watching guide. Extensively illustrated.

Cherfas, Jeremy. *The Hunting of the Whale: A Tragedy That Must End.*
London: The Bodley Head, 1988.
A solid account of historical and modern whaling.

Dale, Stephen. *McLuhan's Children: The Greenpeace Message and the Media.*
Toronto: Between the Lines, 1996.
An attempt to understand how Greenpeace operates in the political and media arenas.

Day, David. *The Whale Wars.*
London: Routledge & Kegan Paul, 1987.
The battles, by activists and scientists alike, against commercial whaling.

Ellis, Richard. *Men and Whales.*
New York: Knopf, 1991.
A huge, comprehensive account, well written and extensively illustrated, of the frequently intertwined, and rarely mutually beneficial, histories of our species and the seventy-plus species of cetaceans.

Evans, Peter G. H. *The Natural History of Whales and Dolphins.*
London: Christopher Helm, 1987.
Informative and comprehensive; still useful, sixteen years after publication.

Fothergill, Alistair. *A Natural History of the Antarctic: Life in the Freezer.*
New York: Sterling, 1995.
Nicely written and illustrated with exceptional photographs, this is the companion volume to an outstanding BBC series, *Life in the Freezer.* The book is one of the better general introductions to the Antarctic, and the TV series is a must-see.

Francis, Daniel. *A History of World Whaling*.
New York: Penguin, 1990.

A concise, readable, useful review.

Friedheim, Robert L. (ed.). *Toward a Sustainable Whaling Regime*.
Seattle: University of Washington Press, 2001.

The common thread running through this collection of pro-whaling papers is that the IWC is no longer a credible organization and should be in some way adjusted, revised, or rejected and replaced.

Frost, Sydney. *The Whaling Question*.
San Francisco: Friends of the Earth, 1979.

The Australian government inquiry into whales and whaling, chaired by Sir Sydney Frost, which prompted that country to adopt a position of opposition to commercial whaling on ethical grounds.

Hart, Ian B. *Pesca: A History of the Pioneer Modern Whaling Company in the Antarctic*.
Salcombe, England: Aidan Ellis, 2001; revised edition, 2002.

Thoroughly researched and comprehensive account of the first Antarctic whaling operation.

Hince, Bernadette. *The Antarctic Dictionary: A Complete Guide to Antarctic English*.
Collingwood, Victoria, Australia: CSIRO Publishing/Museum of Victoria, 2000.

As fun as it is useful, this dictionary includes terms from "macaroni penguin" and "loose pack" to "ahhh" (a command for a sled dog to halt). Each entry is accompanied by historical examples of its use.

Horwood, Joseph. *Biology and Exploitation of the Minke Whale*.
Boca Raton, Florida: CRC Press, 1990.

Since superseded in parts by genetic studies that have revealed the existence of at least two separate minke species, this nonetheless remains the standard scientific monograph on the minke whale.

Hoyt, Erich. *The Whale Watcher's Handbook.*
New York: Doubleday, 1984.
Whales and where to watch them. A classic.

Hunter, Robert. *Warriors of the Rainbow: A Chronicle of the Greenpeace Movement.*
New York: Holt, Rinehart & Winston, 1979.
The founding of Greenpeace, including the early whaling campaigns, as recounted by the organization's first president.

Hunter, Robert, and Rex Weyler. *To Save a Whale: The Voyages of Greenpeace.*
San Francisco: Chronicle, 1978.
A short, illustrated book describing the first anti-whaling campaigns.

Joyner, Christopher C. *Governing the Frozen Commons: The Antarctic Regime and Environmental Protection.*
Columbia: University of South Carolina Press, 1998.
This semitechnical work covers the Antarctic Treaty, the Environmental Protocol, CCAMLR, the IWC, and so on.

Kalland, Arne, and Brian Moeran. *Japanese Whaling: End of an Era?*
London: Curzon Press, 1992.
Although this book is dismissive of the environmental rationale for the anti-whaling campaign, and overly keen to portray that campaign as an anti-Japanese conspiracy, it includes an interesting overview of historical and contemporary Japanese whaling.

Knight, Stephen. *Icebound: The Greenpeace Expedition to Antarctica.*
Auckland: Century Hutchinson, 1988.
A chronicle of the 1986–87 MV *Greenpeace* expedition, which established World Park Base.

Komatsu, Masayuki, with Shigeko Masaki. *The Truth Behind the Whaling Dispute.*
Tokyo: Institute of Cetacean Research, 2001.

The title is, to put it mildly, misleading; this is an apologia for Japan's whaling program and the arguments of the Fisheries Agency of Japan.

Laws, Richard. *Antarctica: The Last Frontier.*
London: Boxtree, 1989.

Extensively illustrated, accessible introduction to the Antarctic.

Leach, Nicky (ed.). *Whale Watching.*
Bethesda, Maryland: Discovery Channel/Insight Guides, 1999.

Includes chapters on cetaceans, human impacts on cetaceans, and where to watch cetaceans in North America.

Leatherwood, Stephen, Randall R. Reeves, and Larry Foster. *The Sierra Club Handbook of Whales and Dolphins.*
San Francisco: Sierra Club Books, 1983.

More than a decade (and a couple of newly described species) later, still one of the best guidebooks to cetaceans available.

Martin, Stephen. *A History of Antarctica.*
Sydney: State Library of New South Wales Press, 1996.

Accessible account of exploration, from the ancients to modern times.

May, John. *The Greenpeace Book of Antarctica: A New View of the Seventh Continent.*
London: Dorling Kindersley, 1988.

Attractive review of the natural history, exploration, and exploitation of Antarctica, with a Greenpeace perspective and some useful information on the Antarctic Treaty system and the various scientific bases on the continent.

McGonigal, David, and Lynn Woodworth. *Antarctica: The Complete Story.*

Noble Park, Victoria, Australia: Five Mile Press, 2001.

Comprehensive, beautiful, extensively illustrated overview of the Antarctic, with a few comparative sideways glances at the Arctic. Comes bundled with an interactive CD-ROM.

McNally, Robert. *So Remorseless a Havoc: Of Dolphins, Whales and Men.*

Boston: Little, Brown, 1981.

One of the first books I read on whales and whaling (and many other aspects of cetaceans and their interactions with humans), and still one of my favorites.

Mickleburgh, Edwin. *Beyond the Frozen Sea: Visions of Antarctica.*
London: The Bodley Head, 1987.

Literate look at Antarctica, its exploration and exploitation. Includes references to, and photographs of, the first Antarctic voyage of the MV *Greenpeace*.

Mitchell, Barbara, and Richard Sandbrook. *The Management of the Southern Ocean.*

London: International Institute for Environment and Development, 1980.

Since superseded by political developments, this 162-page summary of a much longer report is nonetheless very interesting for its perspectives on Southern Ocean conservation and management more than two decades ago.

Mulvaney, Kieran. *At the Ends of the Earth: A History of the Polar Regions.*
Washington, D.C.: Island Press, 2001.

An environmental history of exploration and exploitation, including whaling, in the Arctic and Antarctic regions.

Mulvaney, Kieran, and Mark Warford. *Witness: Twenty-Five Years on the Environmental Front Line.*
London: André Deutsch, 1996.

A photographic history of a quarter-century of Greenpeace campaigning, with introductory text by me and a foreword by the Dalai Lama.

Payne, Roger. *Among Whales.*
New York: Scribner, 1995.

One of the most knowledgeable, erudite, and influential advocates of whales, writing about whales, whale research, whale-killing, and whale-saving.

Perrin, William F., Bernd Würsig, and J.G.M. Thewissen (eds.). *Encyclopedia of Marine Mammals.*
San Diego: Academic Press, 2002.

Huge and comprehensive, with 284 essays on just about everything to do with marine mammals. Not cheap, but highly recommended for the serious student.

Reeves, Randall R., Brent S. Stewart, Phillip J. Clapham, and James A. Powell. *Sea Mammals of the World: A Complete Guide to Whales, Dolphins, Seals, Sea Lions & Sea Cows.* Illustrations by Pieter A. Folkens.
London: A&C Black, 2002.

The new standard in marine mammal species guides: a 500-plus-page overview of all known marine mammals, including—in addition to those listed in the subtitle—sea otters and the polar bear.

Reynolds, John E. III, and Sentiel A. Rommel (eds.).
Biology of Marine Mammals.
Washington, D.C.: Smithsonian Institution Press, 1999.

Collection of scholarly but accessible essays on such topics as communication and cognition; behavior; reproduction; and sensory systems.

Rubin, Jeff. *Antarctica: A Lonely Planet Travel Survival Kit.*
Oakland, California: Lonely Planet, 1996.

Designed primarily for the growing band of Antarctic tourists, this is a very nice pocket-sized guide to Antarctica, its wildlife, its exploration and exploitation, and topics such as Antarctic science and environmental issues.

Sanderson, Ivan T. *A History of Whaling.*
New York: Barnes & Noble, 1993.

Originally published as *Follow the Whale*; a classic account of commercial whaling.

Simmonds, Mark P., and Judith D. Hutchinson (eds.). *The Conservation of Whales and Dolphins: Science and Practice.*
Chichester, England: Wiley, 1996.

Comprehensive, in-depth review of the issues facing cetaceans worldwide.

Small, George L. *The Blue Whale.*
New York: Columbia University Press, 1971.

Classic, authoritative, National Book Award–winning paean to the largest of the whales, and powerful critique of the excesses of the whaling industry.

Soper, Tony. *Antarctica: A Guide to the Wildlife.* Illustrations by Dafila Scott.
Chalfont St. Peter, England: Bradt, 1996.

Very nice paperback pocket guide to the wildlife most likely to be encountered south of the Convergence. Includes a glossary of snow and ice terms, and a code of conduct for visiting the Antarctic.

State of the Ice.
Amsterdam: Greenpeace International, 1994.

Review of the political issues surrounding Antarctic conservation.

Stewart, John. *Antarctica: An Encyclopedia.*
Jefferson, North Carolina: McFarland & Company, 1990.

Two-volume guide containing thousands of entries on Antarctic natural and human history. Includes extensive bibliography and a chronology of Antarctic expeditions.

Stoett, Peter J. *The International Politics of Whaling.*
Vancouver, British Columbia: UBC Press, 1997.

Balanced, scholarly overview of modern whaling politics.

Stonehouse, Bernard (ed.). *Encyclopedia of Antarctica and the Southern Oceans.*
Chichester, England: Wiley, 2002.

Contains fewer entries than the Stewart encyclopedia listed above, but many entries are more scholarly and through. The appendices and study guides that take up the final 80 pages are especially useful.

Szabo, Michael. *Making Waves: The Greenpeace New Zealand Story.*
Auckland: Reed Books, 1991.

Interesting account of the growth of Greenpeace in one country; includes a chapter on the first Antarctic expeditions.

Taylor, A.J.W. *Antarctic Psychology.*
Wellington, New Zealand: Science Information Publishing Centre, 1987.

Psychologist, and consultant to the New Zealand Antarctic Program (and Greenpeace expeditions), examines the many psychological stresses and strains caused by spending prolonged periods in this most harsh of environments.

Tonnesen, J. N., and A. O. Johnsen. *The History of Modern Whaling.*
London: Hurst, 1982.

The definitive history, this 800-page tome is a much shortened (but nonetheless exhaustive) version of the original Norwegian account, which was published in four volumes between 1959 and 1970.

Twiss, John R., and Randall R. Reeves. *Conservation and Management of Marine Mammals.*
Washington, D.C.: Smithsonian Institution Press, 1999.
Includes essays on the International Whaling Commission and on the Antarctic Treaty system.

Watson, Lyall. *Whales of the World.*
London: Hutchinson, 1987.
Notwithstanding the author's insistence on renaming most of the species included, this comprehensive guide remains a classic.

Whales, Dolphins and Porpoises.
Washington, D.C.: National Geographic Society, 1995.
A big, beautiful, and informative publication, written by a team of experts in the field.

Whaling Issues and Japan's Whale Research.
Tokyo: Institute of Cetacean Research, 1993.
The company view of Japan's Antarctic research whaling program, with a few barbs thrown at the MV *Greenpeace* campaigns, and an account, from on board the *Nisshin Maru*, of the 1991–92 expedition.

Wilkinson, Pete, with Julia Schofield. *Warrior: One Man's Environmental Crusade.*
Cambridge: Lutterworth Press, 1994.
The inside story of the earliest Greenpeace Antarctic expeditions, along with some other Greenpeace history.

Williams, Heathcote. *Whale Nation.*
London: Jonathan Cape, 1988.
Inspirational poetry, beautiful photographs, and an eclectic anthology of cetacean literature.

ACKNOWLEDGMENTS

This book is on one level a history of commercial whaling and the efforts of those who have opposed it, particularly over the last decade. It is also a very personal account of a series of voyages on which I embarked almost by accident, but which came to dominate ten years of my life. Although this book obviously reflects my interpretation of events, the experiences on those voyages were shared in total by more than eighty campaigners, captains, cooks, cameramen, radio officers, deckhands, scientists, pilots, mates, mechanics, medics, electricians, and engineers, without whom none of the experiences in these pages would have been possible. Untold thanks and appreciation to all of those with whom it was my great pleasure and good fortune to sail on one or more of the expeditions. The names of those involved are listed in the cast of characters in Appendix A; special thanks, however, must be given to captains Bob Graham, Arne Sørensen, and Andy Troia for their expertise, insight, patience, and support.

Many other people in Greenpeace deserve credit, particularly John Frizell, who conceived the idea of a season-long expedition, who consistently provided welcome and incredibly useful help, advice, and support from shore, and who also happens to be a great guy; Walt Simpson, who conceptualized and organized just about every aspect of every expedition, and who took every opportunity to lobby the necessary people in Amsterdam to send Greenpeace to the Antarctic "one more time"; Louise Bell, my former office companion and fellow listener to obscure Dutch radio stations; John Bowler, Angela Congedo, and Matthew Gianni, who brought me out of "retirement" and oversaw the 2001–2 expedition; and Anne Dingwall, without whom I would never have gone to the Antarctic in the first place.

Thanks are also due to the various folks in Greenpeace Communications over the years: Elena Adams, Martin Atkins, Cindy Baxter, Andy Booth, Sue Cooper, Kate Davison, John Goldblatt, Elkie Jordaans, Mim Lowe, Robert Maletta, Desley Mather, Elizabeth Mealey, Rachel Munday, John Novis, Blair Palese, Dawn Pearcey, Peter Sibley, Liz Somerville, and Mark Warford; at Greenpeace in Australia and New Zealand: Linda Apps, Margaret Baker, Curtis Barnett, Denise Boyd, Stephen Butler, Catherine Delahunty, Nicola Easthope, Henk Haazen, Toby Hutcheon, Peter Gill, Robbie Kelman, Cindy Kiro, Pia Mancia, Daniel Mares, Stephanie Mills, Beth Powell, Nikki Searancke, Michael Szabo, Rob Taylor, and Jon Walter; at Greenpeace's Marine Division and Marine Services: Lieke Bannenberg, Willem Beekman, Jon Brouwer, Simone van Brug, Jeannette Haagsma, Sjoerd Jongens, Marci Malloy, Sharon de Meneges, David Roy, Mijarca Schuyt, Gijs Thieme, and Tanya Whitford; and the innumerable others throughout Greenpeace, especially the Antarctic and whaling campaigns, including Lisa Beale, Leslie Busby, the late Lesley Scheele, and John May, who conspired to hire me in the first place; Ken Ballard, Paul Bogart, Natalie Brandon, Alison Cox, Duncan Currie, Janet Dalziell, Mario Damato, Geert Drieman, Barbara Dudley, Steve Erwood, Trina Fely, Tracey Frauzel, Mikiko Fukuda, Monique Harthoorn, Alan Hemmings, Kevin Jardine, Tom Johnson, David de Jong, Ulrich Jurgens, Frank Kamp, Elaine Lawrence, Gerry Leape, Gerd Leipold, Isabel McCrea, David McTaggart, Peter Melchett, Regina

Monticone, Connie Murtagh, Mamie Mutchler, Motoji Nagasawa, Michael Nielsen, Naoki Ohara, Andy Ottaway, Richard Page, Martina Peschen, Alan Pickaver, Maj de Poorter, Peter Pueschel, Iain Reddish, Simon Reddy, Kelly Rigg, Alison Ross, Sue Sabella, Steve Sawyer, Sandra Schoettner, Sanae Shida, Jenny Stannard, and Julia True.

Many others assisted and guided me over the years before I joined Greenpeace, especially Horace Dobbs, Bill Jordan, Virginia McKenna, Dan Morast, the late Sir Peter Scott, the late Bill Travers, Margaret Whyte, and Sean Whyte—and, of course, my parents, who have given me nothing but support, encouragement, and love.

For helping me come to grips with the whaling issue throughout the years, I would particularly like to thank Leslie Busby, Justin Cooke, John Frizell, Ray Gambell, Sidney Holt, Bill de la Mare, Dan Morast, Vassili Papastavrou, and Cassandra Phillips. For his sheer brilliance and inspiration, I will remain forever indebted to the late David McTaggart.

Portions of this book draw on my reporting for *BBC Wildlife* magazine and on publications I have written, researched, or edited for, among others, Greenpeace, the International Fund for Animal Welfare, the Third Millennium Foundation, and the World Wildlife Fund/World Wide Fund for Nature.

The manuscript was reviewed in whole or in part by Leslie Busby, Angela Congedo, Steve Erwood, John Frizell, Matthew Gianni, and Sidney Holt; many thanks to them for their comments and criticisms.

This book has had a long genesis, beginning in 1994 when I pitched the idea to Richard Ballantine; thanks to him for seeing the promise in my proposal and helping it along its way. Sharon Curtin took on a raw manuscript and a raw author; because of her influence, I rediscovered myself as a writer, and produced a book that I hope is worthy of her investment. Finally, fortunately, the book was accepted by Island Press, to whom as ever I owe a great many thanks, particularly to Amelia Durand, Chuck Savitt, and of course my editor Jonathan Cobb. I remain constantly amazed by

Jonathan's ability to look at what I was convinced was a perfect piece of prose and gently propose ways to make it clearer and better. It is a privilege and a joy to work with him.

Thanks to the team at SeaWeb for its constant help, support, encouragement, and friendship, particularly Susan Boa, Tom Johnson, Bruce McKay, Connie Murtagh, and especially Vikki Spruill.

For their friendship and support, in Alaska, in Amsterdam, and at various rest stops around the world, I would particularly like to thank Johnny Armstrong, Erin Culley-LaChapelle, Laura Dennison, Alysia Gould, Jennifer Kragness, D. J. LaChapelle, John LaChapelle, Stephanie Lasure, Bruce McKay, Deb McKinney, Paul Morley, Warren Rhodes, Dan Ritzman, Sallie Schullinger, Ken Waldman, Tanya Whitford and, above all, Melanie Duchin, Paula Huckleberry, and especially Sam Walton. Authorship can be a lonely process; it makes life a lot easier knowing that, when the isolation becomes too much, I have such a wide range of friends waiting with smiles, hugs, encouragement, and warmth. I can never thank them enough.

Kieran Mulvaney
Anchorage, Alaska
March 2003

INDEX

ABOUT THE AUTHOR

Kieran Mulvaney is the author of *At the Ends of the Earth: A History of the Polar Regions* (Island Press/Shearwater Books 2001) and has written more than 200 articles on science and the environment for publications including *The (London) Sunday Times Magazine*, *New Scientist*, *BBC Wildlife*, and *E Magazine*. He was previously founding director of the Whale and Dolphin Conservation Society, founding editor of *Sonar* and the *International Whale Bulletin*, and a campaigner and spokesperson for Greenpeace. He is presently editor of *Ocean Update*, a monthly newsletter produced by SeaWeb, which seeks to raise awareness of ocean issues. He lives in Anchorage, Alaska.